MODERN FRENCH PHILOSOPHY

MODERN FRENCH PHILOSOPHY

Vincent Descombes

Translated by L. Scott-Fox and J. M. Harding

Cambridge University Press

CAMBRIDGE
LONDON   NEW YORK   NEW ROCHELLE
MELBOURNE   SYDNEY

Published by the Press Syndicate of the University of Cambridge
The Pitt Building, Trumpington Street, Cambridge CB2 1RP
32 East 57th Street, New York, NY 10022, USA
296 Beaconsfield Parade, Middle Park, Melbourne 3206, Australia

Originally published in French as *Le Même et L'Autre*
by Les Editions de Minuit, Paris, 1979 and
© Les Editions de Minuit 1979

Now first published in English by the Cambridge
University Press 1980 as *Modern French Philosophy*
English translation © Cambridge University Press 1980

Set, printed and bound in Great Britain by
Fakenham Press Limited, Fakenham, Norfolk

British Library Cataloguing in Publication Data

Descombes, Vincent
Modern French philosophy.
1. Philosophy, French – 20th century
I. Title
194   B2421   80–40768
ISBN 0 521 22837 9 hard covers
ISBN 0 521 29672 2 paperback

Contents

Foreword

A generation ago few students (or even professors) of philosophy on either side of the English Channel knew very much about the philosophy that was being produced, studied and debated on the other side. Nor for the most part had they any interest in seeking to find out. Indeed, they felt in general fully justified in their ignorance by a settled conviction of the frivolity, superficiality and lack of any rigorous intellectual value of that of which they were accordingly more than content to remain ignorant.

Now – happily – times seem to be changing. On both sides of the same Channel signs are multiplying of a serious desire to learn about what has been and is going on on the other side, and even to participate in it; and, beyond the often still persisting incomprehension, there is an increasing return to the goodwill of mutual recognition and respect.

It would be wrong to exaggerate. It takes more than the few proverbial swallows to make a summer; and reciprocal ignorance, fortified by all the weight of recent tradition and the inertial power of institutions such as the academic syllabus, is still formidable enough. Moreover, in a situation in which ignorance has been for so long so entrenched it becomes genuinely difficult for anyone, however inquiring and however 'open-minded', to know exactly how to set about remedying his situation. One needs a guide – if at all possible, a native guide, one with expert knowledge of his own terrain, but yet capable of real communication with the strangers whom he leads into and through it.

Vincent Descombes sets out in this book to act as just such a guide through the territory of contemporary French philosophy.

No one could be better equipped for such a task. He has taught in Canada, travelled in the United States and even paid more than one visit to Oxford. He is also, and above all, a leading member of the new generation not indeed of 'new philosophers' but, quite simply, of French philosophers as such. For the past few years he has been teaching at the University of Nice and is now moving back to the University of Paris; he has already two books to his credit before this one;[1] he is a member of the editorial committee of the monthly review *Critique*; and this, his third book, although written on the commission of the Cambridge University Press and directed explicitly towards the English-speaking reader, has already proved a philosophical best-seller in its original French version, published[2] in natural slight advance of the necessary English translation.

As Descombes himself would be, and indeed is, the first to stress, his is to be taken simply as one man's view of the terrain. Not only is there and could there be no such thing as the one true and definitive view; not only might other French philosophers take other and equally legitimate views of the context within which they find themselves; Descombes himself for different purposes, or even for the same purposes fifteen years back or fifteen years hence, might view or have viewed his terrain differently, paying more attention to some philosophers and less to others than he has done from his perspective at this particular moment.

It should go without saying, but may be said nevertheless, that if this book is already to be read more as a guide than as an introduction to a certain central range of contemporary French philosophy, it in no way sets out to function as an introduction to philosophy as such. Its tacit presuppositions are not very exorbitant; simply – so to speak – a certain limited knowledge of the history of philosophy and of its dominant themes as they have appeared, above all, in the writings of the ancient Greeks and in those of the principal philosophers of the period delimited by the names of Descartes and Kant. Clearly, a certain knowledge of Hegel would also be of considerable help; but by those with the necessary basic grasp of the preceding period, the essentials of

---

[1] *Le platonisme* (Paris, P.U.F., 1971); *L'inconscient malgré lui* (Paris, Les Editions de Minuit, 1977).
[2] By Les Editions de Minuit, Paris, 1979.

what is here relevant can for the most part be gleaned from the text itself.

The nature of these dominant themes may be recalled through the re-posing of certain familiar questions. What, if to speak in this traditional way may be accepted as intelligible, is the nature of Being? Is it all – that is to say, the universe, the complete or incompletable totality of things actual and possible – of one kind, of two kinds, or more? If it is of one kind alone, does that mean that consciousness must in the last resort recognise itself to be all that there is? If so, who or what could the owner (or the subject) of such a consciousness be taken to be? Or is consciousness able or even bound to consider itself as no more than a derivative special instance of something that, as such, is not conscious at all? If, on the other hand, Being is of two kinds (or more), how can consciousness coherently represent itself as being aware of something altogether outside – other than – itself? Yet how, without reference of some sort to this essentially other than itself, can consciousness come to be self-aware of its own identity as such, let alone aware of its continuing identity through different moments of (historical) time? And how, without the peculiar 'negating' ability of consciousness to distinguish between what *is* and what might have been but is in fact *not* the case, could the objective world be conceived of as having any particular or recognisable character at all?

Put now in these terms, these may be recognised as questions and themes not only of ancient, but also of classical Cartesian and Kantian preoccupation. What Descombes manages to show with admirable economy and verve is how a certain pursuit of these very same themes, handed on and received through the modulations of a further, and double, German heritage, has remained characteristic of the peculiar modern French branch of the great western tradition of philosophical thinking, a pursuit which has been accompanied by a perhaps more idiosyncratically persistent tendency to seek immediate translation of all positions of debate in terms of very contemporary politics.

This does not pretend to be a book that those to whom it is addressed should expect to read with instantly effortless ease. If such a book were to be written, it could scarcely claim to be taken with any seriousness. But nor, in another sense, is it a book that resists its reader. It is, on the contrary, witty, incisive and, in the deepest sense, remarkably clear. It will almost certainly prove infinitely clearer to the uninitiated – and even perhaps to many of the initiated – than many, if not most, of the texts with which it deals. It repays in any case much more than one reading, not only for its information and its intellectual stimulus, but also for the sheer pleasure to be derived from it. It is, moreover, not only a guide to contemporary French philosophy but at the same time a commentary on and a highly personal contribution to it. It is a contribution that, in its particular manner and perhaps even content, could only have been made in this way – by way, that is to say, of primary address to an audience wholly outside and other than that to which French philosophy normally and paradigmatically addresses itself.

And this too may provide much food for further thought.

Balliol College, Oxford   Alan Montefiore
April 1980

Note on abbreviations and translation

Abbreviations in the footnotes refer to the works listed below. English translations are given if available. Those titles marked with an asterisk are cited by the translators in the text, as is Merleau-Ponty, *Signs*, trans. R. McCleary (Evanston, Ill., Northwestern U.P., 1964). All other quotations in translation are their own. All French works are published in Paris.

AD   Merleau-Ponty, *Les aventures de la dialectique* (Gallimard, 1955); trans. Joseph J. Bien, *The Adventures of the Dialectic* (Evanston, Ill., Northwestern U.P., 1973)

AŒ   Deleuze and Guattari, *Capitalisme et schizophrenie*, vol. I, *L'anti-Œdipe* (Minuit, 1972); trans. as *The Anti-Oedipus* (New York, Viking, 1977)

CRD   Sartre, *Critique de la raison dialectique*, prefaced with *Questions de méthode*, vol. I, *Théorie des ensembles pratiques* (Gallimard, 1960) *Critique de la raison dialectique*, trans. A. Sheridan Smith, *Critique of Dialectical Reason* (London, New Left Books, 1976)

Dérive   Lyotard, *Dérive à partir de Marx et Freud* (10/18, 1973)

Disp. puls.   Lyotard, *Des dispositifs pulsionnels* (10/18, 1973)

DR   Deleuze, *Différence et répétition* (P.U.F., 1968)

ED   Derrida, *L'écriture et la différence* (Seuil, 1967); trans. Alan Bass, *Writing and Difference* (Chicago U.P., 1978)

Eco. lib.   Lyotard, *Economie libidinale* (Minuit, 1974)

EN   Sartre, *L'être et le néant* (Gallimard, 1943); trans. Hazel Barnes, *Being and Nothingness* (New York, Simon & Schuster, 1956; London, Methuen, 1969)*

G   Derrida, *De la grammatologie* (Minuit, 1967); trans. Guyatri C. Spivak, *Of Grammatology* (Baltimore, Johns Hopkins U.P., 1976)*

HF   Foucault, *Histoire de la folie à l'âge classique*, 1st edn (Plon, 1961); trans. R. Howard, *Madness and Civilisation* (London, Tavistock, 1967)*

Intr. Hegel   Kojève, *Introduction à la lecture de Hegel* (Gallimard,

	1947); trans. James H. Nicholls Jr, ed. Allan Bloom, *Introduction to the Reading of Hegel* (New York, Basic Books, 1969)*
LC I and LC II	Althusser, Balibar, Establet, Macherey, Rancière, *Lire le Capital*, vols. I and II (Maspero, 1965) (2nd edn. Althusser and Balibar, *Lire le Capital*, trans. Ben Brewster, *Reading 'Capital'*, London, New Left Books, 1970)
LS	Deleuze, *Logique du sens* (Minuit, 1969)
Marges	Derrida, *Marges de la philosophie* (Minuit, 1972)
MC	Foucault, *Les mots et les choses* (Gallimard, 1966); trans. A. Sheridan Smith, *The Order of Things* (New York, Random House, 1973; London, Tavistock, 1974)
NPh	Deleuze, *Nietzsche et la philosophie* (P.U.F., 1962)
OG	Husserl, *L'origine de la géometrie*, translation and introduction by Derrida (P.U.F., 1962); Derrida, *Edmund Husserl's 'Origin of Geometry'. An Introduction*, trans. John P. Leavey (Boulder, Col., Great Eastern, 1978)
PM	Althusser, *Pour Marx* (Maspero, 1965); trans. Ben Brewster, *For Marx* (London, New Left Books, 1969)*
PP	Merleau-Ponty, *Phénoménologie de la perception* (Gallimard, 1945); trans. Colin Smith, *Phenomenology of Perception* (London, New York, Humanities, 1962)*
SC	Merleau-Ponty, *La structure du comportement* (P.U.F., 1942); trans. Alden Fisher, *The Structure of Behaviour* (Boston, Beacon, 1963)*
SNS	Merleau-Ponty, *Sens et non-sens* (Nagel, 1948); trans. Hubert and Patricia Dreyfus, *Sense and Non-sense* (Evanston, Ill., Northwestern U.P., 1964)*
VP	Derrida, *La voix et le phénomène* (P.U.F., 1967); trans. David B. Allison, *Speech and Phenomena: And Other Essays on Husserl's Theory of Signs* (Evanston, Ill., Northwestern U.P., 1973)*

Throughout the present work, the word *l'étant*, itself a rendering of the Heideggerian *Das Seiende*, has been translated as '(the) be-ing'.

In Chapter 1, Section 8, 'The Question of Enunciation', the word *énonciation* has been translated as 'enunciation', and the word *énoncé* as 'statement'. The verb *énoncer* has been translated as 'to state' or 'to enunciate', according to which of the two cognates (*énoncé*, *énonciation*) it distinguishes. Where this distinction is not in play, *énoncé* and *énoncer* have sometimes been rendered as 'utterance' and 'to utter'.

In general, where the word *moi* is not preceded by the definite article, it has been translated as 'myself'. *Le moi*, however, has been translated as 'the self' or as the Freudian 'ego'.

The translators wish to thank the author for his clarification of numerous points, and also E. McArdle for help and suggestions throughout.

Introduction: Philosophy in France

Can the colour of time be described? Who could say what the atmosphere of a period was?

At the outset of this survey I should define its inevitable limits.

French philosophy is the philosophy which is articulated in French, even when it is to state Greek, Latin, English or German thoughts in this language. French philosophy was born when Descartes undertook to reply, in French, to Montaigne's *Essays* with his *Discourse on Method*, followed by three *Essays with this method*. But it was more than French philosophy that appeared with Descartes's challenge to Montaigne. According to the most considerable authorities, for once in agreement – Hegel and Heidegger for example – the pursuit of a truth that has the character of absolute certainty marks the inauguration of modern philosophy.

The following pages are intended to be an *introduction to contemporary French philosophy*. A survey of French philosophy as a whole would start with Descartes (replying to Montaigne). A survey of modern philosophy would begin in the same way. The title of the study whose first page you are reading now proposes a more modest undertaking: to acquaint a reader whom I assume, for the sake of hypothesis, to be as exterior as possible to French philosophical traditions and modes, with the language and issues of what is known as philosophical debate in France today.

'Contemporary French philosophy' cannot be identified with a philosophical *period* or with a *school*. It is coincident with the sum of the discourses elaborated in France and considered by the public of today as philosophical. These are the circumstances (place, dates) which limit the substance of my exposition. It will seem at first that such circumstances are external to philosophy proper. It will perhaps be objected that philosophy, once imbued with the atmosphere of a period, might thereby be reduced to mere *opinion*.

The public is not necessarily the best judge. Its very definition is that it cannot be infallible – a point which should be stressed, inasmuch as our programme undertakes to introduce the reader to *that which was spoken about*, in a given territory and during a given period, or, when all is said and done, to retain only what created a stir among the widest possible audience. This *clamorous* approach to philosophy is necessarily unjust, since it leaves aside whatever – though sometimes worthy of attention – has gone ignored by the public, or has not received attention to a sufficient degree. It must be understood that the texts with which I shall be dealing are not necessarily the most interesting ones to have been published during the contemporary period. It is not even certain that all of them are interesting. For the entire bibliography to be considered falls into four groups:

I. Those texts which everybody quotes and which everybody holds to be worthy of quotation.

II. Those texts which everybody quotes and which some judge to be insignificant.

III. Those texts which are quoted by a few, or by only one person, but which these persons hold to be superior to texts in both the preceding categories.

IV. Those texts unknown to everybody except their respective authors.

It goes without saying that these divisions would have no sense in an introduction to *philosophy in general*, where the only standard for the appreciation of a text's philosophical value, irrespective of its audience, would lie in its exposition of the philosophical issue. But in an introduction to the *French philosophy of today*, we may include only writings from groups I and II. In setting groups III and IV to one side, we must be aware of the fact that we are eliminating not only the mediocre and the insignificant, but also texts which have a genuine public, at least outside France; and those whose time is, or may be, still to come.

Finally, and as a last limitation, the (happily) restricted space at my disposal does not permit me to refer to all the names and titles that have been discussed by the public. This work does not purport to be the *Who's Who* of French philosophy, nor even its *Gotha Almanac*. I shall therefore make no attempt to render certain nuances, or the occasional small divergence within a school, and shall offer only one version of each philosopheme. Here again, it will be the version to have received the greatest acclaim, and not necessarily the most ingenious one. Needless to say, I shall refrain from naming those who in my own personal view deserved greater recognition, who will no doubt obtain this recognition in the near future, or should do so some day. The rhetorical criterion in philosophy is undeniably sound and fury.

It remains to state, however briefly, the circumstances of time and place.

How far does what we take to be our present extend back in time? In many respects, we would be justified in beginning with the French Revolution, or even with Descartes. Thus we may as well start with the *present day*. The great undertaking of each generation is to settle the debts handed down by the preceding one. *The sins of the fathers are visited upon the sons*. In so doing, each generation calls into existence the obstacles that are to confront its descendants. So to situate what is for us the present requires that we take two generations into account: the contemporary one, demonstrably active today, and also its direct predecessor.

In the recent evolution of philosophy in France we can trace the passage from the generation known after 1945 as that of the 'three H's' to the generation known since 1960 as that of the three 'masters of suspicion': the three H's being Hegel, Husserl and Heidegger, and the three masters of suspicion Marx, Nietzsche and Freud. This is not to say that the Hegelians or the Husserlians vanished abruptly from the scene in 1960. But those who persisted in invoking the three H's, or any one of them, after that date, would have been the first to admit that their position was no longer dominant. In argument, they were thus obliged to take the common *doxa* into account, and to defend themselves in advance against the objections likely to be raised in the name of the new trinity. Our object, then, will be to account for this change. Why were the tutelary figures who had reigned from 1930 to 1960 simultaneously deposed during the 1960s to make way for the new arrivals? It should be noted that the grouping of authorities into successive triads is a rhetorical fact. The objections which the conscientious historian of philosophy may raise to such patterns do not alter the fact that an entire generation drew the same conclusions from its reading of Hegel, Husserl and Heidegger, for example. It is also significant that the texts most quoted after 1930 were often difficult of access, either because they had not been translated by that date (the *Phenomenology of Mind* was translated in 1947 and *Being and Time* is still untranslated in 1978), or because they had not even been published (thus, with Husserl, the texts to receive the greatest acclaim were precisely the *inédits*, or unpublished manuscripts, at Louvain). Such circumstances are particularly conducive to productive transformation of the quoted thought by the reader, a transformation that is always manifestly at work in the making of an authority. It should not be believed that the authority a work may carry is the result of its having been read, studied and finally judged convincing. The reverse is true: reading derives from a prior conviction. Works are preceded by *rumour*. As Maurice Blanchot wrote, public opinion is never more purely opinion than where rumour is concerned; opinion is, for instance, 'what can be read in the newspapers, but never in this or that one in particular'; such is precisely the essence of rumour, since 'what I learn from rumour, I have necessarily heard already'.[1] By a kind of Platonic recollection, the text with which *we fall in love* will be the one wherein what we know already can be learned and relearned. Merleau-Ponty recognised this:

> We shall find in ourselves and nowhere else the unity and true meaning of phenomenology. It is less a question of counting up quotations than of determining and expressing in concrete form this *phenomenology for ourselves* which has given a number of present-day readers the impression, on reading Husserl or Heidegger, not so much of encountering a new philosophy as of recognising what they had been waiting for.[2]

It is not our business here to inquire whether or not the interpretations which will be given of Hegel, Husserl, then of Marx or Nietzsche are faithful to the thought they seek to render. Clearly

---

[1] *L'entretien infini* (Gallimard, 1969), p. 26.
[2] PP, p. 11.

they betray it, but perhaps this betrayal is only a way of highlighting what Heidegger called the 'not-thought' inherent in that thought.

A final word on the characteristics of the *domain in which philosophical utterance circulates*.

This space has proved remarkably stable, at least until recently when some creakings became audible, induced by the advent of powerful mass media (television, etc.) to add to the networks of communication already established since the end of the last century.

The *university site* of philosophy is marked by its concentric, highly centralised formation. The *lycées* provide the universities with the bulk of their audience in the form of future secondary-school teachers. These *lycée* teachers are, in theory, recruited by the State by means of a competitive examination system. Given that the content of these examinations (*agrégation*, CAPES) is a function of the sixth form (*classe de philosophie*) syllabus, the teaching of philosophy in France is more or less determined by the nature and function of that syllabus. Officially, the Syllabus, this masterpiece of rigour and coherence, is fixed by unanimous consent. In reality, it is the outcome of a compromise between the various prevailing tendencies, and this is why the much celebrated Masterpiece is so frequently overhauled. Charged by some with propagating a reactionary ideology, by others with eliminating whatever still remained of authentic philosophy in the preceding syllabus, successive versions reflect the momentary balance of *political forces*, not only within the teaching body itself, but also in the country at large.

Few people claim to be satisfied with the syllabus as it stands, and many call for its reform. Nobody, however, questions the need for a syllabus of some sort. This cult of the Syllabus, which never fails to astonish foreigners, is explained by the French veneration for the institution of the *baccalauréat*, that incarnation of the egalitarian ideal. As regards philosophy, to sit the *baccalauréat* consists in the following: on the same day, at the same hour and for the same length of time, all candidates are required to commit similarly worded answers to identical sheets of paper in response – until quite recently – to a single question drawn from the Syllabus. These uniform products are then corrected by the teaching body in compliance with express directives unfailingly provided by the ministry for the occasion. The impartiality of correction is ensured by organising a rota of examiners from town to town, so that no candidate may be known in person by his examiner. Hence the necessity for a single Syllabus, the same for all French *lycées* on the planet Earth and others too, if need be.

The recruitment of teachers, which I cannot go into in detail here, works – needless to say – on similar principles. The *concours d'agrégation* is a veritable initiation rite, severing candidates from everything vaguely deemed to be evil (the provinces, the 'soil', local particularisms) to turn them into civic-minded State missionaries. In this respect, the predominant role of the president of the *jury d'agrégation* is worth stressing. Directly nominated by the minister, he selects the other members of the board, presides over the deliberations, and decides on the subjects for examination (taken from the Syllabus of the *classe de philosophie*); these subjects in turn will determine the syllabus in philosophy departments preparing students for the examination. The very style of French philosophy is perpetually being affected by this chain of events. At the time when neo-Kantianism, in the person of Léon Brunschvicg, presided over the *jury d'agrégation*, the immense majority of students applied themselves to assimilating the thoughts of Plato, Descartes, and Kant, read in that order, as the progression of consciousness towards Mind. But as regards those authors whom neo-Kantianism rejects, such as Aristotle or Hegel, no more than a summary refutation was required.

Teachers of philosophy being civil servants in France, it follows that the discipline has inevitable political repercussions. These are negligible in periods of national stability, but become determinant when the State appears threatened. At the beginning of the Third Republic, university philosophy was entrusted with a mission by the State – to impress upon students the legitimacy of the new Republican institutions. Two doctrines contended for this role: Durkheim's sociological positivism, and neo-Kantian rationalism (deriving from Renouvier, later personified in Brunschvicg). The second was to prevail in the end. Although opposed to each other, both these doctrines teach that mankind, from its distant origins onwards, has not ceased to progress towards the agreement of all human beings upon certain reasonable principles – precisely those on which Republican institutions are based. We shall see how, for the generation of 1930, the starting point was a desire to escape from this optimistic view of history.

But it is, of course, in the extra-university domain (newspapers, reviews, mass media) that philosophies are immediately called upon to divulge their political significance. In France, the development of a political position remains the decisive test, disclosing as it does the definitive meaning of a mode of thought. It is as if the heart of the matter had not been reached until, from suppositions about the One and the Many, or about the nature of knowledge, the subject shifted to the issue of the next elections or the attitude of the Communist Party. Especially surprising here is the abruptness of the leap from the Idea of good to palpable good. In fact, despite heavy over-investment in the political dimension of philosophical debate, almost no important political thinking as such can be seen to thrive within it. The major works of political philosophy in French can be counted on the fingers of one hand. Thus the existentialists, for example, have made innumerable political declarations and taken innumerable political stances; yet their writings are innocent of the least theory of the state, or of any reflection on modern forms of warfare. It is as though this or that philosophical statement might be instantly attributed to this or that political party. Curious reputations are made and unmade. Until 1968, epistemology was broadly to the left, and metaphysics to the right; but with the present emergence of ecological preoccupations, epistemology appears reactionary, whereas metaphysics takes on a subversive aspect.

Such reversals of political values on the opinions market do little to clarify discussion. However, the undeniable evidence here is that the relation of philosophy to *opinion*, in France, is a relation primarily to *political* opinion, and secondly to *literary* opinion, or to literary groups (for example the *nouveau roman*, or *Tel Quel*). Since, for their part, these groups also advertise their political positions, the various relations of alliance and opposition intersect. At a certain period, the *Tel Quel* group, for instance, advocated 'support for the Communist Party', and the reader who shared its views on modern literature would be pro-Communist at the same time. But the same reader would either have to renounce this literary doctrine, or else break with 'support for the P.C.F.' when at a later date *Tel Quel* became pro-Chinese. And according to whether the reader bought the magazine *Tel Quel* at one or other of these periods, he would or would not find in it articles by Jacques Derrida.

This survey will therefore be obliged to take occasional account of the political context, although, needless to add, only where philosophical discourse itself has chosen to connect with such a context.

1

The humanisation of nothingness

The generation of the three H's was the first generation of the twentieth century. Chronology shows that the spokesmen of this generation were born at the beginning of the century (Sartre in 1905, Merleau-Ponty in 1908) and that they made themselves known during the years immediately preceding the Second World War. Older writers, already established by this date, belong to the nineteenth century; this applies to the Bergsonian generation (Bergson himself was born in 1858, and had published his doctoral thesis in 1889).

The Interpretation of Hegel

It may well be that the future of the world, and thus the sense of the present and the significance of the past, will depend in the last analysis on contemporary interpretations of Hegel's works.

(Alexandre Kojève)

There is no clearer sign of the changes in mentality – the revolt against neo-Kantianism, the decline of Bergsonianism – than the triumphal return of Hegel. Banished by the neo-Kantians, he curiously, and suddenly, became a vanguard writer, quoted with respect in leading circles. Two reasons seem chiefly to account for this resurgence. One was the renewal of interest in Marxism that occurred in the wake of the Russian Revolution – part of the prestige surrounding the Bolshevik leaders reflected back upon Hegel, in so far as Lenin, for instance, had actively recommended

him for study. The other was the influence of the course given by
Alexandre Kojève at the Ecole Pratique des Hautes Etudes,
beginning in 1933 and lasting until 1939. The text of this course,
which was followed by most of the protagonists of the generation
of the three H's, was published in 1947 under the editorship of
Raymond Queneau[1].

Nothing could be more characteristic than the change in connotation undergone by the word *dialectic*. Before 1930 it was understood pejoratively; for a neo-Kantian the dialectic was the 'logic of
appearances', whereas for a Bergsonian it could engender nothing
but a purely verbal philosophy. After 1930, on the contrary, the
word was almost always used in a eulogistic sense. It was now
thought proper to transcend 'analytical reason' (the Kantian
Verstand) or again 'mechanism', by means of the dialectic. The
Dialectic became such a lofty concept that it would have been
offensive to request a definition. For thirty years it was almost the
God of negative theology – beyond formulation, it could only be
approached through the explanation of what it was not. Thus
Sartre was to write in 1960, after so many years of dialectical
thinking:

> The dialectic itself... could never be the object of
> concepts, since its movement engenders and dissolves
> them all.[2]

Certainly a disappointing assertion, when it is found in a volume
of close on eight hundred pages devoted, if the title is to be
believed, to explaining precisely in what the dialectical mode of
thinking might consist.

This prestige attaching to the dialectic only began to fade with
the advent of a second generation (after 1960). Burning the idol
venerated until now, this generation denounced the dialectic as
the supreme illusion, from which it sought to free itself through
recourse, this time, to Nietzsche.

---

[1] Queneau evokes this period in his article in homage to Georges Bataille:
'Premières confrontations avec Hegel', *Critique*, nos. 195–6, Aug.–Sept.
1963. Among the list of those who regularly attended the course given
by Kojève (or Kotjenikov) the names of Raymond Aron, Georges
Bataille, Alexandre Koyré, Pierre Klossowski, Jacques Lacan, Maurice
Merleau-Ponty, Eric Weil and Father Fessard are to be found; and also,
less frequently, that of André Breton.

[2] CRD, p. 106.

In the report which he had drafted for the congress on Hegel in 1930, concerning *the state of Hegelian studies in France*[3], Alexandre Koyré began by confessing to the slenderness of his survey. He apologised for having so little to say: in France, there was no Hegelian school. During the ten years which followed, the position altered so greatly that, by 1946, Merleau-Ponty was able to write in the Hegelian terms which surprise us once more today:

> All the great philosophical ideas of the past century – the philosophies of Marx and Nietzsche, phenomenology, German existentialism, and psychoanalysis – had their beginnings in Hegel; it was he who started the attempt to explore the irrational and integrate it into an expanded reason, which remains the task of our century... If we do not despair of a *truth* above and beyond divergent points of view, if we remain dedicated to a new classicism, an organic civilisation, while maintaining the sharpest sense of subjectivity, then no task in the cultural order is more urgent than re-establishing the connection between, on the one hand, the thankless doctrines which try to forget their Hegelian origin and, on the other, that origin itself.[4]

In writing this, Merleau-Ponty had undoubtedly not the least intention of paradox, but only of expressing the common view of a well-established fact. By virtue of what secret genealogy is Hegel at the origin of such 'thankless doctrines' as psychoanalysis or the thought of Nietzsche? Merleau-Ponty did not specify at the time. But, however ambitious the aims of this appraisal may seem, it is of great interest to us. It points to the place where the multiple references of the period converged; it reveals the desire for a *common language*, which it seemed at the time would have to be Hegelian.[5]

[3] Republished in his *Etudes d'histoire de la pensée philosophique* (Armand Colin, 1961), pp. 205–30; in his postscript of 1961, Koyré observes that Hegel's position in France 'has changed beyond recognition'.
[4] SNS, pp. 109–10.
[5] Such 'truths' die hard. At the Colloquy on Bataille organised by *Tel Quel* at Cerisy-la-Salle in 1972, Sollers could still declare that Nietzsche, Bataille, Lacan and Marxism–Leninism were to be understood as the effects of 'the explosion of the Hegelian system' (*Bataille*, 10/18, Union Générale d'Editions, 1973, p. 36).

In 1930 Hegel was a Romantic philosopher who had been refuted long ago by scientific progress (this was Brunschvicg's view, which Koyré did not omit to quote in his *Report*). By 1945 Hegel had become the apex of classical philosophy and the origin of all the most modern achievements in the field. Then the wheel revolved again. The thesis of Gilles Deleuze, published in 1968, begins by evoking the 'atmosphere of the period'; in it we find the Heideggerian 'ontological difference', 'structuralism', the *nouveau roman*, etc. He goes on to say that

> all these signs may be attributed to a generalised anti-Hegelianism. Difference and repetition have replaced the identical and the negative, identity and contradiction.[6]

Foucault too, in his inaugural address at the Collège de France in 1970, observes that

> whether through logic or epistemology, whether through Marx or Nietzsche, our entire epoch struggles to disengage itself from Hegel.[7]

In 1945, then, all that was modern sprang from Hegel, and the only way to reconcile the contradictory demands of modernity was to advance an interpretation of Hegel. In 1968, all that was modern – that is, Marx, Freud etc., as before – was hostile to Hegel. The difference separating the two generations lies in the inversion of the sign that marked the relationship to Hegel: everywhere a *minus* was substituted for the *plus*. The reference point itself remained the same, but in the one case the concern was with drawing towards it (returning, like the prodigal son, to the Hegelian hearth), whereas in the other it was with drawing away (putting an end to the tyranny of Hegelianism).

Those who see in Hegel's work a monument of rationalism will no doubt be surprised at the respect accorded to Hegel by the future French 'existentialists'. If existence is wholly absurd and unjustifiable, how can the notion that 'all that is real is rational'

---

[6] DR, p. 1.
[7] *L'ordre du discours* (Gallimard, 1971), p. 74.

have been accommodated? Merleau-Ponty's diagnosis, quoted above, offers a good explanation of this state of affairs. The expansion of reason may be understood in two ways. It is tenable, certainly, that reason enlarges its empire, and gains sway in areas hitherto foreign to it (history and its violence, existence and its contingency, the unconscious and its stratagems). But equally we might respond to the critique of reason-as-it-exists implicit in the phrase 'to expand reason', and see in this expansion much more than a mere extension – rather a thorough metamorphosis of thought. The ambiguity encountered here is the essential difficulty which the interpretation of Hegel must confront – an interpretation very much in demand, first in a positive sense ('Hegel will draw us together'), then in a critical sense ('Deliver us from Hegelianism'). Non-dialectical thinking would hold to the opposition between the rational and the irrational, but any thinking which aspires to be dialectical must, by definition, induce in reason a movement towards what is entirely foreign to it, towards *the other*. The whole issue now rests upon whether *the other* has been returned to *the same* in the course of this movement, or whether (so as to embrace rational and irrational, the *same* and the *other*, at once) reason will have had to transform itself, losing its initial identity, *ceasing to be the same* and *becoming other with the other*. For the other of reason is unreason, or madness. Thus the problem is raised of the passage of reason through *madness* or aberration, a passage which would precede all access to an authentic *wisdom*.

Kojève, who preferred to speak of wisdom rather than of rationality, inclined towards the last hypothesis. According to him, Hegel came very close to madness at the moment of attaining to absolute knowledge. And, in general terms, far from emphasising the reasonable and conciliatory side of Hegel's thought, his reading dwells on its paradoxical, excessive, violent and, above all, sanguinary features. In the face of the events of 1968, Kojève is reported to have said that, since there had been no bloodshed, nothing had happened ... His commentary on the *Phenomenology of Mind* presents it as an account of universal history in which bloody strife – and not 'reason' – is responsible for the progress of events towards the happy conclusion. He loses no opportunity of recalling the cannon fire that Hegel is supposed to have heard as he ended his manuscript at Jena. This explains why we find, among the most assiduous followers of Kojève's course, the very figures who were to supply most of the ammunition for the 'generalised anti-Hegelianism' which Deleuze observed around him in 1968; among others, Bataille, on whom the influence of Kojève was decisive,[8] and Klossowski.[9] In the version advanced by Kojève, Hegel's thought presents a number of features that might well attract a Nietzschean. It contains an element of risk and adventure; it endangers the thinker's very person, his *identity*; it reaches out beyond the generally accepted measure of good and evil. Hegel had declared that philosophical speculation aimed to reconcile and unite 'the working days of the week' with 'the Sunday of existence'; in other words, life's *profane* aspects (work, family life, conjugal fidelity, professional responsibility, savings account, etc.) with its *sacred* aspects (play, sacrificial spending, delirium, states of poetic exultation).[10] Raymond Queneau, editor of the course, called one of his novels *Le dimanche de la vie*. There is little doubt that what so held the attention of Kojève's listeners was his ability to compromise philosophy – in the sense that we speak of 'compromising acquaintances' – by forcing it to traverse areas of existence on which it had not impinged until then: political cynicism, the virtue of massacre and violence, and, in a global way, *the unreasonable origins of reason*. Through Kojève's gift of eloquence, these aspects of Hegel's work, which had long been treated as the regrettable side of his philosophy, now came to be seen as the measure of its value. Reality is a fight to the death between men for ludicrous stakes – people will risk their lives to defend a flag, to obtain satisfaction for an insult, etc. – and any philosophy that neglects this essential fact is an idealistic mystification. In brutal terms, this was Kojève's teaching.

Kojève bequeathed to his listeners a *terrorist conception of history*. The motif of Terror recurs in each successive debate up to the present day. It appears in the title of the book written by Merleau-Ponty in 1947 to justify a policy of 'support for the P.C.F.' in spite of the Moscow trials (*Humanisme et terreur*). It

---

[8] See Bataille's article on Kojève, 'Hegel, la mort, et le sacrifice', in *Deucalion*, 1955, no. 5, pp. 21–43.

[9] Klossowski explains this transition from Hegel to Nietzsche in his book *Nietzsche et le cercle vicieux* (Mercure de France, 1969), p. 32.

[10] This opposition lies at the core of Bataille's thinking (cf. *La part maudite*, Minuit, 1949).

appears in Sartre's analyses of the French Revolution in his *Critique of Dialectical Reason* (the theme of 'fraternity–terror') as well as in his apologia for violence. It appears finally in the great examination of conscience undertaken by the intelligentsia which led it, in the form of the New Philosophers, 1977–8, to confess to the fascination exercised over intellectuals by the most sanguinary powers, precisely because, unhampered by scruple, the latter are prepared to demonstrate what power is. André Glucksmann has written a book accusing all philosophers, without exception, of consummating in their speculative works a drive towards domination, which would explain the complicity of philosophers and tyrants.[11] Such an obviously excessive indictment shows the extent to which Kojève's teaching has been assimilated and continues to dominate our thinking. For it was Kojève who wrote that there is no essential difference between the philosopher and the tyrant;[12] no doubt life is too brief for one man to be both philosopher and tyrant at the same time, but the difference arises from this fact alone, so that the tyrant is never anything but a statesman attempting to realise a philosophical idea in the world. Since the truth of a philosophical notion is judged, explains Kojève, by its realisation in history, the philosopher cannot reproach the tyrant for tyrannising in the name of an idea, as is always the case with modern tyrannies, where those in power consistently claim to represent an ideology. The basis of terrorist philosophy is not merely, then, as Glucksmann believes, the 'desire to know', but rather *the pragmatic definition of truth* ('the true is the outcome'), a definition which would certainly not win unanimous agreement from all philosophers. This suggestion can be observed in the following passage from Kojève:

> What then is the morality of Hegel? ... What exists is good inasmuch as it exists. All action, being a negation of the existing given, is therefore bad, or sinful. But sin may be forgiven. How? By its success. Success absolves the crime because success is a new reality that *exists*. But how

[11] *Les maîtres penseurs* (Grasset, 1977).
[12] *Tyrannie et sagesse* (Gallimard, 1954), p. 252.

can success be estimated? Before this can be done, History must have come to an end.[13]

This is the reason why revolutions are necessarily bloody.

The Search for a Concrete Philosophy

The generation of 1930 has several times given an account of its apprenticeship. In revolt against academic idealism, it demanded, as it said, a 'concrete philosophy',[14] which later acquired the name of existentialism. 'Idealism', however, may be understood either in the popular or in the metaphysical sense.

A man is an idealist, in the popular sense of the word, when he assumes as his guide in life an 'idea' or an 'ideal'. By 'idea' we mean a 'mental vision', one which does not originate in sight, therefore, and cannot be reduced to any 'lesson of experience'. It is well known that the lessons of experience are bitter, and lead more readily to 'realism', or to 'cynicism', than to idealism. The error of the idealist, if indeed it is wrong to be one, is that he takes no account of what life might teach him, and behaves as if things occurred in reality just as they ought to occur according to the *idea* that he entertains of an ideal world. The idealist's error is known as *abstraction*. He begins by ignoring the irreducible difference between the reasonable world, commensurate with the good, of which he speaks, and the unsettled world, impervious to reason, of which he speaks much less. The world he talks of is one in which people talk; in it, words are exchanged, not blows or cannon fire. Hence the demand for a *concrete* philosophy to abolish the lie of idealism.

The limitations of such a critique of idealism are immediately apparent. The idealist is accused of acting as if the world as it should be, regulated and reasonable, were already here now. He must then be an ingenuous dreamer, if he is not a cunning conservative, or a professor in the throes of academic dotage. It is not his ideal with which he is reproached. Far from being considered stupid or extravagant, it is accepted as the accurate definition of good. What he is reproached with is his belief, exempting him

[13] *Intr. Hegel*, p. 95.
[14] CRD, p. 23.

from all action, that this idea has already been accomplished in the present.

The result is that the victory of concrete philosophy over abstraction amounts to a chronological adjustment. Since the good has yet to be achieved, the idealist, for whom we have no time today, will be right tomorrow. *The error of today* will become *the truth of tomorrow* – a dialectical *tour de force* to be accomplished by action, or *praxis*, to use a would-be Marxist term. Indeed, this word *praxis* was to be one of the key words of the years 1950–60. Use of the word *praxis* where previously the word *action* had served arose incontestably from assiduous study, during this period, of the writings of the young Marx. It is Merleau-Ponty's constant theme in speaking of Marx: *praxis* is the 'locus of meaning', and this was Marx's immense discovery.

> What Marx calls *praxis* is the meaning which appears spontaneously at the intersection of the actions by which man organises his relationship with nature and with others.[15]

In his enthusiasm for *praxis*, Sartre even wrote:

> All that is real is praxis and all that is praxis is real.[16]

After 1965, so as to take their distance from this 'existential' version of Marxism, people no longer said 'praxis' but 'practice'. Writing, for instance, became 'signifying practice' and philosophy a 'theoretical practice'.

At the end of the day, that is, at the *end of history*, idealism would be the true philosophy. In the meantime, this philosophy was false and misleading, since it discouraged action. To act, in this case, could only mean one thing: to oppose whatever impeded the real from being the ideal, in other words, to attack the *reality of the real*. In its critique of idealism, 'concrete philosophy' arrives at an activist position. Philosophy, as revolt against the very reality of the real, fuses with a practical programme of opposition. Indeed, opposition is an understatement – we should speak of an *opposition within the opposition*. For the opposition to which the existentialist belonged was marked out for him by all that he opposed, by the

---

[15] *Eloge de la philosophie* (Gallimard, 1953), p. 69; *In Praise of Philosophy*, trans. James E. Edie and John Wild (Evanston, Ill., Northwestern U.P. 1963).
[16] Quoted by Merleau-Ponty in AD, p. 179.

reality which he abhorred: bourgeoisie, family, institutions etc. If the established order led him to think that its most dangerous enemy was the P.C.F. or the U.S.S.R., then the existentialist satisfied the imperative of betrayal by making known his sympathy for communism. He could not, however, carry this as far as membership of the party, for such an initiative would have amounted to sanctioning the measure of *reality* which existed in communist organisations, or in socialist countries. This is why he created an opposition within the opposition, so as always to awaken its destructive potential. Yet it was enough that the existentialist's enemy (namely *his own person* as he detested it in the form of his class background and way of life) should fix on another privileged adversary for existentialist politics to be turned upside down. He would condemn the organisations that he had hitherto defended, reproaching them for their betrayal, discovering his sympathy with others which, henceforth, were to embody for him the purity of negation. In this way, the hopes of existentialist *commitment* migrated from the U.S.S.R. to China, from proletarian internationalism to the nationalism of the ex-colonies, from Algeria to Cuba or vice versa, from workers to students, from men to women etc. All these successive positions, contradictory yet always peremptory, made a weather vane of existentialist politics, susceptible to the least breath of wind. Such a fundamental lack of resolution at the heart of the resolve thought of as 'commitment' was well explained by Merleau-Ponty's formula in *Humanisme et terreur*: the communists have values in spite of themselves, this is why we support them. In other words, the grounds of approbation, and eventually of condemnation, are external to what constitutes the object of these successive judgments. After 1968, for example, Sartre levelled the charge of bureaucracy against Soviet socialism. But it had been no less bureaucratic when he was undertaking its defence during the 1950s, under Stalin. What had changed in the meantime was not the U.S.S.R., nor even Sartre, but world politics (the transition from the Cold War to peaceful co-existence).

By virtue of its very principle, the doctrine of *praxis* lacks all means of orienting or of judging action. It maintains that the idealist's ideal is a mystification now, but that it will have a meaning in the future. Meanwhile, then, a 'morality of realism', drawn from experience, will have to suffice as grounds for action.

It will not, therefore, be possible to look to philosophy for a rule of action. No *idea* can direct the philosopher of *praxis* in his actions, except the idea that he must act. Action becomes completely indeterminate. The revolt against idealist abstraction gives rise only to an *abstract* apologia for action and violence. The resolution is there to act against ills in general, but in a specific situation – and all situations are specific – the same set of premises can justify any decision whatsoever. Sartre's drama, as well as his political articles, provides ample illustration of this difficulty. The numerous disputes within the editorship of the magazine, *Les Temps Modernes*, have always been of a political rather than a philosophical order. Although thought should, in theory, commit itself in a concrete situation and arrive at a political position, this particular way of thinking actually remained abstract, since it was able to prove both the *for* and the *against* of any position without the least modification of its premises.

Taken in the metaphysical sense of the term, 'idealism' is the name of the doctrine which holds *being* and *being-known* as equivalent. This is the definition offered by Brunschvicg, in Lalande's *Vocabulaire de la Philosophie*,[17] under *'idéalisme'*:

> Idealism maintains that metaphysics may be reduced to theory of knowledge. The affirmation of being rests upon the determination of being as being-known; an admirably lucid thesis (pending further analysis of the word *known*) in contrast with realism, which rests upon the intuition of being as such.

Since idealism equates *being* and *being-known*, it is possible to detect the first signs of the existential revolt against abstraction in Kant's critique of the ontological proof of the existence of God. His analysis of the example of the hundred thalers is well known. In the hundred real (*wirklich*) thalers, there is nothing more than in the hundred possible thalers. The amount is the same in each case. Consequently, the real holds no more than the merely possible. Yes, but we must be specific: no more, that is, from the point of view of the concept, of logic. The hundred thalers that I speak of, when for instance I lament their absence, are of course the same

---

[17] This *Vocabulaire* (Presses Universitaires de France), revised and re-edited several times, constitutes an invaluable document on the state of language and mentality before the existentialist irruption.

hundred thalers whose presence in my pocket is desirable. The *being-known* of the hundred thalers is the same in both cases. Now should these hundred thalers eventually reach my pocket, they will be the very ones whose presence I desired. The concept remains unaltered, then, by the passage from the possible (concept) to the real (existence); and yet my wealth is thereby altered. Their *being* is therefore not the same. And *being* is therefore not identical to *being-known*. In terms of the Kantian definition of existence – unanimously and uncritically adopted by the existentialist generation – existence is not a predicate of the thing. It eludes the concept, and passes into the realm of the inconceivable, whence the complicity of existence with all forms of the inconceivable: contingency, chance, the unjustifiable, the unforeseen. And since the most thorough distinction must be made between having and not having the hundred thalers, between presence and absence, it follows that the concept is indifferent to the most fundamental of differences. The *same* concept will hold for the thing, whether absent or present, ignoring this *otherness*. It was therefore necessary to abandon the concept in order to state the definitive issue – existence or non-existence, being or non-being. This was the reason for the extensive use of literary (fictional) forms of discourse – drama, confessional autobiography, novels etc. – as opposed to theoretical forms.

The Objection of Solipsism

If 'being' = 'being-known', it must be ascertained by whom this being is known. Is it myself, a specific individual, distinct from my fellow men? Can it be anybody? Thus idealism comes up against the problem of solipsism. It is accused of having to admit the absurd thesis whereby whoever pronounces the *cogito* can only conclude, 'My existence is certain, yours is much less so.' And, more radically, 'I am, therefore you are not.'

At a session of the French Society of Philosophy, during which Brunschvicg had developed the arguments of the idealist position, one of the participants, André Cresson, put to him the question of the existence of others. If being may be asserted only in so far as it is known, what is the being of others? For the 'knowing' subject, Brunschvicg for example, what is the existence that should be attributed to others, for example to André Cresson? In the minutes of the session, the following exchange is recorded:

> BRUNSCHVICG: The idea that I have of his consciousness is a component in the system of my judgments about existence.
>
> CRESSON: I cannot accept that I might be reduced to a judgment in Mr Brunschvicg's consciousness, and I doubt whether those present, for their part, would be prepared to accept this either. Moreover, to be consistent, Mr Brunschvicg ought to declare that his is the only consciousness, and that the sole aim of knowledge is to draw up a harmonious table of its representations for the purposes of his solitary ego.[18]

If the 'plurality of consciousnesses', as it was known, may be posed as an objection to idealist metaphysics, this is clearly because the nature of the knowing subject, raised to the status of arbiter of being by means of the equation of being and being-known, has not been sufficiently determined. Brunschvicg was fond of saying that the history of Egypt was actually the history of Egyptology. The Egyptians would ultimately owe their existence, then, to the Egyptologists. And, quite generally, the weakness of neo-Kantianism may have been to invoke some nebulous 'Mind', represented more or less as a community of men of goodwill, with no further definition of what was, after all, to become the mainstay of the world. Did the knowing subject resemble a learned society, or the League of Nations? Might it be envisaged as some kind of association of candidates for the Nobel Prize? Would such a world-principle be adequate to the responsibility involved?

If Brunschvicg's work-table or his pen – objects whose status in his doctrine is, equally, that of phenomena integral to the sum of his judgments concerning existence – could talk, they would no doubt protest with the same vigour as André Cresson against their reduction to such a purely intentional status. The only privilege remaining to the interlocutor is therefore to voice his disagreement, in words, with the idealist philosopher. The phenomenon protests against synthetic *a priori* judgments! The

---

[18] *Bulletin de la Société française de philosophie* (1921), p. 51.

idea of his own person which the interlocutor harbours is in no way consonant with the version proposed by the idealist. The existence of a second consciousness thus calls the idealist equation into question, as it becomes impossible to say whether the being-known of that second consciousness is its otherness as perceived by the first, or the knowledge that it has of itself.

The 'problem of the other', which furnished the writings of French phenomenology with their principal subject matter, is essentially only one particular instance of the reduction of being to representation. The *esse* of others becomes reduced, like every other *esse*, to the *percipi*. The difficulty arises from the fact that, inasmuch as he endorses the idealist theory, the other will claim for himself the privileges of the *percipiens*, and will demand to be recognised, not only as the logical subject of a judgment concerning existence in any given consciousness, but also as the subject of the very consciousness within which this judgment is being articulated. Clearly then, the objection of solipsism may be raised with one of two contrary purposes: either to contest the premises of idealism by demonstrating the absurdity of its end-result, or to contest the idealist's optimism by demanding that he accommodate this dramatic end-result within his doctrine. The second possibility defines the 'concrete philosophy' of the 1930s.

The conflict of consciousness exists in embryonic form within the Cartesian *cogito*. For what was known as 'the philosophy of consciousness', that is, for the Cartesian tradition, the 'I think, I am', was at once the *origin* and the *rule* of all truth. It is the first truth, the truth which inaugurates all others; it is the exemplary truth. The *ego*, as it is given in *ego cogito, ego sum*, is the *absolute* to which all else is *relative*; its truth, independent of any other, is the condition of all others. The word 'absolute', destined for a brilliant career in modern philosophy, is the one used by Descartes in the *Regulae ad directionem ingenii*. Now there can never be several simultaneous absolutes. A second absolute (an other) is necessarily a rival of the first (myself, *ego*). The movement from the *cogito* to the *cogitamus* is not at all the same as the movement from the 'I' in solitary meditation to the 'we' of the Republic of minds. In the plural, absolutes are no more than *pretenders* to the absolute, competitors clawing over one another for the throne.

The limit to the ambitions of concrete philosophy is already apparent. By describing itself in such a way, it certainly revealed the modesty of its revolt against its forerunners, since it assumed the essential feature of their teaching, namely the *cogito*, the so-called inevitable departure point of all philosophy. For what is a 'concrete philosophy' but an abstract philosophy completed by the very thing of which it had made abstraction? Academic idealism had failed to take into account the rivalry inherent in the very notion of the *subject*. Henceforth the status of the subject appeared to be threatened, forever on the point of being overcome by a new arrival and having to be defended against all intruders. As a new version of the story of Crusoe's encounter with Friday, the phenomenology of the other constantly presents multiple facets of contradiction: the other is a phenomenon *for me*, but I am no less a phenomenon *for him*; manifestly, one of us will have to renounce the role of subject and content himself with being *for himself* what he is *for the other*. In such circumstances it is easy to understand the success of the Hegelian dialectic of Master and Slave, which the generation of 1930 never tired of quoting, and which Kojève had made the key to his interpretation of the *Phenomenology of Mind*.

The Origin of Negation

In a concrete philosophy, consciousness may no longer be described as a sequence of representations accompanied by, as Kant said, an 'I think'. Consciousness is no longer the simple representation of oneself, but rather the representation of the self as a being confronted by the outside world, whose identity is precarious, and which must struggle in order to exist. *The other* endangers *the same*. The new status of consciousness may be summarised in one word: *negativity*. The being of consciousness was said henceforth to be conceived as a 'dialectical' being.

The question of the negative is very characteristic of the evolution of French philosophy. It is worth indicating the various ways in which it has been posed in the course of the twentieth century. No one denies that the negative appears in judgment and in the form of the negation 'not'. The difficulty is to ascertain from where this negation 'not' could possibly have sprung. Consider the statement 'Jane is not there'. In what does the possibility of such a statement reside? Perhaps we assume that the status of negation is no different from that of affirmation; in either case, any judgment will be the expression of a state of affairs. This hypothesis would force us to concede the existence of negative states of affairs, facts of absence or of non-being, capable of expression as such. Or, alternatively, we may deny that negation is the simple record of a matter of fact, for example that Jane is indeed not in the same place as the author of this negative judgment. The second hypothesis would have the negation express a conflict between the observable state of affairs and some discrepant state of affairs, both opposed in the mind of the person who formulates the negation. In short, we must either attribute to non-being the paradoxical ability to *present* itself, or consider that man is able to introduce non-being by virtue of the mind's capacity to set itself against what is. At the beginning of the century, the most common position was that which derived nothingness from negation. Being nothing at all, 'nothing' is excluded from the scheme of things. A negative judgment – of the type 'It's nothing' – does not correspond to anything negative in the thing's manner of being or of appearing. The thing is content to be what it is; as for the nothing, it stems from the freedom of the mind, a freedom which must be defined by the power to oppose a *no* to whatever is simply given. Such is the most classic thesis of post-Kantian idealism, of which this example, afforded by Lachelier, prefigures Sartre's developments:

> If to exist is to be posited by the mind, the mind can with the same freedom posit any being, or refuse to posit anything at all (or at least, conceive of itself by abstraction as positing nothing; conceive of its own freedom outside any actual exercise of this freedom...)[19]

The positivity of being, the humanity of nothingness, and the negative essence of freedom: these three theses are inseparable. The metaphysics (doctrine of being) of idealism is a positivism: 'to be' means 'to be the case' or 'to be observable data'. As for negation, it testifies to the capacity of the mind to *de-pose* what actually is, or what it has itself judged 'to be the case', in order to *posit* instead what is not (the possible, the future, the desirable).

[19] Under '*Néant*' ('Nothingness') in Lalande's *Vocabulaire*.

This freedom to depose indicates that the *given* is, more profoundly, a *posited*, and that its positive aspect arises from an initial 'position': the given may be deposed (negated) at any time, having come into being through an original affirmation made by the mind for reasons of which it is sole judge. Only that which, upon examination by the subject, deserves the quality of being, will receive as much. It is not hard to retrace the Cartesian origin of these three theses.

Bergson went still further in the annihilation of nothingness. In *L'Evolution créatrice* (1907), he devoted close on thirty pages to the pursuit of this 'pseudo-idea'. Rounding on the 'false problems' set, in his view, by Metaphysics, Bergson demonstrates how such problems presuppose that negative ideas have meaning. Thus the problem of finality – how may order be explained? –presupposes a possible disorder. Leibniz's statement of the metaphysical problem – why is there something, rather than nothing? – clearly shows that the metaphysician sets *nothing* on a par with *something*, or even accords it a certain priority. But in reality, explains Bergson, this *nothing* is an effect of language. Before we speak, we are imbued with the present and deal only with what is. It is language that sometimes inverts this relationship with the *present* into the statement of an *absence*, by way of the negation. We say 'The table is not white' when the table before us may be black, brown or red; it never exhibits the colour 'non-white'. Bergson concludes from this that there is more in the notion of nothing than in the notion of something, since the former entails first the notion of something, then the result of an operation, positive also, which consists in making away with the thing, while at the same time failing to specify what is to replace it. Certainly the space is never left vacant.

Perhaps the problem is merely referred further away. If, as Bergson holds in opposition to all his idealist colleagues, intelligence can only affirm, either directly ('The table is black') or by using an indeterminate form of negative appearance ('The table is not white'), then how can it, for example, deceive itself into positing that which is not as that which is? The answer to this objection is called *desire*. If the operation of negation, in language, is useful, this is because the mind is in danger of confusing the immediate state of affairs, which it might observe if it were less preoccupied or distracted, with a state that has already disappeared (regret) or has not yet arrived (hope). Negation is thus a precaution against self-deception; it is also, in its way, a point of access to the real.

For the Kantians as for Bergson, the origin of nothingness is negation; but what is the origin of negation? The Bergsonian explanation has all the characteristics of a conjuring trick in which the negative is not eliminated, as was promised, but simply palmed. First, the *absence* of something is transformed into a negative judgment concerning the affirmation of its presence ('The table is not white'='You would be mistaken in calling it white'), and then the *negativity* of this negation is transformed into the *positivity* of a desire which is responsible for such apparently negative modes as disappointed expectation, nostalgia, error, etc. The question here is to know whether this desire can be called positive, and to what degree nothingness, far from being generated, has not quite simply become *humanised*. If indeed desire were only the mask of nothingness, then negation itself, supposedly the generator of nothingness, would be its derivation.

Desire as positive or negative? Such is the ground on which Deleuze takes issue with the dialectic. The 'philosophy of desire', as it was known after 1970, whose classic work is *The Anti-Oedipus*, claims its descent from Nietzsche, and adopts one of his directives: 'the overthrow of Platonism'. Deleuze opposes the affirmative notion of a productive, creative desire to the 'Platonist', then 'Christian' interpretation of desire as lack, distress, suffering. However, the debate about the nature of desire is more a settling of accounts between Deleuze, as disciple of Bergson, and the Hegelians (primarily Sartre and Lacan), than a conflict between Nietzsche and Plato. We know that in Plato desire is presented as a composite: though *Eros* is the child of *Penia*, or Lack, his father is *Poros*, the Happy Mean. Eros is thus a lack *here*, engendered by a presence *elsewhere*. For Hegel, desire is not like this. The term is used, in Kojève's commentaries, to translate the word *Begierde* as it figures in chapter IV of the *Phenomenology*. And since chapter IV is, in Kojève's view, the key to the whole work, dialectical philosophy can now be defined as the thinking which identifies desire with pure negativity, and sees in it not only a negation, but a negation of the negation.

The End of History

Alexandre Kojève was a very talented story-teller. In his commentaries, the austere Hegelian *Phenomenology* turns into a kind of serialised philosophical novel, where one dramatic scene follows another; picturesque characters come face to face, reversals of situation keep up the suspense, and the reader, avid to know the end of the story (*la fin de l'histoire*), clamours for more.

In a general sense, Kojève provided an *anthropological version* of Hegelian philosophy. This was at the time a novel approach for the French, acquainted as they were with the 'absolute idealism' and 'panlogism' of Hegel, but scarcely with 'left-Hegelianism'. The final scene in this humanist version of the Hegelian dialectic provides us also with its principle. The last episode in the narrative of the story is understood as corresponding to a final stage in human history itself, beyond which there are to be no further developments. Kojève never failed to insist, provocatively enough, on the startling consequences of this thesis. History is at an end, we enter now into its aftermath:

> In point of fact, the end of human Time, or History – that is, the definitive annihilation of Man properly speaking, or of the free and historical Individual – means quite simply the cessation of Action in the full sense of the term. Practically, this means the disappearance of wars and bloody revolutions. And also the disappearance of *Philosophy*; for since Man himself no longer changes essentially, there is no longer any reason to change the (true) principles which are at the basis of his understanding of the world and of himself. But all the rest can be preserved indefinitely; art, love, play, etc; in short everything that makes man *happy*. [20]

The 'end of history' is none other than the translation into figural and narrative language of what in the language of philosophy is known as absolute knowledge. Absolute knowledge is the science of the *identity* of subject and object (or of thought and being). This metaphysical thesis, undeniably obscure and incontestably 'idealist', was suddenly given a ready meaning, with a

[20] *Intr. Hegel*, p. 435 (in the note).

'realistic' even a 'materialist' look to it. The identity of subject and object, in the unravelling of this tale, meant that man (subject) would encounter nothing outside of himself (in the object) to impede the realisation of his projects. In other words, nature would be mastered and society appeased. Living in the world as if in a garden of flowers, finding a friend in everyone, man would go into retirement, throw over the work of history and become an Epicurean sage, given up to 'everything that makes man happy' (play, love, art, etc.). The end of history would be the end of *adversity*, the term which adequately translates Hegel's *Gegenständlichkeit*. The proposition stating the identity of subject and object which had hitherto been regarded as 'ideological' (mystificatory) would become true:

> ... Absolute knowledge, that is, Wisdom, presupposes the total success of Man's Negative Action. This Knowledge is possible only 1) within a *homogeneous* and *universal* State where no man is *exterior* to another, where there is no social *opposition* which is not suppressed, and 2) in the midst of a Nature that has been *tamed* by the labour of Man, and which, no longer *opposing* Man, ceases to be *alien* to him. [21]

I do not propose to discuss whether, in this narrative translation of the *Phenomenology*, Kojève deforms Hegel's thought, or brings its most profound sense to light. His interpretation claims to be humanist in that it designates human history as the space within which everything that has meaning must resolve itself. There is no truth except in history. There are therefore no eternal truths, since the world undergoes continual modification in the course of history. But there are errors which have the provisional appearance of truth, and those which, dialectically, become truths. For example, the Master in an ancient city state who averred, 'In every city, there are Masters and Slaves', seemed to be telling the truth, since his statement was verifiable throughout the ancient world. But he was to be 'refuted' as slaves became free in the course of human history; whereas the Slave – a Stoic slave – who in an ancient city state declared, 'I am a free man', appeared to be making a false judgment, but owing to history, his error was to

[21] *Intr. Hegel*, p. 301.

become a truth. It is therefore *action* which determines the true and the false. This is why the *dialectic* – in the classical sense, the development of true into false, and false into true – is considered henceforth to be the feature most proper to any conception of history or of action.

Action, not being, supplies the law of truth. This activism may be distinguished from a simple historicism, since a historical relativism is content to immerse truths within history and thereby abolish any criterion of truth. But for Kojève, the criterion exists. That which succeeds is true, that which fails is false. Such a criterion is interior to history. It is 'immanent' and not 'transcendent', as it was said at the time. For this reason, Kojève called his thesis an *atheism*, and defined it as the precise antithesis of Christian theology. It is important to grasp that, for Hegel,

> all that Christian theology says is absolutely true,
> provided it is applied not to a transcendental and
> imaginary God, but to Man himself, living in the world.[22]

The theologian imagines that theological discourse is one in which man (subject) speaks of God (object), whereas it is a discourse in which God speaks of himself, that is, of *man*, but without knowing it. The ultimate significance of an absolute self-consciousness, or wisdom, is that the author of theological discourse discovers the *Other*, of which he was speaking, to be the *same* as himself, the speaker. He recognises himself in that which he had taken for other, and thereby puts an end to *alienation*.

Classical atheism rejected the notion of divine attributes, pronouncing them inconceivable because infinite, or incompatible among themselves. Humanist atheism reclaims them for the human subject, who in this way becomes the true God. It is precisely this substitution, whereby everywhere the word 'Man' is written in to replace the word 'God', which defines *humanism*. And it is in exactly this sense that the title of humanist was adopted by Sartre and his companions after 1945. Existentialism is a humanism, as he said at a conference published under the same title, which popularised the themes of *Being and Nothingness*.

For atheist humanism to be atheist, in the sense that it claims divine status for man, means that it is an inverted theology. We

----

[22] *Intr. Hegel*, p. 571.

even know which theology was requisitioned by humanism in the interests of human beings: Cartesian theology, as Sartre reveals in his preface to a selection of texts by Descartes, explaining that Descartes's genius was to have posited God as the creator of eternal truths. Divine freedom, far from being preceded by an eternal order of truths which define it and thus limit it, is itself the inalienable foundation of being, truth and goodness. Descartes's one weakness was to have ascribed to God a power of creation which, according to Sartre, belongs by rights to ourselves:

> It was to take two centuries of crisis – a crisis in Faith and in Science – for man to recover the creative freedom that Descartes had placed in God, and for this truth, the essential basis of humanism, to be glimpsed: man is the being whose appearance brings the world into existence. [23]

The distinctive feature of humanism is this will to recovery and reappropriation of divine attributes, among them the most precious of all, the power to create and to 'bring the world into existence'. In what sense can human activity be called creative? This is the question that leads us to the core of the speculation upon negativity. Before moving on from the term humanism, we must however mention the two setbacks which it subsequently encountered: Heidegger's clarification in 1947, and the structuralist debate.

In his *Letter on Humanism*, written in response to the questions put to him by Jean Beaufret, [24] Heidegger explains that there is no relation between his own thought and the humanism of Sartre. His *Letter* points out that this 'atheist existentialism', this 'humanism', are not at all what they purport to be, namely the conclusion of a 'phenomenological ontology' (the subtitle of *Being and*

---

[23] 'La liberté cartésienne', *Situations* I (Gallimard, 1947), p. 334.

[24] Written in 1946 and published in German in 1947, Heidegger's *Letter* was translated into French in 1953. A fragment had already appeared in French, in the journal, *Fontaine*, no. 63, November 1947 prefaced by Beaufret's article, 'M. Heidegger et le problème de la verité' (now available in his book, *Introduction aux philosophies de l'existence*, Denoël-Gonthier, 1971). This article put an end to the misapprehensions which had facilitated the existentialist misuse of Heidegger. It was also the first, and for a long time the only readable text in French about the author of *Being and Time*.

Nothingness). For a 'phenomenological ontology', if the expression means anything at all, would be a doctrine of being which reposes exclusively upon a faithful description of appearances, whereas Sartre's atheistic existentialism, his 'humanism', are what they would disclaim at any cost, namely a simple revival of the most traditional metaphysics for the benefit of a 'man' who had asked for nothing of the kind – a metaphysics which saw in creative causality the divine attribute *par excellence*. After Heidegger's intervention, the word 'humanism' ceased to be the flag which it had been such a point of honour to defend. Soon after, as a delayed and unexpected consequence of the *Letter*, the 'debate on humanism' erupted in France (1965–6). Marxists condemning the bourgeois ideology of 'Man'; Nietzscheans despising the doctrine of resentment born in the spent intelligence of the 'last man'; structuralists of a purist persuasion announcing with Lévi-Strauss the programme of the 'dissolution of man'[25] – all these contended with one another in their anti-humanism. 'Humanist' became a term of ridicule, an abusive epithet, to be entered among the collection of derided '-isms' (vitalism, spiritualism, etc.).

It is worth noting that the slogan of the 60s – 'the death of man' – was prefigured in Kojève's lectures, where it also appeared as the ultimate consequence of the 'death of God'. Kojève said:

The end of History is the *death* of Man as such.[26]

In a philosophy of action, or of history, man is defined by the fact that he acts and changes the course of things. If history is at an end, nothing remains to be done. But an idle man is no longer a man. As the threshold of post-history is crossed, humanity disappears while at the same time the reign of frivolity begins, the reign of play, of derision (for henceforth nothing that might be done would have the slightest meaning). It would have been futile to challenge Kojève with the objection that wars and violent revolutions by no means ceased after 1807, any more than they did from 1934 to 1939. He would have replied that history was only concluded in theory, as an idea, with precisely the *idea* (remaining to

---

[25] *La pensée sauvage* (Plon, 1962), pp. 326–7, trans. as *The Savage Mind* (London, Weidenfeld and Nicolson, 1966).
[26] *Intr. Hegel*, p. 388 (in the note).

be achieved, most likely with terrorist methods) of a 'homogene-
ous State' – an expression which for him could apply as much to
Hegel's reasonable State as to Marx's classless society. In order for
this idea to become a global reality, a little more time was
required, just long enough in which to act – an action which
would correspond to the wars and revolutions in which we were
mobilised.

Negativity

The leading role in Kojève's narrative is played by the concept of
negativity. Two routes lead to the understanding of this notion,
the first anthropological, the second metaphysical. I will take
them in that order.

In a philosophy where success evinces the truth of the discourse
of the happy winner, action is all-decisive. The idle have no future
in this kind of thinking. It is on the terrain of human action,
envisaged as equivalent to that of history – by virtue of Vico's
maxim, 'Men make history' – that the recovery of divine predi-
cates will be achieved, and in particular the power to create, or
again, as Sartre has sometimes called it, 'creativity'.[27] But in what
sense is human action at all creative?

Kojève often makes his concept of action explicit by the juxtaposition of 'labour and struggle'. Labour being understood as a
struggle which does violence to nature, both modes of action have
this bellicose characteristic. All action, then, is opposition to an
adversary. And action, by definition, produces some kind of
effect. The state of the world, after action, is no longer the same.
Since no innovation in the world can take place without an action
to introduce it, and since all action is opposition, it follows that
opposition (or negation, contradiction) is responsible for introducing the new into the old.

For Kojève, negativity thus understood is the very essence of
freedom. The productive power of negation is liberating. Any
other definition would be 'naturalist', and would overlook the
difference between the free being of man and the determined
being of the animal:

[27] CRD, p. 68.

> But if Freedom is ontologically Negativity, it is because
> Freedom can *be* and *exist* only as *negation*. Now in order to
> negate, there must be something to negate: an existing
> given. ... Freedom does not consist in *choice* between two
> *givens*: it is the *negation* of the given, both of the given
> which one is oneself (as animal or as 'incarnated
> tradition') and of the given which one is not (the natural
> and social *World*). ... The freedom which is realised and
> manifested as dialectical or *negating* Action is thereby
> essentially a *creation*. For to negate the given without
> ending in nothingness is to produce something that did
> not yet exist; now this is precisely what is called
> 'creating'. [28]

However, nowhere does Kojève question the legitimacy of
defining a concept, in this case that of action, by the conjunction of
two others (labour and war). It is quite obvious that this union is
what generates the paradoxical notion of a fruitful negation, since
labour accounts for the element of production, the transformation
of the state of affairs, and war supplies the element of negation, the
confrontation with an adversary whose overthrow is a matter of
life and death. Only the fable of the Master and Slave could
provide for this association of the two forms of action. The Slave
is primarily a warrior who has been defeated in a 'fight for
recognition'. He is secondarily a worker serving a Master who has
spared his life, and has reserved all enjoyment (*jouissance*) for
himself. This union none the less remains a juxtaposition, unable
to found a genuine concept. War is destruction pure and simple,
and as such it produces nothing at all (if there is a Slave, it is
because the victor has concluded the war and spared the life of the
vanquished). At the very best it may entail a transference of
wealth through pillage. Labour, for its part, is certainly productive but it involves no radical negation. *Useful* labour is always the
utilisation of existing resources, a transformation of the field in
accordance with a preconceived idea (i.e. given prior to action); it
is never an annihilation.

Are things any clearer from the metaphysical angle?

The humanisation of nothingness implies that there is nothing
negative in the world outside of human action. *Nature*, or that

---

[28] *Intr. Hegel*, p. 492.

which produces without man having to act, is wholly positive. Natural being is defined by *identity* (in the ordinary and non-dialectical sense of the term). The thing in nature – dog, stone – is what it is and nothing other than what its nature (its identity) prescribes. Hence Kojève's doctrine that history is dialectical and nature is not. This permits him to make a concession to the neo-Kantians for whom, as we know, the original sin of the Hegelian system was to include a Romantic philosophy of nature, which claims to 'surpass' Newtonian Mechanics. Kojève grants the point: *Naturphilosophie* is a monster that must be jettisoned.

Kojève calls his position a dualist ontology. The word 'being' cannot have the same sense in the case of man and in the case of the thing in nature. The thing in nature, whether it is a stone or a fir tree, is content to be what it is; its ambitions extend no further than the simple perpetuation of itself (the Spinozist *conatus*). Man himself, if he behaves as a simple living being, cannot be said to act; he reproduces. So it can be argued that 'nature has no history'. By this we should understand that the natural process is defined by the fact of things remaining the same at the end as they were at the beginning, all else being equal. Nothing has really happened: nothing has been lost in transit, nothing has been created, except perhaps the chicken hatching from an egg, laying another egg in its turn, and so on.

The ability to maintain relations with *nothingness* is the distinctive attribute of human action, which inherits the divine privilege from Christian theology. It introduces innovation into the world. This innovation, if it is to be genuinely new, must be different from anything seen before. After an authentic action, it should be possible to say, '*Nothing* will be the same again'. The property of action is thus that it inserts a 'nothing' between the initial and the final state of affairs. The result can therefore be said to be *created*, produced *ex nihilo*, and consequently, the protagonist, as soon as he acts, is manifesting not his will to being (to conserve his being), but his will to not-being (his spleen with being as he is, his desire to be another). The philosophy of action sees the protagonist as a kind of dandy for whom the supreme rationale of a gesture is the elegant absence of all natural reason.

Thus, being has two senses:

1. Natural being. Here, 'to be' means *to remain the same*, to preserve identity.

2. Historical being (or 'historicity'). 'To be' is here defined by negativity. The being of the protagonist consists in *not remaining the same*, in will to difference. And 'difference' does not only mean 'to be different' (in the sense that an apple is different from a pear); difference always involves an activity of pushing aside, of tampering. The *world* (as the totality of that which is) falls into two portions. In the natural portion, things are as they are, and becoming is cyclical. In the historical or human portion, nothing remains as it is, no identity is preserved.

Kojève illustrates his dualist ontology with an image frequently revived by Sartre in *Being and Nothingness*. The world, he says, is comparable to a gold ring:

> Let us consider a gold ring. There is a hole and this hole is just as essential to the ring as the gold is; without the gold, the 'hole' (which, moreover, would not exist) would not be a ring, but without the hole, the gold (which would none the less exist) would not be a ring either. But if one has found atoms in the gold, it is not at all necessary to look for them in the hole. And nothing indicates that the gold and the hole *are* in one and the same manner (of course, what is involved is the hole as 'hole', and not the air which is 'in the hole'). The hole is a nothingness that subsists (as the presence of an absence) thanks to the gold which surrounds it. Likewise, Man who *is* Action could be a nothingness that 'nihilates' in being, thanks to the being which it 'negates'.[29]

We should not be dazzled by this brilliant image into forgetting the equivocal nature of the expression 'dualist ontology'. Ontology means the doctrine of being. Dualist ontology should therefore be a doctrine which recognises two senses in the words 'to be'. We think we have understood: there is the first way of being, being in the sense of identity, proper to nature, and there is the second, being in the sense of negativity, proper to man. But the image of the ring does not tell us this. According to this gilded fable there are not two senses to being. There is, on the one hand, *being* (gold) and, on the other, *nothingness* (hole). As for the dialectic, that is, the inclusion of nothingness within being, or of

[29] *Intr. Hegel*, p. 485 (in the note).

difference within identity, it is to be found in the conjunction of the two. The gold (being) has certainly no need of the hole in order to be, but the gold ring (the world) would not be what it is, a gold ring, without the hole.

And thus 'dualist ontology' is no longer dualist at all. It is at last permissible to hold that being should be defined by identity.

Identity and Difference

Now we are getting very warm, as they say in the game of 'Hunt-the-thimble'. We are nearing the heart of the question which for Kojève's interpretation – and also for contemporary French philosophy as a whole – is decisive.

The dialectic has already ceased to be the ineffable notion that Sartre had claimed was undefinable. We are encountering the dialectic in the modern sense of the word. In its modern or post-Kantian sense, the dialectic is an interpretation of the sense pertaining to the copula 'is' in a categorical judgment, e.g. 'S is P'.[30] Modern dialectics inherits the Kantian debate on the distinction between analytic and synthetic judgments. It is opposed to the analytic interpretation of the copula according to which the word 'is' would signify the identity of the predicate P and the subject S. With a gesture whose significance must be clarified, it introduces *difference* into the very definition of *identity*. But this difference is expressed by a negative judgment, 'A is not B'. The dialectical interpretation of being thus makes manifest a certain *not-being*, interior to *being*, which formal logic finds difficult to accommodate. Kojève summarised it humorously enough:

> Parmenides was right in saying that Being *is*, and that Nothingness *is not*; but he forgot to add that there *is* a 'difference' between Nothingness and Being, a difference which to a certain extent *is* as much as Being itself *is*, since without it, if there were no *difference* between Being and Nothingness, Being itself would not be.[31]

In this text, as indeed in all the texts of the period, 'Being' must always be understood as *that which is*, *be-ing*. In Latin, *ens* and not *esse*. Kojève's joke therefore means that difference, although it is a

---

[30] Cf. Hegel's theory of the 'philosophical proposition'.
[31] *Intr. Hegel*, p. 491 (in the note).

form of nothingness – since to differ from something is *not to be* like it – is a part of that which is. This is necessarily the case, for that which is not a part of what is (the *ens*) returns to the not-being, and thus into nothingness. So that a certain inclusion (which remains to be defined) of nothingness within be-ing is inevitable if we would have a difference between them.

It could equally well be concluded, we should observe in passing, that the difference between something and nothing *is not*, at least in the sense that 'to be' means 'to be something'. Because if the difference between something and nothing were itself something, we would require a new difference in order to distinguish that difference, i.e. something, from nothing. As a result, we must say that 'to be' need not necessarily mean 'to be something' (that is, 'to be identical with itself'). And this development of the argument is ignored by Kojève and his disciples.

In his attempt to give a human face to the negative, Kojève is led to distribute identity and difference among the portions of the universe. This is where the difficulties begin.

Everything seems very clear in the portion of the universe labelled 'Nature', where things are what they are and are content to be so. They do not desire to change their identity and so they do not desire at all ... Hence, for a thing in nature, 'to be' and 'to be itself' are equivalent. Being has the analytic sense of identity, meaning that 'to be' implies *'to be the same, always, everywhere, and in every case'*. The day that the identical ceases to be itself, it vanishes. It *is no more*, as they say of the dead.

In the portion of the world labelled 'History', negativity rules. Or, if we prefer, difference. To act in history is to work at *not being* what one is. In short, being signifies identity in nature, and difference in history. The thing in nature *is*, in that it *is identical*. The historical protagonist *is* in so far as he acts, and he acts in so far as he is always *being different*. So we arrive at this trivial and scarcely 'dialectical' result: in nature, 'identity is identity', whereas in history, 'difference is difference'. The following consequence, well known ever since Plato's *Sophist*, is readily apparent. If nothingness is not being, and if 'to be' and 'to be identical with oneself' are identical, then nothingness is never identical with anything – never, nowhere, and in no case. But if nothingness has no identity, if it is only defined by difference, then nothingness must be said to be *different from itself*; otherwise it

would be identical with itself, which runs counter to the previous
hypothesis. Being, on the other hand, defined as it is by identity,
can never enter into a negative judgment. It thus becomes impossible to state that 'being *is not* identical with difference'. Therefore
being, once defined by absolute identity, is identical with anything, and in particular with difference.

So there is identity not only, as formal logic would have it,
between identity and identity, but between difference and
difference; there is a certain *being* in *not-being*. Now, is there the
slightest difference between the identity of identity with identity,
and the identity of difference with difference? Certainly not. For
there is no more *identity* between identity and identity than there is
between difference and difference. And there is no more *difference*
between difference and difference than there is between identity
and identity. And yet identity and difference are clearly different
types of relation. Yes, certainly. So the *identity* between, on the
one hand, the identity of identity and identity, and on the other,
the identity of difference and difference, is the very factor of
difference between identity and difference.

And so, too, it is false to say that the identical is always exclusively identical, since in one respect at least the identical is identical
with the different. Neither is it true that the different is always
different. For the different is different only when it is identical
with itself, a property it *shares* with the identical.

These are some of the consequences to be drawn from the initial
premise that *to be* should always be understood in the sense of *to be
identical*. In the end, far from challenging this determination of a
univocal being whose meaning is firmly grounded in logic (in the
relation between predicate and subject within the attributive
judgment), the dialectic makes it its own. If the dialectic allows
itself the luxury of criticising formal logic and 'analytic reason',
this is not at all to say that it questions the right of logic to decide
on the sense of the verb 'to be'. It simply reproaches formal logic
for defining identity in its own unilateral way, thus making the
very meaning of the copula or of identity impossible. In introducing difference into identity and negativity into being, thus pro-
claiming the *unity of opposites*, the only purpose of the dialectic is to
safeguard the copulative meaning of being. Difference is necessary in order for identity to preserve itself as the first, if not the
exclusive, meaning of being.

Kojève abides strictly by the most profound meaning of the dialectic when, throughout his commentary, he defines being in terms of identity. None the less this same dialectic, as Kojève knows better than anyone, requires the emergence of negativity *out of* the founding position of a being identical with itself. The position of the 'not-self' is necessarily the direct consequence of the position 'self=self'. It could never be a statement made *alongside* the first. And yet the dualist ontology proposed by Kojève is plainly unable to describe the metamorphosis of being into nothingness, of identity into difference, or of self into not-self. It can only juxtapose them. This allows us to speak of a failure on the part of the anthropological dialectic (of the humanisation of nothingness) to constitute itself as *philosophy*. The French phenomenologists, too preoccupied perhaps with their various commitments 'in the concrete', omitted, as we shall see, to go back over this ontological problem.

The Question of Enunciation

The humanisation of nothingness requires a dualist ontology. In Hegel, ontology is presented under the name 'logic' (justifiably, as we have seen). Two logics, according to Kojève, are therefore necessary: one for nature, which boils down to an epistemology of the physical sciences (and would be a 'critique of analytic reason'), and one for history, which, differing from the first, is dialectical. But these words, 'differing from the first', quickly give rise to the need for a third logic in order to say whether this difference between the first two should be understood in the sense of the first (analytic difference) or of the second (dialectical difference, *Aufhebung*). Either the relation of nature and history is analytic or it is dialectical. And since 'nature' and 'history' have been defined as the two portions of the world, the third logic would be that of the totality. Thus we rediscover, at the price of this indispensable clarification, the Hegelian tripartition:

    i. Logic
    ii. Philosophy of nature
    iii. Philosophy of mind.

In the tripartition of the *system*, the same logic applies, whether for nature or for history. But logic, however it is understood, deals with the *concept*. What is a concept? A concept is an *identity*: the concept 'dog', for example, stands for the ways in which all dogs are identical. Logic therefore deals with identity from the point of view of things being the *same*. And logic states that where the identical is nothing but identical, it is indistinguishable from the different. Identity cannot be thought except as differing from the different. *Difference* is what enables identity to be itself. Generally speaking, the *same* cannot be posited except as *other than the other*. It is, then, thanks to the other that the same can be that which it intends and claims to be: the same – whence the passage from the concept to nature. By definition, the concept is *different* from the thing, but if it were 'too different' it would no longer be the concept of this thing (but an erroneous conception of it). This is to say that the concept without the thing would not be *true* (since it would be the concept of nothing, an imaginary representation). If we give the name *nature* to all those things of which the concepts enable us to think in varying degrees of identity – generic, specific, individual – we must conclude, using a kind of ontological argument, that the identity of the concept with itself is conditional upon the existence of natural things outside the concept. The concept would not be *itself* without this *other*. We can therefore say that 'nature' is the position of the concept 'outside itself', in exteriority. But just as the concept, in order to be truly a concept, must 'posit itself' as different from itself, and 'make itself' into the thing – the inverted commas suggesting here that we are dealing with a purely logical process, a relation of conditioned to condition in thought, in 'the element of the concept' – so the thing, in order to be truly a thing, must also be other than itself. Its identity lies in its reality as thing; this identity, like all identity, is dependent upon difference. And that which differs from the thing is precisely the concept. The thing is thus posited as the other of itself, as the concept. And here we no longer need inverted commas, for the position is no longer logical as before, but perfectly natural and real, since it concerns a thing, and not a concept. This passage from nature to logos is what Hegel calls the *emergence* of Mind. Even while it remains a thing, indeed in order to remain so, any thing which is capable of becoming the concept of itself, i.e. is capable of conceiving its own identity, *is certainly the absolute, not only as substance (thing), but as subject (consciousness of self, knowledge of its own identity)*. And that is what Hegel calls *Geist*, or Mind. So

we find at the end, with the emergence of the thinker, the possibility which marked the point of departure – pure thought, the
object of logical science. In other words, the system contains one
part (that part dealing with the emergence of Mind, or
Phenomenology of Mind) in which it is explained how the system is
possible, or how this discourse was capable of being *enunciated*.

Kojève claims that it is possible to humanise this Hegelian
Mind. A nominal definition of Mind might run as follows: he that
recognises himself in the philosophical discourse of absolute
knowledge, as the subject of that discourse. It is important, then,
in philosophy, to ascertain who is speaking; this is what we now
call 'the question of enunciation'. For as long as philosophy is
taken for the *philosopher's* discourse upon the *world*, it falls on the
hithermost side of absolute knowledge, since the subject (author)
of this discourse speaks of *another* than himself, namely the world,
which he is not, or of which he is only a 'part'. In the Cartesian
tradition, on the other hand, the philosopher's knowledge is
reckoned to be *absolute* when he speaks of *himself* (*cogito*). But in so
far as the philosopher cannot speak of himself without speaking
also of the other things to which he is bound and which, accordingly, enter into the definition of what he is, he only really speaks
of himself when speaking also of the 'not himself'. And consequently, the knowledge of the world developed by the
philosopher – his physics – will be absolute knowledge provided
it can be established that it is the knowledge of a subject, of an *ego*.
It is necessary therefore that the subject of philosophical discourse
upon the world should be the world itself, or, if we prefer, that the
object of philosophical discourse upon the world should be the
philosopher himself.

The stake of modern (and not only Hegelian) philosophy thus
lies in the perilous passage from an initial affirmation posing no
problem for common sense,

>   Man speaks of being,

to a proposition which seriously turns the tables,

>   Being speaks of itself in the discourse which man holds
>   upon Being.[32]

---

[32] A summary of p. 416 of the *Intr. Hegel*.

How should we prove that the subject who enunciates a philosophical proposition is not specifically the philosopher's person but the world itself, to which the philosopher merely affords the occasion for speaking out? In Hegel, as reconstructed by Kojève, the circularity of discourse would be the proof that this dangerous passage has been effected. If it is possible to return to the departure point of the discourse within the discourse itself, then proof has been established that the *subject (author) of the enunciation* is identical with the *subject (matter) of the statement*. If philosophical discourse succeeds in showing that the world would not be the world were man not in it, then it may be established that the real philosopher is the world, for, in producing man, the world produces the possibility of the philosopher, who is to speak of the world. Or, as Kojève wrote:

> Real Being existing as Nature is what produces Man, who reveals that Nature (and himself) by speaking of it.[33]

But we should distinguish here the general difficulties encountered by any demonstration of an 'absolute subject', and the difficulties specific to the humanist version of such a demonstration. The first may be grouped under the rubric of that disputed issue, classic in the tradition of Hegelian commentary: what is the relation between phenomenology and logic in the system? Assuming that the one-way journey (from the *Phenomenology* to the *Logic*) is possible, how might the return from the *Logic* to the *Phenomenology* be made?

To discuss the merits of the Hegelian system here would be a digression. We need only observe how Kojève, as he re-orders the system within a dualist framework, raises the problem of enunciation, or in Hegelian terms, the problem of the relationship between *consciousness* (phenomenology) and *concept* (logic). As its title suggests, the *Phenomenology of Mind* is the discourse (logos) concerning the appearance of Mind. This 'appearance' takes place as follows: the philosopher, as he attempts in a *discourse* to state the relationship between consciousness and that which appears to it as other than itself, becomes aware that his discourse would be meaningless if it were not the discourse held by the world itself. The appearance of Mind is thus the revelation of the identity

---

[33] *Intr. Hegel*, p. 448.

between the thing that the philosopher makes the subject of his statement, and himself, the subject of the enunciation. But where does this revelation occur? Precisely in the *Phenomenology*.

This then is how the *Phenomenology* leads to the *Logic*. As for the latter, it elaborates the concept of being to the point at which it acknowledges the supreme being (*ens verum*) in the absolute subject. True to the Cartesian assumptions in this movement of thought, absolute subject means a subject having absolute knowledge of its own identity. The *Logic* is thus truly the knowledge that the be-ing has of itself. What remains now is the problem of a *return* to the *Phenomenology*. If the *ens supremum* is Mind, it should appear to itself, make itself manifest; there should be a 'phenomenon' of mind. But, as Kant showed, all phenomena are spatio-temporal. Mind would therefore have to appear in a discourse to be pronounced, or written, *somewhere*, at a *determinate date*, and by *somebody*. The dangerous stretch on the return journey from concept to consciousness is therefore that point at which the dialectical resources of the concept must allow a 'here' to be deduced from a 'somewhere', a 'now' from an 'at a determinate date', and a 'myself' from a 'somebody'. We will recognise the hallmarks of Circumstance on the first page of the *Phenomenology*: me, here, now. Knowledge of the *constitution of the world* should enable us to indicate the *place* of the appearance of Mind (for example, western Europe or even Germany, even Jena), and the *time* of this manifestation (for example, the modern era, or even the period since the French Revolution). In the Hegelian system it is of course the 'philosophy of nature', inserted between the 'logic' and the 'philosophy of Mind', which permits the gulf separating the logical concept from the person of the logician to be bridged. The statement, precisely because it is dialectical, enables us to predict the circumstances of its being enunciated, by means of an approximation which Hegelians find satisfactory: the era and the language of absolute knowledge are well and truly deducible from the empty concept of being in general.

How do things present themselves if the transition from concept to consciousness no longer passes through the dialectic of nature?

Kojève cites Spinoza's *Ethics* as the example of a philosophical work written without preliminary introduction; it is a system of philosophy which, unlike the Hegelian system, does not open with a 'phenomenology'. It is therefore, Kojève explains, an impossible book. What is written in the *Ethics* may well be true, but in any case we shall never know, because this book *cannot be read* and *cannot have been written*. Indeed, Spinoza posits the true as being eternal, without explaining how eternal truths can be discovered in time, somewhere, and by somebody who knew nothing of them hitherto. This book must therefore have been written, as it must be read, outside time, 'in a trice'.[34] The *Ethics* is a set of statements which it is impossible to enunciate:

> The *Ethics* explains everything except the possibility for a man living in time to write it ... The *Ethics* could have been written, *if it is true*, only by God himself; and let us take care to note – by a non-incarnate God.
>
> Therefore, the difference between Spinoza and Hegel can be formulated in the following way: Hegel *becomes* God by thinking or writing the *Logic*: or, if you like, it is by becoming God that he writes or thinks it. Spinoza, on the other hand, must *be* God from all eternity in order to be able to write or think his *Ethics*.[35]

For Hegel's *Science of Logic* is also an ensemble of divine utterances. As Hegel himself wrote, it contains

> the presentation of God as he is in his eternal being before the creation of nature and of a finite mind.[36]

It is here that Kojève's call for an 'anthropological' interpretation becomes pertinent. For the declaration made by Hegel at the outset of the *Logic* transforms this work into an inhuman text, whose lines cannot have been written by a man. The author is God, or if we prefer, 'Logos', 'Reason'; in any case it is not Hegel. But if it is God who speaks in the *Logic*, how is it that this book is *signed* by Hegel – who by all accounts did actually write it, at the cost of considerable labour? Or perhaps Hegel thinks that he, Hegel, is indeed the author of the book in which the thought of God – before the creation of the world – is uttered (a world of which one fragment bears the name 'Hegel'). But in that case,

---

[34] *Intr. Hegel*, p. 352.
[35] *Intr. Hegel*, p. 354.
[36] *Wissenschaft der Logik*, ed. Lasson (Meiner, 1963) vol. I, p. 31.

Hegel thinks he is God; and as Hegel is notoriously not God, and has not been thinking the *Logic* since the beginning of time, we shall have to accept that Hegel is mad. Or perhaps, to take up the anthropological thesis, Hegel thinks of himself as a writer, human, mortal, who is subject, even in his thinking, to the condition of temporality; in that case his claim is not to be divine or eternal, but to *become* so, and he is no longer mad, even if he brushes with madness. Kojève recalls a period of depression in Hegel's life, between the ages of twenty-five and thirty, and sees in it the effect of the resistance of the empirical individual known as 'Hegel' to the threat of absolute knowledge.[37] By pronouncing the speculative utterance ('I am everything which is'), the thinker abolishes his humanity along with his particularity, since evidently a man, as such, is never any more than a mediocre fragment of the world. This moment of madness has made a strong impression on French writers. Georges Bataille comments on it in *L'expérience intérieure*.[38] Moreover, a whole tradition of French literature associates the reading of Hegel with experiencing the impossibility of writing. We already find traces of this in Flaubert.[39] While reading Hegel at Tournon, Mallarmé also suffered a depression. His letter, written on 14 March 1867 to his friend Cazalis, is well known:

> I have just lived through an appalling year. My Thought has thought itself, and has arrived at a pure Conception. All that my being suffered in this long agony is unrecountable, but fortunately I am perfectly dead . . . I have become impersonal, and am no longer the Stéphane that you knew, but rather an aptitude which the Universe has for seeing and developing itself through what was formerly me.

The question of enunciation is the question of the truth of statements considered with reference to the conditions of their enunciation. A statement is 'false' if its enunciation is demonstrably impossible. Thus it is that the 'I am God' implicit both in Hegel's *Logic* and in Spinoza's *Ethics*, is a statement which annuls

---

[37] *Intr. Hegel*, p. 441.
[38] Hegel, in his experience of being God, 'believed for two years that he was going mad'. (Op. cit., 2nd ed, Gallimard, 1954, p. 140.)
[39] Derrida notes them in ED, p. 12.

itself, in the manner of such classic paradoxes as 'I am asleep', 'I am dead', etc.

Kojève argues from the basis of a humanist plea, close in its style to Feuerbach. The enunciating subject of philosophical discourse is for him identical with an empirical individual, having a proper name, present 'here and now', born in such a town in such a year etc. This plea generally leads to one or another version of relativism, or 'psychologism' as Husserl says. Yet Kojève means to uphold the absolute subject of absolute knowledge. How is this possible? As we have seen, the world necessarily implies man, which allows the philosopher, as he treats of the world, to discover this implication in it, and to accomplish the perilous leap from the 'I speak' to the 'it speaks'. This implication is 'dialectical'; it expresses the identity of subject and object. Now Kojève maintains that his ontological dualism, though it denies nature any dialectical becoming, by no means abolishes the dialectical character of the *totality*:

> If the real Totality implies Man, and if Man is dialectical, the Totality itself is dialectical.[40]

And since the totality is dialectical, the cape of absolute knowledge can be rounded; man knowing the real is the real knowing itself (and discovering that it is the absolute subject). But how can the totality imply man without leaving nature in the dialectical anticipation of its own negation by Mind? Here, without acknowledging it, Kojève operates a kind of phenomenological reduction, in the Husserlian sense. For the *thing*, which man is not, and which must be shown to imply the discourse of the learned man, of which it is the object, he substitutes this same thing as *object* of that learned discourse, the thing therefore as 'intentional object', as Husserl would say, or, for a logician, as referent. Of course the thing, inasmuch as it is spoken of, supposes the discourse in which it is treated, just as in the immense Husserlian tautology, the object in so far as it is a *cogitatum* requires a *cogitatio*:

> Taken separately, the Subject and the Object are
> *abstractions* ... What exists in *reality* – as soon as there is a
> Reality *of which one speaks* – and since in fact we *speak* of

[40] *Intr. Hegel*, p. 483 (in the note).

reality, there can be for us only the
Reality-of-which-one-speaks – what exists in reality, I
say, is the Subject-that-knows-the-object, or, what is the
same thing, the Object-known-by-the-subject.[41]

Thus in one step Kojève grants himself the point which most required explaining, passing light-heartedly over what in every philosophy continues to be the most exacting problem of all, and the difficulty most worthy of consideration. For the issue is not to show that every *object* calls for a subject, but that every *real* is indeed *a real of which one speaks*, that is, an object. The problem was to generate the relation of knowledge itself; but Kojève's solution generates nothing at all. It consists in ignoring the problem. He writes:

In fact, *this* table is the table of which I am speaking at this moment, and my words are as much a part of this table as are its four legs, or the room which surrounds it. One can, to be sure, *abstract* from these words and from many other things besides, as, for example, from so-called 'secondary' qualities. But in doing this one must not forget that then one is no longer dealing with a concrete reality but with an *abstraction*.[42]

This excellent example is the very formulation of the phenomenological question. Is that speech which calls the table 'table' and addresses it by this name, an accident exterior to its essence, a 'secondary quality' as regards the table itself (that is, *for it* and not merely *for us*)? Can the table be the table in a universe of silence? Or is the discourse concerning the table, far from being a type of superstructure added to the already complete reality of the table, and arising from its chance encounter with a creature capable of speech, as essential to it as its four legs? The whole of what is at stake in every conceivable phenomenology lies in this.

But here again, Kojève facetiously evades the issue, affecting this time to speak as a Marxist. The table, he says, necessitates the words of which it is the object to the degree that it only enters the world, only appears there, as a result of human labour, which in its turn implies discourse. It is plain that the difficulty has merely

[41] *Intr. Hegel*, p. 449.   [42] *Intr. Hegel*, p. 483.

been deferred. Of course the table is a product of art. But did the tree which was cut down to supply the wood for the table demand to be transformed into a table, and did it imply the artisan? Is the violence done upon the tree in its encounter with man a regrettable accident in its eyes?[43] Is the man who works the wood necessarily a party to the exploitation of forest resources? Or, by performing a work, might he also be someone whose craftsmanship fulfils the most essential possibilities of nature? These are the questions that should be asked.

APPENDIX

Nothingness in *Being and Nothingness*

In his commentary, Kojève specified that the elaboration of a 'dualist ontology' was the task of the future.[44] It was as if Jean-Paul Sartre had taken upon himself the project of realising this treatise on dualist ontology. Already known before the war for his short stories (*Le Mur*), his novel (*La Nausée*), and his literary columns in the *Nouvelle Revue Française*, as well as for his psychological investigations into the imagination and the emotions, he published *Being and Nothingness*, his first philosophical work, in 1943. The dualism called for by Kojève is already evinced in the title of the book. For the '*and*' which links being to nothingness associates one opposite with another without it being possible to speak of any community of the two. Indeed, Sartre writes:

> In a word, we must recall here against Hegel that
> being *is* and that nothingness *is not*.[45]

Perhaps, but how do we know?

The case is, quite simply, that 'being has no need whatever of nothingness in order to be conceived of',[46] whereas nothingness, since it is the negation of being, needs being before it can posit itself as its negation. Being can dispense with nothingness in order

---

[43] This idea appears again in Lacan, with the story of the elephants (of-which-one-speaks, unluckily for them) which provides the motif for the jacket of *Séminaire*, vol. I (Seuil, 1975).

[44] *Intr. Hegel*, p. 485 (in the note).

[45] EN, p. 51.

[46] EN, p. 52.

to be, whilst nothingness, like a parasite, lives entirely dependent upon being: 'It is from being that it takes its being.'[47]

However, matters are less straightforward than these peremptory declarations lead us to suppose. If it were true that 'nothingness is not', the title of Sartre's book would become absurd. If nothingness is nothing at all, its nullity adds nothing to being (that is, here, the be-ing, the *something* as in 'why something rather than nothing?'). It would have been enough, then, for this essay in 'phenomenological ontology' (the subtitle of the book) to have been called 'Being'. Or perhaps, 'Being, outside of which there is nothing'.

But Sartre's ontology is not at all a doctrine of the *unity of being*, as we might have thought from his refusal to accord to nothingness any participation in being. It affirms the *duality* of being. Nothingness is nothing, which means that it is the negation of being; and the negation, now, is not nothing, but something. Yet negation cannot be derived from a being initially defined by its self-sufficiency. Sartre writes, against Bergson, that negation cannot be engendered out of the fullness of that which is. This is why nothingness (which is not) must be *added* to being (which is): $1 + 0 = 2$, not 1.

Just as nothingness supposes negation, so negation in its turn supposes the negator. The humanisation of nothingness is complete:

> Man is the being through whom nothingness comes into the world.[48]

But how can man, since he is part of *something*, be the occasion of *nothing*? This is only possible provided that, unlike all other beings, man is dependent on negation in order to be in the manner of man. Although things need only be in order to be, it is indispensable for man *not to be* in order to be (note that 'to be' = 'to be something' throughout). This paradox lures the reader towards the negative definition of freedom, the essence of freedom as negativity, or in Sartre's words, the power to 'nihilate'.

The duality of being as proper to the thing and being as proper to man has replaced the duality of 'being and nothingness'. The two terms in the pair have become the two senses of being. The

[47] *Ibid.*   [48] EN, p. 60.

problem of the unity of these two senses is now posed, and Sartre refers to it in passing:

> Although the concept of being has this peculiarity of being divided into two regions without communication, we must nevertheless explain how these two regions can be placed under the same heading. That will necessitate the investigation of these two types of being, and it is evident that we cannot grasp the true meaning of either one until we can establish their true connection with the notion of being in general and the relations which unite them. [49]

It is evident . . . In spite of this evidence, any search for the meaning that being may have had prior to the schism into two 'regions without communication' is postponed. Sartre prefers to start off with the 'investigation' of one and the other region. But in fact, of the 722 pages in the treatise, *things* are entitled to no more than four (pp. 30–4). The remainder are given over to what the title refers to as 'nothingness'.

The two 'regions' are now denominated 'being in itself' and 'being for itself'. These Hegelian categories refer, in the case of the thing – which need only be in order to be – to its self-sufficiency considered as a complete *identity* with itself; and in the case of man, to the *difference* which prevents him from being likened to a thing, a difference which originates in the fact of *consciousness*. Now consciousness here means the *examination of conscience*, which is to say that, in turning back upon himself (or reflection), man is not content simply to *perceive* himself (to be *for himself* in the sense of 'appearing before oneself'), but judges himself, approving or condemning whatever this examination may reveal to him, giving or withholding his consent. If we admit that 'to be' is no more than 'to appear', as Sartre posits in the first sentence of his book, we are then obliged to credit the examination of conscience with an unlimited and infallible acumen. Far from floundering in the labyrinths of subjectivity, the gaze of consciousness probes heart and soul with rigorous inflexibility. But this is necessarily the case, since *esse* = *percipi*. Any error about oneself is thus in reality a lie, attributable to 'bad faith'. This is why man, who is

[49] EN, p. 31.

already *for himself* in the first sense, of his own self-perception, is also *for himself* in the sense that he is nothing other than what he is in his own eyes. 'Being for itself' is thus the ontological designation appropriate to consciousness.

If four pages suffice to describe 'being in itself', then there can hardly be very much to say about it. In fact, the reader cannot help feeling that even these are four too many. Sartre effectively defines 'being in itself' in terms of absolute identity: 'being is what it is'.[50] But to speak of identity in such a case is to go too far, for given that identity is a relation, it requires at least an incipient difference, or reflection. But the *in-itself* is so well enclosed within itself that it relates to nothing, not even to itself. We arrive at a description of 'being in itself' which is reminiscent of the first hypothesis in Plato's *Parmenides*:

> It is what it is. This means that by itself it cannot even be what it is not; we have seen indeed that it can encompass no negation. It is full positivity. It knows no *otherness*; it never posits itself as *other* than another being. It can sustain no connection with the other.[51]

If Sartre had not dispensed here with quoting the *Parmenides*, it would doubtless not have escaped him that his 'fully positive' being was defined with recourse to a series of negations. And in a 'phenomenological ontology', you are what you seem. If 'being in itself' appears to us by way of the negative, it must contain a certain negativity after all. What is more, a being that can sustain no relation with anything whatever cannot be said to be identical especially if it is incapable of distinguishing itself from that which it is not. Finally, and by the same token, it may be endowed with 'neither name, nor discourse, nor science, nor sensation, nor opinion', as Plato wrote of *the One which is only One*. Having no relation, it certainly cannot *appear*, or *be known* (enter into a relation of knowledge), all of which is inconvenient to say the least, if we recall that this page purported to define the being of the phenomenon.

'Being for itself' is described, for its part, as the exact antithesis of 'being in itself'. The *for-itself* is all difference and opposition. 'Being in itself' is so much identical with itself that it thereby loses

[50] EN, p. 33.   [51] EN, pp. 33–4.

even the relation of identity; 'being for itself' is so negative that it is in perpetual flight before itself, incapable of stopping anywhere.

But with all this, we still do not know what the word *being* means. Yet the question acknowledged to be decisive on page 31 is not taken up again until page 711: what relation is there between the two regions of being? In what ways are they both regions of being? Sartre describes the problem of the link between the *in-itself* and the *for-itself* as *metaphysical*, although he does not explain why. He puts it as follows: why does the *for-itself* emerge out of the *in-itself*? The task of metaphysics is to examine this emergence, this 'source of all history'.[52] We recognise the problem encountered by the humanist interpretation of Hegelian idealism: how does history emerge out of a nature which supposedly knows nothing of history or of negation? It was exactly at this point that Kojève's efforts to establish that man is implied by the world ran into difficulties.

Furthermore, the *in-itself* and the *for-itself* have been defined as the two regions of being ('being' = 'the totality of that which is'). They must therefore have something in common, namely *being*. The philosophical question has been posed at last. In the conclusion to his book, Sartre inquires into the possibility of considering the *in-itself* and the *for-itself* *together* – an inquiry into the meaning that a synthesis of his thesis (in–itself) and his antithesis (for–itself) might have. But no synthesis is possible, because the relationship is unilateral. The *for-itself* cannot do without the *in-itself*, whereas the *in-itself* requires the *for-itself* only in order to appear to it; but, as Sartre explains, the *in-itself* does not need to appear in order to be. Consequently, man is not implied by the world. Sartre toys momentarily with the hypothesis whereby at the 'origin of history' there was an attempt by the *in-itself* to undergo the 'modification into for–itself', so as to rise to the 'dignity of the in- and for–itself'. This obscure phrase, which as Sartre immediately points out, conceals a profound contradiction, serves for a Sartrian cosmology: if the *in-itself*, or the world of natural things, wished to emerge from its stupor of identity, it would have to acquire difference so as to enter into a relation with itself and achieve consciousness. This *in-itself* would be at once being (like

---

[52] EN, p. 715.

the thing), and consciousness (like man). And on account of the voluntarist definition of consciousness which presides throughout the work, this being, with its consciousness of self, would be the *ens causa sui* (in post-Cartesian philosophies, the definition of God).

All this amounts to saying that, aside from his dualism, Sartre can envisage only one philosophical possibility (the very one he desires to avoid) – that of a metaphysical pantheism which would describe the birth of humanity on the planet Earth as the means employed by the Universe in order to perceive itself; in the human species it creates the mirror (*speculum*) of its own reflections. But Sartre objects that in order to experience the desire which would lead it to 'posit itself as other', the *in-itself* would already have to possess an inkling of consciousness or of will. It follows that the *for-itself* is not entitled to consider itself as the route taken by the universe to achieve the consciousness of its divinity. The passage from *human* subjectivity ('I speak of the world') to absolute subjectivity ('the world speaks of itself') is prohibited. This prohibition is without doubt the last and most consistent word in Sartre's thought. In 1961, in his article on Merleau-Ponty, he reproached the latter for having adopted, finally, the philosophy of synthesis:

> Where exactly was he going, during those dark years that changed him within himself? One would sometimes think, to read him, that being invents man in order to be *manifest* through him. [53]

The conclusion of *Being and Nothingness* adjourns the matter with an 'as if':

> It is as if the world, man, and man-in-the-world were only able to produce an abortive God. [54]

This conclusion does not surprise the reader of *Being and Nothingness*; it was foreseeable in the introduction. Given that being is the identical which is no more than identical, whereas consciousness is the difference which must never attain to identity, the relation between the two is necessarily a non-relation, and

---

[53] 'Merleau-Ponty vivant', *Les Temps Modernes*, no. 184–5, 1961, p. 366.
[54] EN, p. 717.

the synthesis a failure. However, the reader may well hold the opinion that what has proved abortive in this affair is less the deification of man than Sartre's ontology itself. For, having reached the end of the book, he will still be ignorant of what being and nothingness are, or in what way they are linked.

2

The human origin of truth

Kojève explained to his listeners that the aim of philosophy was to account for the 'fact of history'.[1] He said that this question, stifled by the 'monist ontology' inherited from the Greeks, had been posed for the first time by Kant and Hegel. In *Being and Nothingness*, Sartre too assigns to metaphysics the task of answering the question, why is there history? But the only answer he could envisage was a kind of pantheistic myth in which he claimed not to believe. It is impossible, he explained, for nature to give rise to consciousness.

Merleau-Ponty points out that the opposition of subject and object, or in Sartrian language, of *for-itself* and *in-itself*, makes any understanding of the 'fact of history' (something much in demand) impossible. Once denaturised by virtue of the negative definition of freedom ('to be free' = 'to be able to say no'), man is in opposition to things. Being and freedom are understood as antithetical. But in these conditions, historical action is not possible, for such action is distinguished from futile agitation by the fact that it leads to results, that it modifies the course of things, that it leaves behind it a work. And the possibility of historical work is excluded by the antithesis which confronts the stubborn identity of being with the freedom of nothingness. Either the work is on the side of freedom (but then it is arrested at the level of a *project* opposed to the world as it exists), or else it is real, and takes place in the world, but then it passes into the region of the *in-itself*, and is no longer in any way human.

[1] *Intr. Hegel*, p. 366.

Rejecting the Sartrian antithesis, Merleau-Ponty pioneered what has been known in France as 'existential phenomenology'. The programme of this phenomenology was to describe precisely what lies *between* the 'for–itself' and the 'in–itself', between consciousness and the thing, freedom and nature. It favoured the terrain of the '*entre-deux*' (between-the-two), as it was called at the time:

> The synthesis of *in itself* and *for itself* which brings
> Hegelian freedom into being has, however, its truth. In a
> sense, it is the very definition of existence, since it is
> effected at every moment before our eyes in the
> phenomenon of presence, only to be quickly re-enacted,
> since it does not conjure away our finitude.[2]

These lines contain – 'in a sense' – Merleau-Ponty's entire philosophy.

1. The alternatives of classical philosophy are rejected: man as he exists (here we come back to 'concrete philosophy') is neither pure 'in–itself' (a thing, a material body in the scientific sense), nor pure 'for–itself' (a *res cogitans*, a sovereign freedom). Hence that feature of Merleau-Ponty's style, reminiscent of Bergson: whatever the subject being broached, an antithesis is sketched only to be rejected (Neither ... nor ...).

2. But in its turn the solution of antitheses is found *neither* in a synthesis which might reconcile the two points of view, *nor* in a rejection of the assumption which gives rise to the antithesis. The solution is sought 'between the two', in a 'finite' synthesis, that is, an unfinished and precarious one.

The fact of history proves that the synthesis which Sartre had judged impossible is taking place every day. Neither thing nor pure mind, man appears

> as a product/producer, as the space in which necessity can
> turn into concrete freedom.[3]

It is here that Merleau-Ponty looks to Husserl – more precisely, to the author of *Krisis*. In Merleau-Ponty's version, phenomenology would be, definitively, the project for a description of the foundations of history, namely *human existence*, as it is *lived*; never, then,

[2] PP, p. 519.
[3] SNS, p. 237.

as all black or all white, but as mixed and variegated. What must be described is this composite: product/producer, active/passive, instituted/instituting; or, in all these guises, a subject/object.

The Soul and the Body

To bridge the divide between things and consciousness calls for the elaboration of a philosophy of nature. Merleau-Ponty sets out this philosophy in his short thesis, *La structure du comportement*. French taste, however, would have difficulty in accepting an excessively romantic work on the odyssey of the mind through natural forms. This is why Merleau-Ponty adopts a more French approach, discussing the classic problem of the unity of soul and body. From Descartes to Bergson, the definition of matter and the philosophical basis of physics are played out in the relationship of body to mind (for this reason French philosophy reserves a seat of honour for *psychology*, which is reputed to study that relationship). In Merleau-Ponty's thesis, discussion of the methods of contemporary psychology (which he defines as the study of behaviour) is only there in order to facilitate 'an understanding of the relationship between consciousness and nature' (the first stage of the book). But the point at which consciousness enters into contact with nature in general is none other than the body of the conscious being. It is therefore necessary to look at the 'relations of soul and body' (the title of the closing chapter).

Merleau-Ponty seeks to show that 'behaviour' (for which the French, '*comportement*', is simply the translation of the word 'behaviour' as defined by the Behaviourist school) must be explained 'dialectically' and not 'analytically'. In general terms, the analytic explanation reduces the complex to the simple, starting from the principle that the whole is the result of the combination of parts supposedly exterior to one another (cf. the *partes extra partes* in the Cartesian definition of matter). In a return to the Romantic inspiration which maintained that the whole is greater than the sum of its parts, Merleau-Ponty brings to light something which is lost in analytic explanations: the wholeness of the whole, the complexity of the complex. Any behaviour pattern, whether human or not, is a 'structured whole'; it may not be reduced to the mere effect of the constellation of contextual factors. A behaviour pattern is not the *reaction* to a *stimulus*, but rather the *response elicited* by a situation. The faculty of apprehending the situation as a question to which it will reply must thus be ascribed to the organism whose behaviour is under observation. And therefore *soul*, which the grand dualism of Descartes had refused them, must be given back to animals and even to 'inanimate objects'. Beings in nature are not wholly in exteriority: they have an interior. Or again, behaviour is no longer the effect of a *milieu*, but a relation between thing and *milieu* which Merleau-Ponty sees as dialectical. Behaviour patterns, he says, 'have a meaning'; they correspond to the living significance of situations. There is therefore meaning and dialogue in nature. And this is what it was necessary to show. Q.E.D.

Merleau-Ponty calls this philosophy of nature a 'philosophy of structure',[4] a word which is not at all to be understood in the later sense of structuralism. Here, 'structure' is the equivalent of *Gestalt*, much prized by the 'psychology of form'. Nature presents itself as a 'universe of forms', arranged in hierarchical order. Physical forms (inert matter) are only imperfectly formal, while living forms are more so, and human forms are entirely so. With this triad, Merleau-Ponty accepts the legacy of what has held, in France, the role of a *Naturphilosophie*, via the reading of Aristotle by Ravaisson (who also corresponded with Schelling):

> Matter, life and mind must participate unequally in the nature of form; they must represent different degrees of integration, and, finally, must constitute a hierarchy in which individuality is progressively achieved.[5]

The notion of form, which this philosophy of nature appears to borrow from a school of psychologists, finally discovers its true meaning in the mission it receives: to make conceivable a transition from *nature* to *consciousness*:

> The notion of *Gestalt* led us back to its Hegelian meaning, that is, to the concept before it has become consciousness of self.[6]

Starting from there, Merleau-Ponty takes up what he calls the 'problem of perception'. He defines it in terms of the following

---

[4] SC, p. 143.   [5] SC, p. 143.   [6] SC, p. 227.

difficulty: what are the relations of 'naturised consciousness' and 'pure consciousness of self',[7] or again, 'in Hegelian terms', of 'consciousness in itself' and 'consciousness for itself'?[8] *Pure consciousness of self* is consciousness reduced to the 'I think' as defined in the idealist tradition. *Naturised consciousness* is 'perceptive consciousness', the 'I perceive'. And the difference between the two is this: while the 'I think' is given over to itself in complete abstraction from all circumstance, the 'I perceive' is necessarily incarnate and cannot overlook the fact. In order to see anything, we must be somewhere, preferably in daylight, or equipped with a reliable lamp, etc. – whence the strict analogy that as the soul is to the body, so the *cogito* is to the *percipio*. To show that the 'I think' is founded upon the 'I perceive' would therefore be to provide an account of the unity of soul and body, and thus also of 'mind' and 'nature', which is to say, finally, an account of history.

The Earth does not Revolve

Any attempt to question the Cartesian division of substance into thought and extension is necessarily also a critique of the science which is conditional upon this division. Hence a conflict, highly characteristic of French philosophy, between the two camps, phenomenology and epistemology (in France, the name taken by that philosophy which maintains that it is for science to tell us what is, the rest being 'poetry', or, as it is believed, subjective expression). For phenomenology, as Merleau-Ponty understands it, tries to re-establish a method of communication between things and the mind, and this would be the sense of the word *phenomenon*:

> The experience of a real thing cannot be explained by the action of that thing on my mind: the only way for a thing to act on the mind is to offer it a meaning, to manifest itself to it, to *constitute* itself vis-à-vis the mind in its intelligible articulations.[9]

How can a thing 'offer a meaning'? Would it be a text to be read, a speech to be heard? Absolutely. In his critique of behaviourism

---

[7] SC, p. 241.   [8] SC, p. 191.   [9] SC, p. 215.

Merleau-Ponty had already likened the relation of organism and milieu to a 'debate'; the milieu poses questions and the organism replies by its behaviour (for example, such and such a situation offers the signification 'danger', to which the organism replies with gestures which in their entirety signify 'struggle', or 'flight'). Henceforth, phenomena are considered as statements, which is doubtless the key to this phenomenology. Taking the perceptual experience of a 'lovely spring morning', to say that I experience with joy a certain quality in the sky would be the same thing, for the phenomenologist, as to say that the sky 'offers me the meaning' of a lovely morning. *That which shows itself to me* is measured in terms of *that which it is possible for me to say about it*. A phenomenon is thus identified with the sayable.

Hence the definition of phenomenology as description. Its task is not to *explain* but to *make explicit*, or to reproduce in discourse the statement which preceded the discourse, and which is the phenomenon. Merleau-Ponty readily quotes the following lines from Husserl:

> It is the pure and, so to speak, still dumb experience
> which must be brought to the pure expression of its own
> meaning.[10]

These words indicate clearly that 'meaning', before being that of 'the expression' – in this case the statements that tell of an experience – is, more primarily, the meaning of this experience itself, which for all its dumbness has much to say. To speak is therefore to give a voice to that which does not know how to speak. It is a hopeless enterprise in some respects: discourse may well adhere to experience, but it will always be discourse *upon* experience, or speech following on, with what Derrida calls an 'originary delay'. Thus phenomenology embarks upon a task which it itself describes as 'infinite' (a discreet way of saying that it is unrealisable, for a promised land which we will reach at the cost of an 'infinite journey' is indistinguishable from a land which is eternally prohibited). It seeks to found the 'I think' upon the 'I perceive', and understands the *cogito* in accordance with the most classical tradition, in the sense of an 'I judge', or a predicative enunciation. The aim is therefore to found predicative activity on

---

[10] *Cartesian Meditations*, § 16.

an 'ante-predicative'[11] activity. But given that the means to this
end is to relate in discourse that which precedes the discourse, the
ante-predicate can never be reconstructed as it was, in its dumb
purity, before being made explicit. The relationship of the 'I
perceive' to the visible world corresponds to what Husserl calls
'the world of life'. As Lyotard has put it:

> In so far as this life-originating world is ante-predicative,
> all predication, all discourse, undoubtedly *implies* it, yet is
> *wide* of it, and properly speaking nothing may be said of it
> ... The Husserlian description ... is a struggle of language
> against itself to attain the originary ... In this struggle, the
> defeat of the philosopher, of the logos, is assured, since the
> originary, once described, is thereby no longer originary.[12]

---

[11] It is here that 'the Earth does not revolve'. Merleau-Ponty had been
deeply interested by Husserl's text of the same title (which he quotes in
PP, p. 491). It is certainly a striking illustration of the phenomenological
step which marks a return to the *lived world* as being at the origin of
everything we know, and even the original origin, *die Ur-Arche*. At first
sight we tend to think that the question of the earth's motion must be
decided by astronomy, i.e. by a science dealing with the planet as one
celestial *object* among others. Since astronomers have adopted the
Copernican solution, we *live* in one world in which we both see and say
that 'the sun rises', and we *think* in another, where we know that the
earth revolves around the sun. Conflict exists between the lived world
(*Lebenswelt*) and the known world, between the *percipio* and the *cogito*.
Phenomenology invites us to resolve this conflict by ceasing to identify
the real with the objective, and the lived-through with the apparent. It
sets out to show how the lived world lies at the origin of the known, or
the objective world. And if the lived world lies at the origin of the *true
world*, it must, in its way, be more truthful than the true one.
  Science deals with the earth as an object and ascribes to it a movement
in space. But this science was born *on the earth*, and it was *here* on this
earth that it provided 'objective' definitions of motion, rest, space, and
objectivity in general. Scientists' statements, for example the Copernican
statement, take their meaning from experiences acquired here. The *here*,
which is the place of this first experience, is not therefore a place in
space, since it is the place of origin of the very notion of space. On this
'refutation of Copernicus' see Derrida's comments (OG, p. 78–9) and,
from a standpoint hostile to phenomenology, those of Serres (*Le système
de Leibniz et ses modèles mathématiques* (2 vols, P.U.F. 1968) vol II, pp.
710–12).
[12] *La phénoménologie* (P.U.F., 1954), p. 45. This short introduction to
phenomenology is a significant document which well illustrates the
preoccupations of the fifties. The interest of phenomenologists has
shifted from mathematics to the human sciences, from the
anti-historicist polemic to the search for a common ground with
Marxism.

Experience is still *dumb*; it is not coincident with discourse. If the 'expression' by which the experience is rendered in discourse is indeed the expression of the *meaning* of that experience, then it is the expression *of* that experience. Discourse simply manifests externally (ex-presses) that which, dumb and implicit, was already present internally. Some of Merleau-Ponty's formulations tend in this direction:

> It is true that we should never talk about anything if we were limited to talking about those experiences with which we coincide, since speech is already a separation ... [But] the primary meaning of discourse is to be found in that text of experience which it is trying to communicate. [13]

The text of experience: if experience affords a meaning, it must in its way be a text, of which 'texts', in the sense of books, are only approximate reproductions. But if experience is a text, by whom is it written? For Sartre, there is no room for doubt: the scribe is man, the being through whom 'meaning comes into the world'. By the same token, the world has no meaning by itself (meaning must be imparted to it). Merleau-Ponty, of course, cannot give this answer, since he challenges dualism. The question must therefore be put to him.

Does the Dark Side of the Moon Exist?

For Merleau-Ponty, the fact of the unity of soul and body shows that the antitheses so abundant in philosophy are transcended *in fact*. The task of philosophy is to say how: to describe this unity, as it is testified to by perception. Reviving a theme of Gabriel Marcel's, Merleau-Ponty points out that the body of the idealist philosopher is the living refutation of the doctrine he professes, for the philosopher can make it neither into an element of his 'self' (defined by the abstract 'I think') nor into a fragment of his 'not-self'. The body is not an object; it is never at any remove, never offered totally to the person who inhabits it. Now the *ego* of the *ego percipio*, unlike the *ego* of the *ego cogito*, cannot masquerade

[13] PP, p. 388.

as pure mind; it is necessarily an 'incarnate subject'. On this point, the antithesis is already defeated; it is essential for the *perceiver* to be incarnate, hence visible, perceived/perceiving. The foundation of the 'I think' upon the 'I perceive' would thus be the return to the concrete after which modern philosophy was hankering. The 'I think' tends towards abstraction. No sooner is it stated in its purity than it claims universality, since whoever says 'I think' thereby ascribes to himself a certain *thought*, and it can be maintained that this thought is the same regardless of who thinks it. The 'I perceive', on the other hand, is not capable of ready universalisation. If two people say 'I perceive' at the same time, we already know that they are not perceiving the same things. Each has his own perspective (deriving from his *situation* in space). The subject of perception is individuated; he looks out from *here*, today, etc.

It is useful to refer to the favourite example of phenomenologists, that of the cube and its six sides. By definition, a cube has six sides, but nobody can see them all at once. The six sides are never simultaneously before my eyes. When I say 'This is a cube', I attribute to it more than I can see: namely the sides that I would be able to see if I were to move around it. So there is referral to another experience, either past or future, in each immediate perceptual experience. The thing which is *present* to me and which 'offers a meaning' to me – as if to say, 'I am a cube' – is never fully revealed. I assume that the hidden faces of the cube are present on the other side, where I am not, but in point of fact, I do not know this at the moment. As a result, perception, which, according to a philosophy of the *percipio*, is the very experience of truth, always involves the possibility of being invalidated or gainsaid by an ulterior perception. The phenomenology of perception echoes the intransigence of Thomas the Apostle: 'I will believe in the resurrection of Jesus Christ on the day I can *see* and *touch* him.' Truth only has a meaning in the present. Only that which is present to me here and now *is*, truly, absolutely and beyond doubt. However, Thomas the Apostle is not infallible. Perhaps when he saw, he was mistaken. Thus what is true today runs the risk of being overthrown as soon as it becomes 'yesterday's truth'. As Lyotard suggests, the phenomenological definition of truth does away with eternal truths and makes truth into a question of *history*:

> There is thus no absolute truth, the postulate common
> both to dogmatism and scepticism; truth is defined in its
> becoming, as the revision, correction and surpassing of
> itself – a dialectical operation which always takes place
> within the living present (*lebendige Gegenwart*).[14]

And, incidentally, it is easy to understand the fascination exercised over a whole generation by the then unpublished manuscripts of Husserl on the 'Living Present' (capital letters were eagerly added!). The phenomenological concept of time, as Husserl was reputed to have developed it in his later philosophy, was considered the key to the question of history (the philosophical stake of the generation). But it was precisely from this inclusion of the *absent* within the *present* (the *yesterday* and the *tomorrow* within the *today*) that Derrida was to launch his offensive against phenomenology.

The example of the cube allows us to measure the distance between the *percipio* and the *cogito*. The six-sided cube is the cube as an object of predicative statements. As for the perceived cube, it can never have six sides at once. This, then, is the meaning of the 'primacy of perception in philosophy' (the title of a lecture by Merleau-Ponty): just as the earth, in a sense, does not revolve, so the real cube does not have six sides, for the *real cube* is the cube which is present, and a cube will never present all of its six sides at once:

> The cube with six sides is not only invisible, but
> inconceivable; it is the cube as it would be for itself; but
> the cube is not for itself, since it is an object.[15]

In more general terms, phenomenology maintains that the only meaning which 'being' can have for myself is 'being for myself'.[16] Consequently we must include the actual conditions under which the object is given to us in our definition of it. Just as the trip to the holiday home is part of the holiday, the route towards the object is a part of the object. This is the fundamental axiom of phenomenology. And so perspective, for example, should not be considered as the perceiving subject's point of view upon the object perceived, but rather as a property of the object itself:

---

[14] *La phénoménologie*, pp. 40–1.   [15] PP, p. 236.
[16] PP, p. iii.

Perspective does not appear to me to be a subjective deformation of things but, on the contrary, to be one of their properties, perhaps their essential property. It is precisely because of it that the perceived possesses in itself a hidden and inexhaustible richness, that it is a 'thing'.[17]

Once this axiom is established – which consists in rejecting the Kantian distinction between the phenomenon and the thing, while subjugating the phenomenon to the subject – paradoxical consequences abound, and Merleau-Ponty does not shy away from any of them. It was necessary to say, for example, that the world is *uncompleted*, for the perceiving subject, always situated, can never have more than a partial view of the world.[18] *Man*, too, *is uncompleted* as long as history has not reached its conclusion. *God himself is uncompleted*, for he is the name of the infinite distance separating man from his fellow men, the *ego* from the *alter ego*. In an article written in 1947 to defend Sartre against his critics at the time, Merleau-Ponty said:

If humanism is the religion of man as a natural species or the religion of the completed man, Sartre is now further away from it than ever.[19]

Real humanism, the humanism of Sartre, to which Merleau-Ponty here subscribes, is therefore that of the uncompleted man. There is nothing to stop us seeing in this humanism *a religion of the uncompleted man* for, as Merleau-Ponty specifies in an article on Marxism, religion is after all no more

than the fantastic effort of man to reunite with other men in another world.[20]

The Phenomenon

All these forms of incompletion have been assembled under the heading of ambiguity, and everywhere Merleau-Ponty has been presented as the 'philosopher of ambiguity'. However, when Merleau-Ponty is reproached for failing to commit himself (Neither ... nor), he replies that it is not his thought which is

[17] SC, p. 201.   [18] PP, p. 465.   [19] SNS, p. 80.
[20] SNS, p. 226.

equivocal, but the thing itself, of which he seeks to give a faithful account – the lived world, existence.

Let us suppose, however, that the famous phenomenological cube is a can, and that I propose to use this can for carrying wine to my cellar. It matters to me greatly that this can should not, like the 'lived cube' of phenomenology, be a 'unit of meaning' which is merely presumed or anticipated by means of the series of 'profiles' it offers in succession to the eye. This can would only have its six sides at the end of an infinite labour of verification, and a 'limit-idea' of the can is of no use to me at all. I require a *completed* can, and no one would tolerate his ironmonger trying to sell him a phenomenological can, uncompleted and leaking everywhere. But my experience of the can I use is as unassailable as the experience of the phenomenologist, who is content to perceive it. It is the experience of a *given* cube with all its sides at once. In the same way, the road perceived by the phenomenologist is a 'perspective being', whose sides converge and meet in the distance; but fortunately the road along which he drives is not. Why should the most privileged relation to the thing be one of perception?

More generally, the issue is to know whether phenomenology should be a *question* about the phenomenon, or whether it is only a way of refusing certain questions as 'bereft of meaning' because they are 'contrary to the hypothesis'.

Now Merleau-Ponty evidently opts for the second path, at least in the *Phenomenology of Perception*.[21] The hypothesis which supports the entire edifice is that 'being' means 'being for myself'. As studied by the phenomenologist, the phenomenon is the 'being for myself', the appearance before myself. But what, in this relation, is meant by *myself*? Is it the phenomenon which gives 'myself' its meaning? Or is it 'myself' which decides the phenomenon? Which of the two is to measure the other?

In fact, the phenomenologist shares his use of the word 'phenomenon' with the posivitist, who insists that 'being = being

[21] Later, Merleau-Ponty recognised a certain inadequacy in the starting point of his *Phenomenology of Perception*. His death interrupted that trend in his thought which was leading him towards quite a different philosophy. Under the title, *Le visible et l'invisible*, Claude Lefort has published certain passages in final draft form, and some notes for a book, which Merleau-Ponty had been working on for several years (Gallimard, 1964). See Lefort's commentaries in *Sur une colonne absente* (Gallimard, 1978).

for myself', but views this as a regulating factor of his discourse. For him, phenomenality coincides with the relativity of the observed fact to the observer. Only the observable can give rise to an affirmation, the rest being 'conjecture' or 'speculation'. It remains, of course, to settle the conditions for what would be deemed acceptable as 'observation': the characteristics of witnesses, recording procedures, various kinds of apparatus etc. None of this affects the thing itself, nor would the positivist claim that the rules by which he chooses to abide have any bearing on the thing. Auguste Comte remarked that if the earth were slightly nearer the sun, it would be enveloped in perpetual fog, the sky would not be visible and thus astronomy, the firstborn of the sciences, would have been impossible. The heavens could not be observed, and yet they would not exist any the less for that. The positivist, therefore, distinguishes 'in itself' and 'for us'. But the phenomenologist admits of no 'in itself', for his initial operation is not one of a reduction to the observable, but one of a *reduction to meaning*. If there is to be anything unobservable for ourselves, we must be able to refer to an *experience* in which consciousness is aware of what presents itself as unobservable, or else we would not know what we were talking about. Consequently, the unobservable is in all likelihood only provisionally so, and may be observable *in the future* or *elsewhere* – unless it is that quota of obscurity inherent in experience, in so far as experience is incomplete. Here the unobservable would be another name for the inexhaustible future of observation.

In other words, phenomenality (the meaning of the phenomenon) as understood by the phenomenologist, far from being a relativity, names *the appearance of the absolute*. In Hegel as in Husserl, phenomenology relates one thing only: this appearance of the absolute, which is the *absolute subject*. And Merleau-Ponty seems to place himself within this tradition when he writes, 'I am the absolute source.'[22]

In that case, why was so much emphasis given to the fact that the foundation of the *cogito* on the *percipio* put an end to the absolute claims of consciousness, consigning it to the realm of the unfinished and the uncertain? Does the 'primacy of perception' generate positivism or absolute knowledge? The perceiving

[22] PP. p. iii.

subject is particular, incarnate, situated, committed etc. – in short, a subject that appears relative to all kinds of conditions. But is this subject in a position to defend its humanity when it inherits at one and the same time the absolutist ambitions of the *cogito* and the title of *true subject*? By raising the relative to the absolute, it would seem that Merleau-Ponty is engaged in an ambiguous undertaking. Does the subject become relative, or does perception become absolute? Perception becomes absolute; for ourselves, it becomes absolute knowledge. Merleau-Ponty is thus led to encumber the unlucky *percipiens* with the last thing it wanted: the crushing attributes of the 'absolute subject'. A ludicrous potentate, thrust onto a throne too high for it, the perceiving subject sees its empire disintegrate around it. Cubes shed their sides, things dwindle away into the distance, becoming minuscule; faces have an 'ambiguous' air, others only exist in the infinite, the world frays at the edges ... In truth, the kingdom of sensible things demands another sovereign: it rejects the imposition of this equivocal prince.

Merleau-Ponty's work is open to a double reading. A new 'philosophy of consciousness', as it was called, could as readily be found there as an attempt to surpass this type of philosophy. A 'philosophy of consciousness' consists in the doctrine that the *origin of truth* is the *cogito*. Merleau-Ponty insists on the return to a 'true *cogito*', namely the 'I perceive' beneath the 'I think'. The origin of truth is particular, relative, *human*. But then the phenomenon is only a semblance, or the opinion that I, *myself*, situated *here*, *in the present*, can hold about things. Yet his phenomenological premises prohibit any distinction between being in itself and being for myself. Although it is human, the origin of truth is 'the absolute source'. The oscillation between relative and absolute, between 'I am writing the text of my experience' and 'the world itself is writing this text, I do no more than hear its voice'; the hesitation between the principle of *subject* and the search for a more ancient origin, for a more originary neuter (*ne-uter*, neither ... nor ...), the source common to both subject and object – all these waverings are present within the circularity of the starting point: the only meaning 'being' can have for me is one of 'being for myself'. Should this be taken to mean that any other form of being is altogether beyond me? Should it be understood on the contrary as an imperious declaration to the effect that the only meaning of the word 'being' is the one it has for me? This circularity is patent in propositions such as the following:

> The double meaning of the *cogito* is the fundamental
> metaphysical fact. I am sure that there is being – provided
> we look for no other kind than being-for-myself. [23]

The Phenomenology of History

Merleau-Ponty writes that, in the authentic *cogito*, the 'I think' would neither contain nor maintain the 'I am', but that conversely,

> the 'I think' . . . is re-integrated into the transcending
> process of the 'I am', and consciousness into existence. [24]

These words clearly express the ambitions and the limitations of 'existential phenomenology': a return to existence, since the 'I am' has priority over the 'I think'; an inversion of idealism, for which the 'I think' gives all its meaning to the 'I am' – but an inversion that remains on the ground of the *cogito*, therein respecting the essence of what has been taught in philosophy since the time of Descartes.

The only novelty is that the subject – absolute as ever – is credited with a 'transcending process' which in the language of the day denoted a movement going *beyond* the given or the present. The subject is perpetually in flight before itself. If it knows, it does not know that it knows, and if it knows that it does not know, it cannot even be sure of knowing this. If it believes, it does not believe that it believes. [25] The perceiving subject, unlike

---

[23] SNS, p. 164.

[24] PP, p. 439.

[25] A NOTE ON THE UNCONSCIOUS. Merleau-Ponty suggested interpreting the Freudian notion of the unconscious in terms of the ambiguity of consciousness. In a lecture given in 1951, he rejected the unconscious itself. What psychoanalysts call the unconscious, he said, can cover only an 'unrecognised, unformulated knowledge, that we do not wish to assume' (*Signes*, Gallimard, 1960, p. 291; trans. R. McCleary, *Signs*, Evanston, Ill., Northwestern U.P., 1964). He added: 'In an approximate language, Freud is on the point of discovering what other thinkers have more appropriately named *ambiguous perception*. It is by working in this direction that we shall find a civil status for this consciousness which brushes its objects (eluding them at the moment it is going to designate them, and taking account of them as the blind man takes account of

the identical Self of idealism (Myself = Myself), is defined in terms of the definitive impossibility of any 'coincidence with oneself'. Plunged back into existence, the subject is affected by an internal difference which Merleau-Ponty calls by turns non-coincidence with self, non-possession of self, opacity, etc. The false *cogito* is the absolute consciousness in which a subject recognises itself as being identical to what it thinks. But if someone were able to say that he was identical with himself, he would be outside time. The true *cogito* is human consciousness, marked as it is by an 'interior distance'. And finally, *time* must be recognised in this distance, where 'to be myself' is always 'to be outside myself'. The 'I' is never altogether an 'I'. It is unfinished, or as Deleuze says, *'fêlé'* ('cracked'). (In southern French, a *'tête fêlée'* is someone who is 'a bit cracked'.) In the *ego*, there is thus always an impersonal, or pre-personal, factor, over which the person of the thinker can never entirely return in order to think it out. For example, it is not altogether true to say 'I can see the blue of the sky.'

> If I wanted to render precisely the perceptual experience, I ought to say that *one* perceives in me, and not that I perceive.[26]

obstacles rather than recognising them), which does not want to know about them (which does not know about them, to the extent that it knows about them, and knows about them to the extent that it does not know about them), and which subtends our express acts and understandings.' (*Ibid.*) These 'others', who had spoken of 'ambiguous perception', were the founders of *Gestalttheorie*.

Merleau-Ponty proposed therefore that psychoanalysts should cease to speak about the unconscious and become converted to ambiguous consciousness. The debate of the 1960s, which was to set phenomenology and psychoanalysis in opposition to each other, was undoubtedly the crucial reason for the defeat of the former in the eyes of public opinion. The psychoanalysts had no difficulty in showing that this trading-in of the *unconscious* for *implicit consciousness* entailed the loss of all that was valuable in Freud's discovery. For an idea of the way in which the two sides clashed, see Actes du Congrès de Bonneval, 1960, published by Desclée de Brouwer as *L'inconscient* in 1966. This discussion anticipates the polemic between the Lacanians and Paul Ricœur, sparked off by his *De l'interpretation, un essai sur Freud* (Seuil, 1965); *Freud & Philosophy: An Essay on Interpretation*, trans. D. Savage (Newhaven, Conn., Yale U.P., 1977).

[26] PP, p. 249.

It is not *I* that sees any more than it is *I* that dies; neither sensation nor death are personal experiences of which *I* am the subject. The thinking subject can only apprehend itself as 'already born' and 'still alive': the limits of birth and death elude it. Thought stands out on an obscure ground to which it looks back, which it cannot illuminate, and which is

> a kind of original past, a past which has never been present.[27]

Facing the unfinished subject stands the equally unfinished object. Herein, then, resides the originality of idealism as *reformed*, but not *surpassed*, by Merleau-Ponty: *the identity of subject and object* – the fundamental proposition of idealism – transpires within incompletion, non-coincidence, penumbra.

The philosophy of perception operates a certain displacement of the 'I' towards the 'one' (a displacement which was hastily and mistakenly interpreted as a *surpassing* of the subject, whereas it was evidently a case of transference, a movement from the personal subject-to an impersonal and anonymous one). Here, in Merleau-Ponty's view, is what makes the constitution of a philosophy of history possible. If the 'I' harbours an impersonal subject ('one sees', 'one is born', 'one begins'), then the same holds good for the 'we', and this anonymous collective mind bridges the gulf that separates the *in-itself* and the *for-itself*. For it is this divide that makes the fact of history unintelligible.

In his inaugural lecture at the Collège de France in 1953, Merleau-Ponty said:

> The theory of the sign, as elaborated by linguistics, may imply a theory of historical meaning which can cut across the alternative of *things* or *consciousness* ... Saussure may well have sketched a new philosophy of history.[28]

Merleau-Ponty was probably the first to have actually demanded a philosophy from the *Course in General Linguistics*. Here he invokes its structuralism as against Sartrian dualism. Ten years later, others were to invoke Saussure as they phased phenomenology into retirement. The 'new philosophy of history' drawn from the *Course* was not phenomenological. In this phenomenologico-structuralist imbroglio, we should single out the fact that, in the

[27] PP, p. 280.   [28] *Eloge de la philosophie*, pp. 74–5.

service of his project for a phenomenology of history, Merleau-Ponty mobilised the very authorities which would be invoked against all forms of phenomenology after 1960. During the fifties, Saussurian linguistics and the structural anthropology of Lévi-Strauss were his allies. It is as if these allies in the resistance to Sartrian activism transformed themselves, after Merleau-Ponty's death in 1961, into opponents of phenomenology in general, forming the heteroclite camp which was christened 'structuralism'.

In *Les aventures de la dialectique*, Merleau-Ponty reproaches Sartre with his unawareness of the 'interworld':

> The question is to know whether, as Sartre maintains, there are only *men* and *things*, or whether there is not also this interworld which we call history, symbolism and the truth remaining to be accomplished.[29]

If the subject–object dichotomy were correct, then all meaning would issue from men, and all meaning *for myself* would issue from *myself*. A solipsism of this order cannot conceive of history without holding each individual, at each instant, responsible for the burden of universal history, and this in every one of his decisions. A person cannot say, 'I want' without determining, whether he likes it or not, the meaning of the price of bread, the government's policies, the future of mankind and also its past – Roman civilisation, Indian dances, etc.

The solution is therefore that there should be a meaning, not outside humanity in general, but outside each consciousness, i.e. *among them all* in the form of *symbols*. Meaning is then *outside* myself in so far as it is *for ourselves*, the 'ourselves' being comprised of those persons present (capable of saying 'we want') and the anonymous backdrop of humanity. Here Merleau-Ponty is speaking of 'symbolism' with reference to the works of Lévi-Strauss (about whom I shall say a little in the following chapter). But in fact his conception of 'symbolism' is much closer to Hegelian *objective Mind* than to structural anthropology. In his lecture he asked:

> Having dispensed with the resource of Hegelian objective Mind, how are we to avoid the dilemma of existence as a

thing and existence as consciousness, how are we to understand this generalised meaning which lingers in historical forms and in history as a whole, which is not the thought of any one *cogito*, and which, however, calls to them all?[30]

It is the *structures* of structuralism which supply an answer to this 'how?':

> The presence of structure outside us in natural and social systems, and within us as symbolic function, points to a way beyond the subject-object correlation which has dominated philosophy from Descartes to Hegel.[31]

In 1942, Merleau-Ponty had said this of *Gestalttheorie*. Twenty years later, he enlists structuralism in the same crusade against the antithesis of nature and mind. In other words, Merleau-Ponty understands the 'structures' of structuralism in the same sense as that in which he himself spoke of 'structure' in *La structure du comportement*. He confuses them with *Gestalten*. It is true that he is not alone in committing this error.

Symbolism belongs to the order of language, therefore the possibility of history resides in language. Merleau-Ponty's philosophy of history (his political philosophy) is thus his philosophy of language. But language must be understood, he considers, on the basis of the unity of soul and body as expressed in *gesture*. A gesture, of whatever kind, is invariably *expressive*. A style of handwriting, a way of walking or of lighting a cigarette are all recognisable. Since there is expression, there is also the appearance of a meaning. Of course this gestural meaning is not yet an intentional or explicit signification, unless it obeys a code (as, for example, with the secret signs agreed upon by spies). It is, according to Merleau-Ponty, a meaning in the process of being born, or in the 'incipient state'. Gesture, then, would be the 'institution' of meaning, which is to say that it produces meaning.[32] And in a

---

[30] *Eloge de la philosophie*, p. 73.

[31] 'De Mauss à Lévi-Strauss', *Signes*, p. 155. This article dates from 1959.

[32] Merleau-Ponty's course at the Collège de France in the year 1954–5 was entitled, 'The "Institution" in Personal and Public History'. The summary of the course shows that the notion of institution, 'the remedy for problems of consciousness', should make 'the evolution of phenomenology into a metaphysics of history' possible (cf. Merleau-Ponty, *Résumés de cours*, Gallimard, 1968, pp. 59 and 65).

philosophy inspired by Husserl, history is precisely the history of truth or of meaning, to the extent that it is assimilated to a *tradition*, and that meaning is the only thing which may be transmitted indefinitely.[33]

And so Merleau-Ponty writes:

> in the use of our body and our senses in so far as they involve us in the world, we have the means of understanding our cultural gesticulation, in so far as it involves us in history.[34]

Language explains history, since the meaning of history is that it be the history of meaning. 'Being-in-the-world' or the 'body proper' places us at the origin of language, to the extent that use of the body is expressive. Here then, via these intermediaries, is how the phenomenology of perception translates into a philosophy of *praxis* – a philosophy of history, a political philosophy.

As we can see, linguistic theory (speech, expressive gesture) and political theory (*praxis*, locus of the meaning of history) are indissociable. Thus the two axes, *semiology* (the theory of the sign), and the *theory of history*, came to define the level on which the subsequent evolution of French philosophical discourse would unfold. In what follows, these guidelines will enable us to evaluate the respective positions of those involved.

---

[33] See Husserl's *Origin of Geometry*, and Derrida's important introduction to his own translation of it. Attention will be given to this introduction further on.

[34] *Signes*, p. 87.

3

Semiology

The Intellectual Scene in 1960

The ambition of French phenomenology was to have a dialectical philosophy of history, supported by a phenomenology of the body and of expression. The generation active after 1960, however, condemned dialectics as an illusion, and rejected the phenomenological approach to language. The opposition between the prevailing post-war doctrine and what was soon to acquire for the public the name of *structuralism* appeared to be – or would have sought to be – total.

The dialectic was the promised land of the little existential tribe of 1950. The greatest criticism that could be levelled against a person was that his thinking was not sufficiently dialectical. After 1960, the dialectic continued to be at the centre of discussion, but it had moved into the dock. It had come to be seen as the most insidious form of the 'logic of identity' which in its turn was held to be the supreme philosophical illusion. Here the philosophers of the structuralist era strike a Bergsonian note. What they call the 'logic of identity' is that form of thought which cannot represent the *other* to itself without reducing it to the *same*, and thereby subordinating difference to identity. The logic of identity is countered with a 'thinking based upon difference'. The effects of reading Heidegger[1] are discernible in this change of course, and in the accompanying renewal of interest in Nietzsche.

---

[1] 'For Hegel, the business of thinking is thought as absolute concept. For us, the business of thinking is, provisionally, difference *as* difference.' *Identität und Differenz* (Neske, 1957), p. 37.

Ultimately, the contradiction of French phenomenology lay in its effort to dispute 'objective thinking', which had been responsible for antitheses of the kind, 'soul and body', while attempting to do so by means of a return to an authentic *cogito*. Although 'objective thinking' impoverishes the world by reducing each thing to being the mere *object* of a representation, the 'authentic *cogito*', or *percipio*, is no less objective (or 'objectifying', as it was also said) than scientific judgment. In choosing to remain 'within the Cartesian perspective of philosophies of consciousness',[2] phenomenology is incontestably idealist. It has merely refined the correlation between the thing reduced to *object* and thought reduced to *consciousness*. Whether this object is henceforth a 'perspective object' (Merleau-Ponty), or whether this consciousness is compared to nothingness (Sartre), the essential point, which is the irruption of the self into the equation of *being* and *being for myself*, remains unchanged. Where Parmenides said, 'being is', modern philosophy proclaims that 'being is for myself'.

Phenomenology is thus imprisoned within the 'closure of representation' (as Derrida calls it), inasmuch as it retains the principle of the *subject*. Here the critique of phenomenology links up with the critique of the dialectic. For what is a 'subject'? 'Subject' (or 'suppositum') is the name given to a be-ing whose *identity* is sufficiently stable for it to bear, in every sense of the word (sustain, serve as a foundation for, withstand), change or modification. The subject remains the same, while accidental qualities are altered. Since Descartes, the most subjective of all subjects is the one which is certain of its identity, the *ego* of *ego cogito*. The quality of subjectivity is thus confined to consciousness. But what is the dialectic, if not precisely a superior concept of identity ('speculative identity', or 'identity of identity and non-identity'), which leads to recognition of the *absolute, not as substance but as subject* (Hegel)? The double attack on phenomenological consciousness and the logic of identity is therefore conducted under the banner of a single crusade against the *subject in general*.

---

[2] Jean Beaufret, in *Intr. aux ph. de l'existence*, p. 121. In the same article, dated 1947, Beaufret wrote: 'So long as philosophy maintains the interiority of the being subject, in whatever form, at the root of its own certainties, it is condemned to organise only the invasion of the world by a haemorrhage of subjectivity.'

But what signs will mark the breaking of the chain that binds philosophy within the area from which it seeks to escape – representation, identity, the negative, the subject? It will not be enough, of course, simply to strike these words out of the vocabulary. We must be wary of mistaking the wish to reach the promised land for having already arrived there.

It may happen for example, that the subject is declared 'surpassed' in cases where emphasis has simply been given to the impersonal and anonymous elements of experience, as if 'subject' and 'person' were one and the same. The question of a 'transcendental field without subjects'[3] has figured greatly in recent French philosophy. Here, the origin towards which phenomenological reduction would have us return is not Husserl's 'absolute *ego*' (which has its drawbacks – solipsism, etc.), but a kind of 'one', of neutral origin (neither me nor you) out of which the 'I' might then take shape. Such trends are already discernible in Merleau-Ponty's work. But the absence of a personal subject is equivalent to the presence of an impersonal subject. In fact, it is not hard to detect the promotion of new subjectivities in many of the communiqués announcing victory over THE SUBJECT.[4]

Structuralism

Properly speaking there is no definable structuralist philosophy such as might be opposed, for example, to the phenomenological school. 'Structuralism' is, after all, only the name of a scientific method. The *effect* of structuralism upon philosophical discourse is none the less incontestable, and we should enquire into the reasons for this. *Deconstructions* – and here is the effect – have taken the place of *descriptions*.

[3] The expression seems to belong to Jean Hyppolite. See the reference and discussion in Derrida, OG, pp. 84–5. The whole notion is more or less derived from Sartre's article, 'La transcendence de l'ego' (1938, republished by Vrin, 1965).

[4] Louis Althusser, for example, gives this definition of a non-ideological concept of history: history is a 'process without a subject'. By subject, he means 'person' in the legal sense. This enables him to attribute to none other than Hegel the merit of having been the first to conceive history as a process *without a subject*. Doubtless the word 'Mind', fairly frequent in Hegel's work, had eluded Althusser's 'symptomatic reading' (cf. his contribution to *Hegel et la pensée moderne*, P.U.F., 1970, p. 106).

Phenomenology was the description of phenomena. It chose to confine itself to the phenomenon and to say what distinguished one phenomenon from another. But since it held that 'phenomenon' meant an 'appearing to consciousness', this initial resolve to describe led to a 'bracketing out' of the existence *in itself* of the phenomenal thing, and therefore to the identification of being with meaning. Such was the purpose of 'reduction': the thing is reduced to the 'meaning' that it 'offers' to consciousness. The second stage consisted in demonstrating how consciousness 'builds up' from the given (i.e. from impressions) an object having precisely that meaning (the cube 'outside consciousness', for example).

Why this reduction of being to meaning? Husserl consistently presents it as a free action that one may choose to accomplish. In reality, phenomenologists never succeeded in justifying this initial choice of *epoche*, which however is all-decisive. Thus the notion that it is forbidden to overstep the limits of experience and that experience is always *lived by someone*, is revealed as the prejudice of phenomenological reduction. In other words, it is forbidden to distinguish 'being' and 'being for myself'. Everything that exists must be capable of being described as the meaning offered by the 'lived-through' (*vécu*) of someone or other ('*le vécu*' translates Husserl's *Erlebnis*)[5]. For example my lived-through might have the following meaning: I am perceiving a cube, and I build up the sense-unit 'cube' successively, from the sequence of 'sides' and 'profiles' which I see, etc. Now let us take the dream, madness and myth as instances. How are we to greet what the dreamer, the subject of hallucination or the myth-teller say to us? The dream account, delirium and the language of myth are invariably the *expression* of a particular *experience*: in the first case, oneiric experience of the world, in the second, schizophrenic experience, and in the third, mythical experience. All these are ways of existing, of 'being-in-the-world'. Alongside the two forms of experience, scientific and perceptual, with which we are most familiar, we must set these other 'lived experiences'. And since 'lived experience' is the origin of truth, a phenomenological analysis – of myth for instance – will consist in describing the

[5] In French, the adjective *vécu* has the connotation of on-the-spot journalism, the sensationalist press, literature of the personal testimony ('I was there', 'An hour with De Gaulle', 'I lived through all that').

'mythical consciousness', that is, the meaning offered by the world to anybody with a mythical experience of it:

> [If] the person who experiences something knows at the time what he is experiencing... then the madman, the dreamer or the subject of perception must be taken at their word, and we need merely confirm that their language in fact expresses what they are experiencing.[6]

I insist on these examples of dream, delirium and myth because they are the privileged objects of structural analysis. Shortly we will see how it opposes any attempt to treat the utterance under analysis as the expression of a 'lived-through'.

Deconstruction appears to denote a negative operation, whereas *description* suggests the simple acceptance of the given. In reality, the 'phenomenological positivism' of which Merleau-Ponty speaks was never the 'return to things themselves', nor the 'decision to confine oneself to the given' which it claimed to be, for it is in no way given, like a fact which would simply require description, that the given is given 'to a consciousness', in a 'noetico-noematic correlation' etc. That being should be *for myself* is certainly not what experience tells me: it is an assumption prior to any experience. 'Deconstruction' is a method which results from the unmasking of this phenomenological naïvety. The word 'deconstruction' was first proposed by Derrida, to translate the *Destruktion* of which Heidegger speaks in *Being and Time*, saying that it must not be understood in a negative sense (to demolish), but in a positive sense (to circumscribe). Before Derrida's introduction of the term, which was to be widely employed, it had existed only among grammarians, for whom it designated the analysis of sentence *construction*, which only comes to light when disturbed by deconstruction. The laws of poetic construction, for example, are revealed in the transposition of the poem into prose which, as regards the reference, is equivalent. Similarly, the aim of a 'deconstruction' in philosophy would be to show how philosophical discourses are constructed. Deconstruction thus attempts to propose a 'theory of philosophical discourse' (just as *poetics* is the theory of poetic discourse). Such a programme is clearly critical, for the philosophical statement means to be, or

[6] PP, p. 335.

would claim to be, governed by the thing itself, and seeks only to make manifest the referent which it invokes, to show it, or to 'allow it to exist'. But the deconstruction of philosophical statements destroys this illusion. It is not because it reflects the thing itself, thereby permitting the thing to declare itself to us, that the statement is constructed in the way that it is. The statement is only constituted in this way as a result of the constraints inherent in philosophical discourse. The case is the same here as it is for poetry. If a poetic utterance, for example:

> Oisive jeunesse
> A tout asservie,
> Par délicatesse
> J'ai perdu ma vie.
> Ah! Que le temps vienne
> Où les cœurs s'éprennent
>
> > (Rimbaud)

(Idle youth/Enslaved to everything/With sensibility/I've wasted my life/Let the time come/When hearts fall in love.)

presents the construction that it does, this is not at all because some lived state (regret, desire) has elicited this particular form of expression in which to speak its meaning (including the inexpressible or unsayable elements). The poet listens not so much to the stirrings of his heart as to the prescriptions of the French language, whose resources and limitations engender a poetics which governs the poem. Indeed, the closer that poetic expression claims to be to some spontaneous lyricism of lived immediacy, the more it is codified. The more the poem strives for emotional effect, the nearer it draws to popular forms of expression, whose regularity tends to the stereotype (ditties, refrains, nursery rhymes). So, in this 'pessimistic' poem by Laforgue:

> Quand on est mort, c'est pour de bon,
> Digue dondaine, digue dondaine,
> Quand on est mort, c'est pour de bon,
> Digue dondaine, digue dondon!

(When you're dead, it's for good/Refrain. (Repeated))

The problem encountered at the outset recurs here, but with a new vocabulary. The illusion of 'philosophical discourse', as revealed by deconstruction, is to affirm the transition from the *objective genitive* to the *subjective genitive*, in the 'discourse *of* the thing itself' that philosophy attempts to be. The thing itself addresses you through the channels of philosophical proposition.

But in what way can 'structuralism' raise the question of philosophical discourse? It is useful here to distinguish between three kinds of structuralism:

1. As the method of *structural analysis*, structuralism is older than French phenomenology, and altogether foreign to the present debate.

2. In so far as it merges with *semiology* (the theory of the sign), structuralism throws phenomenology into crisis by triumphantly setting against it another conception of *meaning*.

3. In so far as it is simply a philosophical 'orientation', structuralism is no more than the name that familiarised the public with the conversion of philosophy to the critique of both phenomenology *and semiology* (structuralism no. 3 is conspicuous for its indifference to 'structures').

The fact that contemporary structuralist philosophy also includes a critique of semiology is often overlooked, because it is thought that philosophy may be found already in structuralism no. 2, i.e. in the work of anthropologists. Philosophers themselves have shared and encouraged this error, since few of them have challenged the anthropological conversion of philosophy as it could be seen in 'existentialism' (which has much to say about *human* existence, but very little about *existence* as such), and in the philosophy of *praxis* ('everything which is real is praxis').

If structuralism induced a crisis in phenomenology (still dominant in 1960), it was because the latter had chosen to define itself in relation to what were known in France as the 'human sciences' (above all, psychology and psychoanalysis, with ethnology). According to its advocates, the strength of phenomenology lay in its aptitude for engaging in dialogue with the most active tendencies in anthropological research. The phenomenological generation prided itself on having given rigorous, philosophically acceptable expression to what was expressed only falteringly in the human sciences. Reinforced by the notions of 'behaviour', *Gestalt*, and then 'structure', these sciences rejected the subject–object antithesis and proposed a middle term, 'neither thing nor idea'. In the form of the authentic *cogito* where soul and body are united, phenomenology fulfilled their requirements by providing them with the amphibian that they desired but were unable to articulate.

In itself, structuralism (no. 1) is only a method. This method, not tied in principle to any specific object, aroused interest outside specialist circles as soon as it began to tackle sign systems (no. 2). Semiology, lastly, provoked the philosophical controversy of the sixties, the controversy concerning consciousness and the 'death of Man' (no. 3). We shall look at these various points in detail.

What is a Structural Analysis?

The inventor of structuralist method was probably the Philosopher in Molière's *Le Bourgeois Gentilhomme* (Act II, Scene v). Monsieur Jourdain wishes to write a letter to the Countess, using the following words: *Fair Countess, I am dying for love of your beautiful eyes.* He demands a lesson in rhetoric from the Philosopher and receives a lecture, well before the event, in semiology. 'I tell you, I don't want anything in the letter but those very words, but I want them to be stylish and properly arranged. Just tell me some of the different ways of putting them, so that I can see what I want.' The key-concepts are already recognisable: 'stylish', 'arranged', 'different ways'. The answer to a problem posed in this manner can only be structural – how many love letters may be written to the Countess, including the elements given in Monsieur Jourdain's sentence? There are two stages in the solution to a problem of this kind:

1. To identify the elements , by a procedure of breaking down the given whole (Monsieur Jourdain's sentence) into its constituent parts.

2. To ascertain the various ways in which these parts may be combined so that a variety of messages may be obtained.

This is precisely the Philosopher's approach when he lists the sentences obtainable by a simple repositioning of two parts in the original formula, each of these changes disclosing the possibility of a new message.

	(1)	(2)	(3)	(4)	(5)
I	Fair Countess	I am	dying	for love	of your beautiful eyes
II	I am	for love	of your beautiful eyes	fair Countess	dying
III	Dying	I am	fair Countess	for love	of your beautiful eyes
IV	For love	I am	dying	of your beautiful eyes	fair Countess
V	Of your beautiful eyes	fair Countess	for love	I am	dying

Each of the sentences proposed by the philosopher is what is known in algebra as a *permutation*. The few examples he gives demonstrate that the love letter required by Monsieur Jourdain consists of five successive positions, among which the five parts of the sentence must therefore be distributed (provided we ignore, for simplicity's sake, a variation introduced once: *I am /am I*). Each possible love letter is thus structured by a sequential relation. However, the sum of possible love letters is characterised by a group structure, since it corresponds to the one hundred and twenty possible permutations of five elements, presentable as a table. Let us assume:

a=fair countess b=I am c=dying
d=for love e=of your beautiful eyes.

This may be written,

(I)   a b c d e
(II)   b d e a c
        etc.

This exposition of the algebraic structure is moreover only the first step in an analysis of the love letter in question. The real issue is raised by Monsieur Jourdain's query:

M. JOURDAIN : But which of these is the best?
THE PHILOSOPHER: The one you used yourself, *Fair Countess, I am dying for love of your beautiful eyes.*

To reply as the philosopher does is effectively to have found a solution to the problem of *meaning*. In the code used here, this meaning has nothing to do with a flattering appraisal of the

Countess's eyes, any more than it seeks to inform her amiable person of their effect on Monsieur Jourdain. Dispatched to the Countess, any of these permutations states the same thing, namely, 'This is a declaration of love' – a declaration which is, besides, selected from a conventional set that the philosopher goes on to itemise: 'Fair Countess, the ardour of your glances has reduced my heart to ashes' etc. But from another point of view, the permutations are not equivalent. The structuralist must therefore distinguish the *denotation*, which remains the same in each of the 120 love letters, and the *connotation*, which is modified every time. Convention ascribes to permutation no. 1 the connotation of 'artlessness', and so, in the rhetorical code of the seventeenth century, it is the best. The connotation of 'preciousness' or 'amphigorism' might be attributed by the same classical code to any of the other permutations. To pursue the matter further we should refer to Roland Barthes, who has equated the 'connotative signified' with 'ideology' (to be taken in the sociological, or even Marxist sense of the term):

> The future belongs to a linguistics of connotation, for on the basis of primary systems afforded by human language, society is constantly developing systems of secondary meanings.[7]

These secondary systems are the 'mythologies', the discourses which shape ideology (society's representation of itself). A society articulates itself in its own articulations of fashion, sport, great actresses, power, whence the project for a structural analysis of the 'discourse of fashion', the 'discourse of power' etc.

If reference is made to the numerous Introductions to Structuralism available on the market, the following answer to the question of structural analysis which we are considering here will often be found: that the method of analysis is structuralist when meaning, in the object analysed, is taken to be dependent on the arrangement of its parts. In short, the structuralist is held to have realised that an element may not be isolated from its context and that 'everything is linked'. This definition, restating in effect the perennial definition of the 'framework' so dear to schoolmasters,

---

[7] *Eléments de sémiologie*, IV. 2 (included at the end of *Le degré zéro de l'écriture*, Gonthier, 1965, p. 164); *Elements of Semiology*, trans. Annette Lavers and Colin Smith (London, Cape, 1967).

is clearly inadmissible. Like *Gestalt*, it rests on a romantic notion of the 'living whole'. In reality, the only acceptable definition of structure is the one provided by mathematicians. And so, in France, it is appropriate for us to consult Bourbaki:*

> We can now clarify what is to be understood, in general terms, by a *mathematical structure*. The feature common to the various notions ranged under this generic heading is that they all apply to sets of elements, the nature of which *is not specified*; in order to define a structure, one or more relations involving these elements may be taken … it may then be postulated that this or these relations fulfil certain conditions (to be enumerated), which are the *axioms* of the structure envisaged. To develop the axiomatic theory of a given structure is to deduce all the logical consequences of its axioms, *forbidding oneself any other hypothesis* concerning the elements under consideration (and especially any hypothesis with regard to their particular 'nature').[8]

The only philosopher in France to abide by the structuralist method as defined in this way would no doubt be Michel Serres. For he understands structure neither in the architectural sense (an arrangement of the parts whereby 'everything holds together'), nor in the organic sense ('everything is linked with everything else' in living forms), but in the mathematical sense. He provides an excellent definition of structural analysis as it may be used in the cultural sciences:

> For a given cultural content, whether it be God, table, or basin, an analysis *is structural when* (and *only when*) it presents this content as a model.[9]

In other words, structural analysis begins with the structure, i.e. with relations that, defined in a purely formal way by certain properties, characterise a set of elements, the nature of which is not specified. From the basis of the structure thus estab-

---

* Bourbaki, Nicolas: the collective pseudonym of a group of French mathematicians working, since 1939, on a definitive survey of mathematics. (Trs.)

[8] 'L'architecture des mathématiques' (*Les grands courants de la pensée mathématique*, Cahiers du Sud, 1948, pp. 40–1).

[9] *La communication* (Minuit, 1968), p. 32.

lished, the analysis demonstrates that a certain cultural content (kinship system, or myth) is a 'model' of that structure, or, as it is also known, a 'representation' of it. What, then, has been demonstrated? Neither more nor less than that this content is *isomorphic* to a number of other contents. Structure is precisely that which holds good in an isomorphism[10] between two sets of contents.

Structuralism is, in fact, a *comparatist* method, as much in mathematics (Bourbaki) as it is in anthropology. In France, Georges Dumézil was the first to show, by example, the merits of structural comparison. Instead of examining the gods and legends of different peoples from the point of view of *content*, he found it more fruitful to conduct a formal comparison. Instead of comparing an Indian god with a Roman one, to elucidate the similarities between them – the formula of all religious syncretism, permitting almost any result – he compares one pantheon with another; that is, the sets rather than the elements, the relations rather than the terms. It is these relations between elements, the structures then, which are found to obtain from one set to another within the same cultural domain. Dumézil thus showed how, from one Indo-European people to another, in a great variety of guises, the same *system of functions* organising pantheons and epics was to be found. All the 'contents' analysed appeared as 'models' of a single 'structure' – the trifunctional system of sovereignty, war, and fertility (Jupiter, Mars, Quirinus). The pantheons of the Indo-European peoples therefore correspond. But there is also a correspondence between the pantheon of each people and its representation of the social order (*oratores, bellatores, laboratores*).[11]

It is impossible to speak of the structure of a particular object – a text or an institution. What is structured is not the thing itself, as

---

[10] If we translate the elements, relations, and operations of set E into the elements, relations and operations of set E', we can say that isomorphism occurs between E and E' when the translation of a result which was true for E is also true for E', and when a false result for E translates as false for E' also.

[11] It goes without saying that Dumézil's work belongs to the history of religions. These brief comments in no way claim to account for its value in the eyes of historians, but only to clarify a point of method. The same applies for Lévi-Strauss and Lacan, who will be considered later. It is for ethnologists and psychoanalysts to say what their work has contributed to knowledge. An illuminating commentary on these writers will be found in *Le discours et le symbole* (Aubier, 1962) by Edmund Ortigues.

literary criticism often imagines (so much so that on occasion it will draw attention to the structure as the feature of originality in the work under study), but the set, of which this thing may be considered as one *representation*, in comparison with other sets. This is why structuralism moves from the structure to the model; it reconstructs or reproduces the given that it sets out to analyse. In its productivity, structuralism is the opposite of the phenomenological procedure which, as we will remember, condemned abstraction. Michel Serres notes the minor revolution which took place:

> Meaning is no longer the given, whose obscure language must be deciphered, but on the contrary, what we give to the structure in order to constitute a model.[12]

If, as I have said, Serres is perhaps the only philosopher in France whose work is consonant with the spirit of structuralist analysis, this is because he takes his definition less from Saussure than from Bourbaki. Although Saussure has generally been invoked as the supreme authority of structuralism, he never actually speaks of 'structure', but rather of 'system'. '*In a language, there are only differences.*' This is why knowledge of any one element is conditional upon knowledge of the system. For the value of a term is 'differential', or 'oppositional'; any one term is that which the others are not. Yes, but if this term were opposed equally and to the same degree to every other term in the system, then 'everything would be linked', and the analysis could not begin.

Michel Serres belongs to that French tradition for which philosophy can only constitute itself in relation to science. Philosophy is an epistemology – this thesis is common to every positivism in the world. The originality of the French positivist school is that it conceives of reflection upon the sciences as a reflection upon their *history*. Here the teachings of Kant and Comte converge. For Kant, the business of philosophy is to study reason. This is also the positivist programme, and it gives rise to neo-Kantianism rather than to Kantianism proper because positivists disagree with Kant on the raising of certain 'categories' and 'principles of understanding' to the status of absolutes, when they are valid only in relation

---

[12] *La communication*, p. 33.

to a certain state of positive knowledge. In their view, while he believed in the eternal constitution of reason, Kant unwittingly gave expression to the Newtonian order. We will recall that in his preface to the first edition of the *Critique of Pure Reason*, Kant cautioned against confusing this critique of reason with a simple critique of the books and the systems that had been elaborated in the course of the history of thought. For the neo-Kantian positivists, in spite of this warning, he could not have done better than to convey the rationality specific to the Newtonian system, and thus a particular historical configuration of reason. As far as the French school was concerned, the final chapter of the *Critique* – the 'History of Pure Reason' – became the entire book (whereas Kant had devoted only four pages to it, indicating a gap to be filled later, which gives some idea of how urgently he viewed the historical issue). This 'history of pure reason', having now become the entire critique, demonstrated how philosophy always corresponds to a certain degree of development in positive knowledge, whence the parallelisms dear to neo-Kantians: Plato is explained by the crisis of irrational numbers, Descartes by the birth of modern physics, Kant by Newton. According to this view, the validity of a philosophy is judged in terms of the relevance of the discourse it holds upon the science of its day – a relevance which we are in a good position to assess, situated as we are at a higher stage of history. Thus we learn that Aristotle is gravely mistaken, that Leibniz is everywhere a precursor, that Hegel has the pretension to refute Newton, and Comte to arrest the progress of science, etc.

The originality of Serres's work is that he succeeds in exploding positivist dogma on its own ground. What is this dogma? Since the positivist school is historical, it rejects a finished state of science. Scientific truths are no longer eternal, nor even 'omnitemporal' (as Husserl said), since there is a history of science. Thus the true encounters the false and it is a matter of ascertaining what their relationship may be. Only two answers have ever been given to this question. The first salvages the one unique truth with a theory of historical progress, whilst the second denies that there is progress, and pluralises truth. The first answer is that of the positivist school. According to Comte's 'law of the three states', the untruth, formerly taken for the truth, is in one way or another the *condition* of the truth. This is either because untruth was a garbled attempt at truth – a solution thought naïve nowadays for its supposition of a *continuity* from false to true (such that the false would not be *truly false*) – or it is because truth should be defined as 'surpassed' or 'rectified' error, the so-called 'dialectical' solution, whereby Gaston Bachelard himself thought to 'surpass' Comte's continuist conception with the notion of an 'epistemological break' (between the *untruth* of myth, or of daily experience, or the phenomenological 'lived-through', and the *truth* of science).[13] The other answer is 'perspectivism'. Merleau-Ponty's phenomenology, for example, which in this respect perhaps derives more from Cassirer than from Husserl, restores to aesthetic, mythical, oneiric and perceptive experiences their truth, alongside scientific experience. What is bereft of meaning in one perspective may find it in another.

Use of the comparatist method in his works on the history of the sciences leads Serres to destroy the positivist schema. He observes that positivism's ultimate credential, the history of the sciences, does not exist. In reality, what is offered under this title is sometimes the history of one science, as distinct from others, and sometimes a general history disguised as the history of 'mind' or of 'rationality'.[14] Hence this diagnosis:

> As long as there continues to be no history of the science*s*, that is, of the flow of knowledge as such, and not disintegrated, there will be no practical possibility of elucidating the relations between this formation, since it does not exist, and the others.[15]

Everything therefore must be begun afresh. First a history of the sciences must be brought into existence; the analysis must define periods or 'ages' (in the geological sense) in the history of science,

---

[13] See especially *La formation de l'esprit scientifique* by Gaston Bachelard (Vrin, 1938). Serres points out the puritanical inspiration of this book and its 'Confessor's handbook' aspect in 'La Réforme et les sept péchés capitaux', *L'interférence* (Minuit, 1972). On Bachelard, reference can usefully be made to *Hommage à Gaston Bachelard* (P.U.F., 1957), and in particular to Georges Canguilhem's study, 'Sur une épistémologie concordataire', re-edited by the author in his *Etudes d'histoire et de philosophie des sciences* (Vrin, 1968).

[14] *L'interférence*, p. 205.

[15] *La distribution* (Minuit, 1977), p. 18.

by showing that all the areas of knowledge between one date and another are isomorphic. To do so, the analysis will establish that within those time limits, the areas in question are models of one and the same structure, or again, that they can express one another. For instance, Serres has shown in his thesis that the sciences of the 'classical age' reflect a single theme, that of the *fixed point*. [16] But the success of this operation makes it quickly apparent that there is no reason to restrict oneself to the history of the sciences. The translation of the language of one area into that of another may be performed outside the areas of science. The series of models is not restricted to these disciplines alone, and the theme is to be found, already operative, in literature, in political and religious discourse, etc. The movement, then, leads from the 'cultural formation called science' to the *sum* of cultural formations. The 'modern age', for instance, is no longer the era of the *fixed point*, but that of the *steam-driven engine*; thermodynamics is not a science in itself, but that which reiterates itself in all the sciences:

> Suddenly, all is motor. This is how the world works, the sea, the winds, systems endowed with life and emitters of signals, everything in motion, from the hand-tool to the cosmos, from history to languages. A general philosophy of things from which it is uncertain whether we have emerged, hardly conscious as we are of being in it. [17]

The steam engine is not only reiterated by the natural sciences (with their energetics) but also by Marx with his accumulation of capital, by Freud with his primary process, by Nietzsche with his will-to-power and his eternal recurrence, by Bergson with his two sources, one hot and the other cold; likewise Michelet, Turner's paintings, Zola's novels, etc.

And so there is no value in the separation of literary genres. Learning should not be filed on one side (capable of being true or false) and fiction on the other (neither true nor false). A virtuoso of the isomorph, Serres brings Descartes's *Meditations* out of a La Fontaine fable or a locomotive out of the work of a nineteenth-century thinker, a theorem out of a narrative, a legend out of a

---

[16] *Le système de Leibniz et ses modèles mathématiques* (2 vols., P.U.F., 1968).
[17] *La distribution* p. 286.

demonstration and a demonstration out of a legend. Here it is not at all a matter of hunting for more or less ingenious parallels, but of *translating* word for word. These are not interpretations (the discovery of a content hidden beneath appearances) but formal equivalences (discovery of an isomorphism).

> We play guessing games, penetrate disguises. But nothing has really been done as long as the laws of the transformation, the complete system of its references, and the ordered ensemble of transcriptive operations have not been set in place. [18]

To say that all texts are inter-expressive of one another means that the difference between the *learned text* and the *fictional text* is annulled, not by force but by devising a route which begins at one and leads to the other.

The opposition between truth and error, or alternatively between science and fable, which is at the root of positivism, in the end appears crude and superficial. In the first place, 'the study of legend is a legend, the study of mythology is a mythology'. [19] For it is possible to translate learned discourse (which sets itself up as the 'meta-language' of mythological language) into myth. In the second place and conversely, the myth is already a study of mythology, for the principles of structuralist ethnology, for instance, can be found in a comedy by Molière, and *L'essai sur le don* by Mauss in *Dom Juan*. [20]

Fable is not a stammering prefiguration of science, as the continuist theory of the history of science would maintain. Nor is it the anti-science, the sin hunted down by Bachelard, the superstition which science must combat in order to institute itself (the discontinuist antithesis). Fable is interior to science.

> Knowledge without illusion is an illusion through and through, in which everything is lost, including knowledge. A theorem of it might be sketched like this: *there is no myth more innocent than that of a knowledge*

[18] *La traduction* (Minuit, 1974), p. 265.
[19] *La communication*, p. 226.
[20] Cf. 'Le don de Dom Juan' (in *La communication*).

> *innocent of myth*. I can think of no others, so imbued are
> myths with knowledge, and knowledge with dreams and
> illusions.[21]

The concept of reason must be reformed, then, once and for all.
It is not true that for the Greeks *logos* triumphed over *muthos* (like
good sense over delirium) with a victorious 'epistemological
break'. It is true that reason rehearses order, and asserts that 'the
real is rational'. From the standpoint of this rationality, the universe rehearsed by myth is one of disorder. But it is time to grasp
that order is a particular instance of disorder. Seen in this light, the
real is not rational, although rationality, for its part, is real (but
only as an exception). Myth shows us that the rational is miracul-
ous.[22]

Communication

When structuralism is spoken of in France, one does not as a rule
immediately think of the method of structural analysis as such,
but of the application of this method to sign systems. In theory,
nothing predisposes structuralism to any privileged bearing upon
the sign. Nor does anything oblige the science of the sign to be
exclusively structuralist. There is none the less an affinity between
the method and the field of research. Communication is the
notion by means of which the two – sign systems and analysis in
terms of structure – are brought together.

Signs are made in order to circulate, to be exchanged or *com-
municated*. To communicate, however, it is necessary to have
solved the problem of the transmission of the message under
satisfactory conditions. Communications engineers analyse the
problem in the following way:

1. At the *entrance* to a communication channel. A passage from
the source of information to the message, i.e. to the emission of
certain signals, must be possible.

2. At the *exit*. The message must be capable of being decoded: a
passage from the reception of signals to their interpretation must
be possible. For example, the indicator will light up on the dashboard of a car when the level of oil in the tank falls below a set

---

[21] *La traduction*, p. 259.
[22] See preface to *La distribution*.

critical threshold. The communication established whenever the driver turns on the ignition operates here by means of a *code* whose vocabulary is restricted to two *symbols* (on/off) and which only allows for the emission of two messages. The value of each of the signals is, as Saussure held, 'purely differential'. It is effectively possible to conceive of the indicator at 'On' as meaning 'Nothing untoward', instead of 'Warning'.

This is the way that communications theory approaches sign systems; the properties of any code whatever are already foreseeable.

1. *The code precedes the message.* If to emit a message always consists of 'encoding' and 'transmitting' a piece of information, the code may never be produced by its users during the actual process of communication. The code precedes all its hypothetical uses, and defines all the situations in which it can be used. It remains possible, on the other hand, to transmit one code by means of another (in morse, an agreement might be reached concerning a particular code of visual signals, etc.).

2. *The code is independent of the message.* By definition, the most rudimentary of codes must allow for the emission of at least two messages ('yes'/'no'). The value of an emitted message can be measured; it is the relation of this message to all other messages possible in the same code, from which it follows that an unexpected message is impossible. The message can never entail the unprecedented or the unforeseen. This is the logical result of the starting-point of information theory. The phenomenon of communication is studied from the point of view of the receiver, which is only natural, since the definitive concern of the communications engineer is not with what may be done or said at the entrance to the channel, but with what emerges at the exit. Communication exists precisely to the extent that the message is received as it was emitted, which amounts to saying that it exists in inverse proportion to the alterations and distortions occasioned by the transmission of signals. Whatever the signals – noises, grimaces, gesticulations, vocal intonations – to describe any production of signals as codified is to say that the receiver, registering them in succession, is able to compare what he has received with what he could have received, *what has been said* with *what might have been said*.

3. *The code is independent of the emitter.* Before the transmission

has even begun, the receiver already knows everything that it is possible to say. The only thing he does not know is what will, in fact, be said. We must conclude from this that, however rich the code, the sum of possible messages is finite. By fixing what can be said, the code defines and patterns the situations capable of being signalled, and as a result prohibits any acquaintance with other aspects that it has not selected. For the emitter, to emit a signal is to accept the limits of the code. It would be inaccurate to say that the emitter of a signal expresses himself, or conveys his experience. If we call the source of information (e.g. the monitoring of the oil-level in the tank) 'experience', and the code 'language', the hiatus that separates them should be immediately apparent. While the source passes through all possible states, the code selects certain situations in advance, which it fixes as capable of being signalled. Thus the code of the dashboard selects the difference between 'empty' and 'full', but ignores such states as 'half full', 'nearly empty', etc.

We should bear in mind that the analysis of the material process of communication *favours the receiver* (since the value of the communication is assessed at the receiving end) and that, on the other hand, it emphasises the difficult role of the emitter, who must give account of a situation which is by definition new, while using a code that limits the scope of his expression in advance (and forbids him, in fact, to express himself, in the sense of expressing the 'pure meaning' of his particular experience, which is itself 'still dumb'). If we now consider linguistic phenomena as phenomena of communication, and the so-called 'natural' languages as codes employed by men for the transmission of messages among themselves, we will arrive at semiological structuralism (no. 2). And if, taking a further step, we compare the whole of social life to a process of signals in exchange, we will arrive at structural anthropology as defined by Lévi-Strauss, or the reduction of anthropology to semiology.[23] Generally speaking, the structuralist thesis is embodied in Jacques Lacan's famous formula: the unconscious is structured like a language. *Is structured*, i.e. is the

---

[23] In his inaugural address at the Collège de France in 1960, Lévi-Strauss demanded for his own discipline the place which Saussure ascribed to a putative semiology (cf. *Anthropologie structurale*, vol. II, Plon, 1973, p. 18; *Structural Anthropology*, vol II, trans. Clare Jacobson and Brooke Grundfest Schoepf, London, 1977).

possible object of a structural analysis, which makes it *like a language*. If social anthropology professes to be structural, this is because it rests upon the hypothesis that social life is 'structured like a language' – provided it is clear that here 'language' means a code of communication.

Semiology maintains that human language is analogous to a communication system. Whatever obtains for the codes constructed by engineers will obtain, *mutatis mutandis*, for human language. Thus the three canons of structuralism (no. 2) run as follows:

1. *The signifier precedes the signified.* Language is in no sense a *medium*, a means of expression, a mediation between interior and exterior; for the code precedes the message. There is not, therefore, any initial lived-through situation, or any imperious need to express it, which might lead to inventing a form of expression consonant with this 'lived-through'. The message is not the expression of an experience; rather it expresses the possibilities and limitations, in comparison with experience, of the code employed, whence the difficulty of articulating the unforeseen. How can what falls outside the possibilities of the code be 'encoded'? The answer lies in the second canon.

2. *Meaning arises out of non-meaning.* The code is independent of the message, and the meaning of the message emitted, whatever it may be, is already capitalised in language. But if this were so, would conversation not be reduced to an exchange of ready-recorded signals, classified in a code of convention and good manners? How far would life be enslaved to observances? In such and such a situation, the interlocutor must be addressed in such and such a way, with such and such a turn of phrase, to which he will necessarily reply with such and such another, whatever the respective situations of those concerned. This is why the only way for the speaker to generate meaning is to produce a message bereft of meaning, that the code had not foreseen (a message that could be called 'poetic'). Non-meaning is thus the repository on which we draw in order to produce meaning. Meaning is the effect of non-meaning; this theory of the 'logic of meaning', as Deleuze calls it, is the *pons asinorum* of structuralism. It will suffice to mention the illustrious cases of Lévi-Strauss's 'floating signifier' and Lacan's 'signifying metaphor'.

Lévi-Strauss has explained that all human languages include

'floating signifiers', or expressions which the linguistic community accepts as being properly formed, but which are without
any precise meaning. These signifiers are used, says Lévi-Strauss,
every time the signifier is inadequate to the signified.[24] The
'inadequacy' may be understood in the following way: each time
that the speaker is confronted with the *unknown*, he is at a loss for
what to say, since there is no message in the code that corresponds
to this unprecedented situation, allowing him to impart it to
others. And yet the unknown situation presents itself to the
speaker as unknown, new, mysterious. He does not confuse it
with any of the situations he is capable of articulating unambigu-
ously in the code of the community. How can we explain the
possibility, in man, of perceiving the unknown *as unknown* (and so
of seeking to know it, i.e. make it disappear)? The explanation lies
in the nature of language. It is one thing to have the faculty of
speech, and another to have something to say. At the very instant
that the first man gave utterance, he was put to a decisive test.
Having language at his disposal, he could say everything that his
language authorised him to say (nothing, in his linguistic capacity,
prevented him from embarking on a recitation of the Book of
Genesis or Newton's *Principia*), yet he had nothing to say (for lack
of any knowledge, for lack of a signified). The inadequacy of
signifier to signified was at that moment complete; the entire
realm of the signifier was floating ...

We have another version of this 'logic of meaning' in the
Lacanian notion of metaphor:

> Metaphor is located precisely at the point where meaning
> is produced out of non-meaning.[25]

What is it to speak? If to speak is to say something worth saying,
who will be content with using the code, or with making his
observations and desires known by emitting one of the messages
from the repository of the code? The solution, then, is to emit a
message *other* than the one foreseen by convention, thereby oblig-

[24] This concept of the 'floating signifier', with which Lévi-Strauss accounts
for the non-scientific forms of human thought (art, poetry, myth, magic,
etc.) appears in 'Introduction à l'œuvre de Marcel Mauss', a text by
Lévi-Strauss published in M. Mauss *Sociologie et anthropologie* (P.U.F.,
1950).

[25] *Ecrits* (Seuil, 1966), p. 508; *Ecrits: A Selection*, trans. A. Sheridan (London,
Tavistock, 1977).

ing the words to say something quite different from that which they signify in the 'treasury of language'. In metaphor, Lacan retraces Freudian condensation, *Verdichtung*, the source of all *Dichtung* (poetry or myth), for which the formula is: *one word for another*. And it is also, for a psychoanalyst (as Lacan observes, a receiver in the purest sense) the formula of the *lapsus calami* or the *lapsus linguae* ('Latin words used in ordinary language and which, signifying a slip of the tongue or the pen, convey the speaking or writing of one word in place of another' – Littré). In either case, the conventional signifier, which is not authorised to appear in the statement and is in this sense *repressed*, has been replaced by another, unexpected signifier – the *manifest* signifier. This *quid pro quo* produces what Lacan calls an 'effect of meaning'. The signified of the manifest signifier featuring in the sentence emitted is not at all, contrary to the doctrine of traditional rhetoric, the occulted signifier, but a *new meaning* released with the aid of this exchange of one signifier for another. In this way the subject of the enunciation sometimes communicates that which the convention of language does not authorise him to say – namely the meaning of his desire:

> It is in the substitution of signifier for signifier that a
> poetic or creative effect of signification is produced.[26]

As we can see, the Freudian explanation of the *lapsus*, equally valid for the joke (*Witz*) and for the symptom, also sheds light on what Edgar Allan Poe calls the 'genesis of the poem'.

3. *The subject submits to the law of the signifier.* In dealing with language, phenomenology placed itself on the side of the speaking subject, and saw speech as one means among others of corporal expression. Speech was defined as a gesture, that is, a manner of 'being in the world' through the body proper. In his 'verbal gesticulation', the speaking subject was at the origin of the meaning of his utterances:

> The linguistic gesture, like all the rest, delineates its own
> meaning.[27]

Only then was the language constituted, a language which was no more than the sum of available significations, the repository of expressions already invented in various circumstances by 'speak-

[26] *Ecrits*, p. 515.   [27] PP, p. 217.

ing subjectivities', and which belonged to the 'intersubjective' community. In contrast, semiology places itself on the side of the receiver. The message received by the latter will convey information provided that this message could have been different. To decode the message is, for the receiver, to credit the speaker with the binary choice or choices which have allowed him to select the precise message he has emitted from among all those which he could equally well have constructed with the help of the code at his disposal. Such procedures of construction in no way reflect events at the information source. Nothing suggests that the state of this source lends itself to the requirements of the code. Of course artificial codes are built in such a way as to provide a working knowledge of what occurs at the source. But since we do not know who the author of 'natural' languages may be, there are no grounds for assuming that there is any preordained harmony between language and experience. The code, and not its emitter, decides what shall and shall not be pertinent. If language is a code, it is language which speaks each time that the speaking subject delivers a remark, of whatever kind. Speech is not a gesture which renders the meaning of the experience, 'still dumb', into verbal expression, for dumb experience has no meaning by itself. Meaning appears with the signifier, or with the first opposition between 'yes' and 'no', between 'something' and 'nothing'. The meaning of the message is not the meaning of experience, nor is it the meaning experience would have, prior to all expression, if this were possible. It is the meaning that experience can *receive* in a discourse which articulates it according to a certain code – that is, in a system of signifying oppositions.

Lacan has insisted on the heterogeneity of language and experience. Man is 'the living being who speaks'. This was the Greek definition. But life does not pass into speech intact. Man's obligation to express his *needs* in the form of a *request* addressed to another – and to formulate his request in the language spoken by this other, namely the 'mother tongue' – subjugates him to the signifier. This submission induces an effect of aberration in him (with respect to the norm embodied in the robust simplicity of natural, animal life): *desire*. Man desires in so far as he is a *subject*, which no longer means the 'absolute origin' of meaning, but literally 'subjected to the signifier' (just as in an absolute monarchy one is 'the king's subject'). Indeed once the other (for instance the mother) concedes to the subject's request (for instance, by providing him with the nourishment and care he demands), she does more than satisfy a need, she shows that the demand affords her delight, and her response therefore betrays something of her own 'good pleasure', her desire. This response to the demand is also a testimony of love. Hence a dimension of lack and insufficiency inevitably appears in the relationship between the subject and the other who responds to him. The particular object given in response to the demand may well appease hunger or thirst, but no gift suffices as a proof of love. Every proof of love is 'symbolic' (in the sense that one speaks of the 'symbolic farthing' awarded as damages, which serves to efface a slight of honour). There can never be *enough of it*. As the demand for love is bottomless, extravagant on both sides (first, say, on the mother's side and then on the child's), the mirage of an *absolute object* takes shape – the object of desire – to fill the 'gap' created in man by language:

> Desire is neither the appetite for satisfaction, nor the demand for love, but the difference obtained by subtracting the first from the second.[28]

The opposition between phenomenology and semiology may be summarised in the following way. For the first school, the fundamental problem is that of *reference* (or denotation); for the second it is that of *enunciation*. Phenomenology asks how a statement such as 'the sum of the angles of a triangle is equal to two right angles' can be said to be true, when we know that no perfect triangle exists in the world we inhabit. Since the referent of such a statement does not exist in another world either (the heaven of ideal objects), we must, in spite of everything, look for it here, where we are, and thus reconstitute the genealogy of science by returning to its origin (the perceived). Semiology shifts the focus of attention to the relation of the speaker to the signifying system that enables him, as he produces his utterances, to establish certain bonds between himself and others who speak the same language – the same system. Between the phenomenologist's perceiving subject and the theorem, the signifier is interposed, and this signifier can in no sense be derived from the perceiving body (via such notions as 'gesture' and 'expression'). No gesticulation, no

---

[28] *Ecrits*, p. 691.

grimace, no vocalisation is capable in itself of introducing the opposition between yes and no, between presence and absence, which is at the root of all signifying systems.

Structures

But where is the 'structuralism' in all of this? The origin of the word 'code' is juridical. And indeed the code plays the role of law in communication – it is the rule that must be obeyed if messages are to be produced or received. We must now examine in what ways these rules are systems endowed with structure.

In semiology, the given is constituted by collections of 'messages': recordings of accounts gathered by the anthropologist 'in the field', for instance, or a series of folk tales pertaining to a certain people. To define all these documents as messages is to undertake the task of discovering what code enabled them to be produced – and also others, which are lost or hypothetical. Tailoring the corpus into minimal units, identifying the paradigmatic classes, discovering the rules which obtain in syntagmatic series – all this is daily fare for the semiologist. The procedures are comparable to those of the linguist studying a language which is still not well known. Where is the structuralist bias to be found in this way of proceeding? The linguist who is studying a language for the first time will have finished his work once its grammar and vocabulary have been established. The structural, i.e. the comparative problem, is posed in both instances. The *vocabulary* brings the language under study into communication with the linguist's own; by providing the means of translating the first into the second, it reveals the isomorphism between them. *Grammar*, for its part, poses a similar problem, for short of a naïve application of his own grammatical categories to the language under investigation, the linguist must find a means of making his own categories and those of the other language appear as particular instances of more general functions, as different responses to an identical problem which every language must resolve. Here again, he will have to trace the rules of the transition from one language to the other, and establish correspondences between the morphological laws of one and those of the other.

A code is structured because it is always constituted by an initial convention with reference to another code. The definition of a code is that it should be translatable into another. This definitive property is called 'structure'.

Lévi-Strauss's anthropology claims for itself the title and the attributes of the semiology whose programme had been outlined by Saussure (he referred to it as 'semeiology'). It professes, at the same time, to be structural. In so far as it is semiological, this school of anthropology offers a hypothesis on the nature of social life, a conception which could be described as *exchangist*, and which holds that

> a society consists of individuals and groups
> communicating with one another.[29]

These groups are primarily family lineages, communicating with one another through the exchange of women. The exchange obeys rules of exogamy which, as an ensemble, constitute a kinship system. The rule above all others is the prohibition of incest, or the ban against keeping back the women who are due to the other group. In so far as it is structural, Lévi-Strauss's anthropology sets out to relate the various systems of communication. This may be achieved in two ways. A kinship system may be compared to a different kinship system observed in another culture, or alternatively to a system governing another kind of communication. Lévi-Strauss explains that there are three levels of social communication: women, wealth, and messages proper, whose system is the language.

The ultimate objective of this anthropology is to find a means of expressing such systems in terms of one another:

> The analysis of different aspects of social life will have to
> be pursued until it reaches a level at which the passage
> from one to another becomes possible; that is, elaborates a
> kind of universal code capable of expressing the properties
> common to the specific structures arising from each
> aspect.[30]

If this level were ever reached, then with the *universal code* the invariants of all structures would have been found. The diversity

[29] *Anthropologie structurale*, vol. I (Plon, 1958), p. 326; *Structural Anthropology*, vol. I, trans. Claire Jacobson and Brooke Grundfest Schoepf (London, Allen Lane, 1968).
[30] *Anthropologie structurale*, p. 71.

of cultures, languages, and customs would have been integrally explained, that is, reduced to the unity of human nature. And in order to account for this unity of all cultures which would emerge at the term of structural analysis, we would have to postulate, Lévi-Strauss tells us, an 'unconscious activity of the human mind', one which would consist in the application of the structures to the ever-diverse contents supplied by human experience. The diversity of situations would explain the variety of cultures, and the identity of the human mind would assure their inter-communication.

The notion of the 'human mind' 'unconsciously' elaborating structures is so vague that perhaps it would be wiser not to look for its meaning, particularly since Lévi-Strauss has little more to say on the subject. If it were to be developed further, one would arrive at a variety of pantheism: social structures are the structures of the mind, replicating those of the brain, itself a part of the matter in which the whole of the cosmos is in turn reflected.[31] The significance of this mysterious unconscious hardly matters, as the issue of what Lévi-Strauss's hypothesis might mean will only arise when the 'universal code' is discovered; then there will be no shortage of time in which to provide an account of it. It would be unfair, moreover, to stress these abstruse formulas more than the author does himself, for whom it appears that 'philosophical questions' and questions that are 'provisionally insoluble by scientific means' are one and the same thing.

We have just seen that structuralism, in the semiological sense of the term, is based on the comparison of human language to a code of communication. But this comparison makes light of one obvious difference: a code is constructed, while a language is not. To construct a code, we require a language. In the first place, a 'natural' language, let us say the French language, is not a code on which French speakers have reached an agreement prior to all conversation with the sole intention of exchanging information. Not only did this primordial covenant never take place, but furthermore a language does not have the univocity of a code, in which the semantic value of each symbol is fixed by decree. This is why Lacan ceased to speak of codes and preferred to talk of the 'signifier' (meaning a signifier which is always more or less 'float-

---

[31] *La pensée sauvage*, p. 329.

ing'). [32] In the second place, the construction of the code is always carried out in the natural language.

The paradox of structuralism is as follows. It announces its project (to combat 'the philosophy of consciousness') by showing that the signifier is not at the service of the subject, nor entrusted by the latter with his 'significative intentions' (as phenomenologists say). It wishes to show man's subjection to signifying systems (which precede each of us individually). But this demonstration has recourse to concepts from information theory, i.e. from the thinking of engineers whose goal (so the word 'cybernetics', as they have called their science, suggests) is to invest human beings with total control by means of better communications techniques. Nothing in this project should seriously alarm the 'philosophy of the *cogito*', or the Cartesian tendency in philosophy, unless the *cogito* (a metaphysical position, and the corner-stone of a project for 'mastery and possession of nature') is confused with psychological introspection.

The Humanist Controversy

It will be impossible to understand the intensity of the debate among intellectuals over the issue of structuralism, if one sees it as a mere methodological dispute within the social sciences – 'Questions of Method', as Sartre said in 1961.

It might even be admitted that at first sight, structuralism scarcely seems suited to the part that it was to play for ten years: a devastating gospel, a subversive truth, an intrepid breakthrough, the first counter-thrust to the western logos and its ethnocentrism ... Far from posing as the horseman of the Apocalypse, structuralism first characterised itself more modestly as an expanded rationalism. Its aim as acknowledged by Lévi-Strauss is 'a sort of super-rationalism' [33] (an ambiguous expression besides, since it is not clear whether he means 'an ever more powerful rationalism' or 'something akin to a surrealism of science'). It was this aspect that Merleau-Ponty took up in 1959, in an article commenting on the work of Lévi-Strauss:

[32] See *Ecrits*, p. 806.
[33] *Tristes tropiques* (Plon, 1955), p. 50; *Tristes Tropiques*, trans. J. and D. Weightman (London, Cape, 1973; Harmondsworth, Penguin, 1976).

> Thus our task is to broaden our reasoning to make it
> capable of grasping what, in ourselves and in others,
> precedes and exceeds reason.[34]

As we have seen, this was exactly what Merleau-Ponty had
expected in 1946, from an interpretation of Hegel.

The mission of an expanded reason is to understand the irrational, which impinges on us in two forms: among us, as the
madman (who 'exceeds reason'), and outside us as the savage
(who 'precedes' it). Hence the privileged status enjoyed by
psychoanalysis (which, with its concept of the unconscious, has
introduced unreason to those who had believed they were of
sound mind) and by social anthropology (which studies the
archaic behaviour of 'primitives'). If these sciences can enable us
to understand the irrational – in dreams, delirium, magic or taboo
– then the reason of the western adult male suffers a setback, but
only to the advantage of a more universal reason. Nothing is more
commensurate with the perpetual out-stripping of reason by itself
than structuralism, which is ultimately the quest for universal
invariants. In the anthropological domain, the structuralist is none
other than the representative of the demands of science. Just as the
science of motion (physics) is the knowledge of that which, in the
course of a change, remains unchanged – that is, the invariable
relationship between positional variations of the moving body in
space, and the date of those positions in time – so human science is
the knowledge of that which remains constant in any possible
variation; and here variation corresponds to cultural disorienta-
tion, a voyage to exotic or archaic latitudes.

Where can we find grounds for controversy? The truth is that
behind what seems to be a learned dispute over the merits of this
or that method, there is a political stake, not perhaps for everybody, but for the intelligentsia.

As we have seen, semiology displaces all issues towards the
analysis of discourse and gives pride of place to the relationship of
emitter to code, or, in Lacanian terms, of subject to signifier. The
result is that the origin of meaning can no longer be located where
the phenomenologists had thought to find it, in the author of
discourse, the individual who believes he is expressing himself,

[34] *Signes*, p. 154.

but rather that it lies in language itself. Let us take the narration of a myth. The meaning of this myth is not to be found in the narrator's 'lived-through', it should not be read as the expression of a 'mythical consciousness'. Myth is recitation; the narrative form of the tale has not been invented by the narrator, for it exists prior to the telling, and may be considered as a code allowing mythical messages to be emitted. In order to determine the meaning of the myth therefore, it must be compared to other myths circulating in the same cultural ensemble, and its code must be reconstituted. The narrator is subject to the constraints of this code, and his account owes little to his own imagination. The significance of his characters and their adventures is determined in advance by the grammar governing the tales of his particular cultural domain. If, for example, oppositions such as 'giant/dwarf' or 'princess/shepherdess' should be significant within this code, then the size and occupations of the characters are no longer a matter of choice. Consequently the narrator of a myth is simply actualising the possibilities inherent in the code, or in the signifying system to which he submits in order to speak. In the end, it is indeed the structure that decides what may – sometimes what must – be said on a given occasion.

Not man, but structures are decisive! Man is nothing! Such was the lesson that public opinion drew from the research of structural anthropology; or so we might think, to read the scandalised commentaries of the now-obsolete 'humanists'. But this is not the main point.

We know that, in *Group Psychology and the Analysis of the Ego*, Freud devotes a chapter to two institutions which he calls 'artificial groups' – the Catholic Church and the army. How, Freud asks, can the coherence of these bodies, which continue to withstand the tests of time (persecution, defeat, etc.), be explained? Of course, the source of the strength of any mass organisation is known to everybody: 'discipline is the back-bone of an army', as the saying goes. But what surprises Freud is the meekness of the individuals who submit to the discipline, sacrificing their independence and even their lives. He considers that *love* is the only force capable of leading an individual to such disdain for his own interests. The cohesion of 'artificial groups' must therefore be libidinal. Soldiers and believers love their leaders and fraternise by virtue of this common passion.

Lacan, who has commented several times on these passages, remarks that the bond of love between members of the Church or comrades in arms was established by discourse.[35] The bond is *symbolic*. Institutions – churches, armies – maintain themselves to the precise degree to which they maintain their founding symbols, i.e. a signifying system. In such organised communities, orthodoxy is synonymous with a strict observance of forms. It is important to speak in a certain way, to use 'consecrated' words. In every orthodoxy, the identity of the signifiers is decisive; beyond this, everyone is free to understand them as best he can.

Thus, as Mallarmé thought, to disturb language and signifying forms would be to subvert the community.[36] In his seminar of 1970, Lacan affirmed that social bonds are founded by discourse. This formula is doubtless the best expression given so far to what was at stake in the structuralist debate.

It should be remarked that in 1921 Freud chose the German army and the Catholic Church for his examples, which at the time were the most obvious (although he does suggest that political organisations such as the 'Socialist Party' might in the future replace religious organisations). But in France in 1960, the 'artificial groups' which an intellectual was likely to encounter were more often the Communist Party (or again the small Far-Left groups who longed to appropriate its role as the 'revolutionary leadership of the proletariat'), and the various psychoanalytic societies.

In this context, the principal semiological thesis acquires a political significance, and calls into question the power which such institutions exercise over their members. If it is true that the signifier is exterior to the subject, then the various political discourses of industrial society are analogous to the mythical narratives of so-called primitives. In both cases, the individuals are preceded by a language which sustains the community, enabling everyone to relate the things that befall him, not perhaps exactly as they occur, but in such a way as others understand. The satisfaction that a party member experiences when he hears the speeches of his leaders or reads *L'Humanité*, the Communist Party daily, is comparable to the relief which the sick Indian feels when

---

[35] See 'Situation de la psychanalyse en 1956', in *Ecrits*, p. 475.
[36] 'On a touché au vers' (*La musique et les lettres*).

cured by the tribal *shaman* in Lévi-Strauss's paper on 'symbolic efficacy'.[37] In both cases, an individual is reintegrated within his community by the workings of the symbol. Lévi-Strauss, who for his part compares the Indian *shaman* to the psychoanalyst in western societies, concludes in the following terms:

> The shaman provides the sick woman with a *language*, by means of which unexpressed, or otherwise inexpressible, psychic states can be immediately expressed. And it is the transition to this verbal expression – at the same time making it possible to undergo in an ordered and intelligible form a real experience that would otherwise be chaotic and inexpressible – which induces the release of the physiological process, that is, the reorganisation, in a favourable direction, of the sequence to which the sick woman is subjected.[38]

The semiological theorem of the exteriority of the signifier has thus a political corollary. The self-styled 'political ideologies' of our societies are, very precisely, myths, and their symbolic efficacy (the trust of the faithful, the adherence of the masses) is no guarantee of their correspondence with the reality which they claim to describe. Lévi-Strauss is explicit on this point. 'Nothing resembles mythological thought more than political ideology.'[39] A myth is the account of a founding event, of a privileged episode belonging at once to a certain time (its origins) and to all time (since festivals are given over to repeating it). This, as Lévi-Strauss observes, is exactly the place held in France by an event such as the French Revolution, both in generalised political ideology and, for example, in Sartre's thought, as found in the *Critique of Dialectical Reason*:

> an ethnographic document of the first order, which it is indispensable to study if we wish to understand the mythology of our time.[40]

With semiology, the very notion of a 'meaning of history' becomes obscured. Not without nostalgia, Merleau-Ponty had

---

[37] *Anthropologie structurale*, I, ch. x.
[38] *Anthropologie structurale*, I, p. 218.
[39] *Ibid.*, p. 231.
[40] *La pensée sauvage*, p. 330.

spoken of the 'sublime points', the 'perfect moments' at which each individual, fleetingly, is consonant with the course of the world, and experiences universal history as his own.[41] The ethnologist has no trouble recognising in these privileged instances of collective ferment an equivalent of the *festival*, during which archaic communities revive their unanimity in a ritual rehearsal of the founding myth. Lévi-Strauss concludes that the *lived* meaning of history is necessarily its *mythical* meaning.[42]

By revealing the heterogeneity of signifier and lived experience, semiology was thus making a political point. It demonstrated that the hold of institutions over individuals can be traced to the ascendancy of language. In its way, it foreshadowed the riots of May 68, by showing that a dominant discourse is the imposition, not so much of certain truths (dogmas, 'signifieds') as of a certain language (formulas, 'signifiers'), which the opposition itself is obliged to employ in order to make its objections known. Episodes such as the cure of a sick person by the witch doctor or of a hysterical woman by the psychoanalyst show that the crucial questions unfold at the frontiers of the dominant language. The witch doctor's patient believes in the myths and traditions of his tribe, yet he experiences an intolerable and incongruous suffering in his body. The community entrusts its witch doctor with the resolution of the problem posed by this discrepancy between the discourse of the community (myth) and the individual's experience. Here, pain is that insubordinate, senseless, unacceptable element with which the patient is helpless to deal, and by which he is *excluded* from communal life, 'but which the *shaman*, calling upon myth, will re-integrate within a whole where everything is meaningful'.[43]

To temper the brutal element of existence, to absorb the heterogeneous, to give meaning to the senseless, to rationalise the incongruous; in short, to translate the *other* into the language of the *same* – these are the functions of myths and ideologies. Semiology thus paves the way for a critical study of dominant discourse in the West, which would disinter the conflicts that lie beneath the soothing solutions and rational postures, 'where everything is meaningful'. Shared language, forms with univer-

[41] AD, pp. 99 and 122.
[42] *La pensée sauvage*, p. 338.
[43] *Anthropologie structurale*, I, p. 218.

salising pretensions, unanimous communities are all falsehoods. The generation of 1960 renounced the ideals defended by Merleau-Ponty in 1964 of a 'new classicism', an 'organic civilisation'. It no longer believed that the task of the century was to *integrate* the irrational within an expanded reason. The task now was to deconstruct what was understood as the principle of the dominant language in the West (the logic of identity), and to provide a critique of history, henceforth to be approached as a myth, that is, an efficient solution – but devoid of truth – to the conflict between the same and the other. It is useful to distinguish two aspects: the critique of history, and that of identity. Whilst political minds are more at home with the first, and metaphysical minds with the second, it goes without saying that most of the important writings will include, in varying proportions, elements belonging to both.

4

The critique of history

History is the western myth.

Such a statement clearly implies a critique of history. This critique, however, does not consist in denying that there is history, contrary to the charge brought by Sartre against the structuralists. Speaking of Michel Foucault's (highly successful) book, *Les mots et les choses* (*The Order of Things*), Sartre says:

> Foucault supplies people with what they have been needing: an eclectic synthesis in which Robbe-Grillet, structuralism, linguistics, Lacan and *Tel Quel* are each invoked in turn so as to demonstrate the impossibility of historical thought.
>
> Behind history, of course, the target is Marxism. This is an attempt to constitute a new ideology, the last bulwark which the bourgeoisie can still erect against Marx.[1]

The Order of Things, 'last bulwark' raised by the 'bourgeoisie' against 'Marx' . . . Unfortunately for Sartre, his judgment here is a strikingly clear testimony to the mythical nature of his conception of history. Nobody seeks to 'deny history'. Our only concern is to ascertain whether a sober conception of it may be reached after the twilight of the Hegelian idol.

Nihilism

Like several philosophers of his generation, Foucault comes from the French positivist school, for whom philosophy is a function of

[1] 'Jean-Paul Sartre répond', in *L'Arc*, no. 30, Oct. 1966, pp. 87–8.

the history of concepts at work in the various learned specialist fields. Having set out to write a history of psychiatry, i.e. a study of the distinction made by doctors between the *normal* and the *pathological*[2] in the field of mental health, Foucault finishes by writing his *Histoire de la folie à l'âge classique*.[3] The initial theme would have been of the most traditional kind in French epistemology, retracing the formation of the fundamental concepts of a given discipline, their variations in time, the 'epistemological obstacles' that had to be overcome in order to 'produce' them, etc. The gradual shift towards the second title provides the thesis of the book: the psychiatrist speaks of the mad person, but the mad person himself does not speak.

> I have not sought to write the history of that language,
> but rather the archaeology of that silence.[4]

If history is defined as the past, then the archaic is the past of that past, the other city buried in the groundworks of the old city, the pagan temple beneath the medieval cathedral, the bones in the unknown burial ground, etc. The disappearance of the archaic is the condition of the appearance of the historical. Foucault intends to sound the limits of what we can recognise as *our* history. At the interior of this history of ours, as of all history, identity presides; within it, a single culture enables a number of human beings to articulate a collective 'we'. This identity – here is what must now be demonstrated – is constituted through a series of exclusions. If all cultures are finite or limited, this is not to be explained in negative terms by the fact that no one culture could succeed in universalising itself. It is because in an initial decision (a first 'division'), each culture rejects a certain number of alternatives. In his preface, Foucault cites some of the 'divisions' which gave the western *ratio* its identity: the opposition of East and West, dream and reality, tragic and dialectical. But all these splits are summed up in the great opposition of *reason* and *unreason*.

Foucault goes further and asserts that the history of madness is the history of the possibility of history. 'History', as we

---

[2] We may recognise the title of Canguilhem's doctoral thesis in medicine, *Le normal et le pathologique* (1943; 3rd edn, P.U.F., 1966).

[3] I shall quote from the 1st edn of Foucault's thesis, which differs in certain respects from the later ones.

[4] HF, p. ii.

understand it, implies in effect the accomplishment of works and the transmission of words endowed with meaning. Now madness, according to Foucault, is defined by 'the absence of works'. The mad person's gestures culminate in nothing, his delirious talk refers to nothing; his life is fundamentally work-less and inoperative. The possibility of history rests upon the decision that all gestures and words which afford no positive significance be rejected as unreason. Madness surrounds history on all sides; it is there *before* history and it is still there *after* history. History must here be understood in the sense imparted to it by dialectical thought; man is what he does, and his 'praxis' defines reality. In neo-Hegelian doctrines, history is the 'work' *par excellence*. Madness is everything which can find no role to play in the drama of history and which makes no contribution to the 'end of history'. Yet madness has the last word:

> The great work of world history is inescapably accompanied by an absence of work, renewed at every moment but running on unaltered in its inevitable void throughout history; before history, since it is already there in the primitive decision, and after it again, since it will triumph with the last word that history pronounces.[5]

The end of history is indeed the triumph of meaning, as Hegelians believe. It may be final reconciliation, universal recognition or even, in certain versions, a generalised embrace (or simply the embrace of the real by the thinker alone); in any case, a higher synthesis, the annihilation of the negative in a victorious negation of the negation, the presence of truth and the truth of presence. However, it is also the apogee of non-meaning. For there is nothing left to be done (therefore all action is absurd), nor anything left to be said (therefore all speech is insignificant). At the end of history, the human species enters into an irremediable idleness, an aimlessness without end. This was Nietzsche's doctrine. By announcing the 'death of God' and 'the aimlessness of the last man', he invokes the great modern utopia of a 'close of history'.[6] Kojève had already said that the end of history was equivalent to the death of man. In all his works, Blanchot

---

[5] HF, p. vi.
[6] MC, p. 275. The famous passage on the impending disappearance of man can be found on pp. 396–8.

described this life after death which is the lot of man in the aftermath of history, and to which modern literature, in his view, is the supreme testimony. After the end of history, said Georges Bataille, human negativity does not disappear – it only becomes 'unemployed'. Blanchot comments on this remark as follows:

> For everyone, in one form or another, history is running out ('in all but the outcome') . . . Yes, all things considered, we are each living more or less in the perspective of a finished history, already seated on the banks of the river as it ebbs and flows, content with a contentment which should be that of the universe, each of us God then, by our beatitude and knowledge. [7]

And yet man, who ought to be content, is not at all content and declares as much. Instead of having attained supreme wisdom as scheduled, he is left to undergo the experience of his bewilderment.

This absurd situation of man's dissatisfaction, attested to by literature (literature 'of the absurd', as it was known for a time), presents theory with a problem. Evasive answers must be put to one side, for instance that of Eric Weil:[8] the discontented are those who have not understood the reasons why they should be happy; they must learn to reason better. That of the Marxists: the discontented are right, and Hegel's dates were incorrect (out of idealism, needless to say). The end of history is not for now but for later, at the price of a few historical vicissitudes. Indeed the dissatisfaction of which Bataille and Blanchot speak proceeds less from any misunderstanding than from an all too lucid grasp of the situation. The problem, if we like, is one of a dissatisfaction resulting from the very obligation to proclaim one's satisfaction. Nor does it arise from the fact that the work of history is still unfinished, for it raises no objections to this postponement, this delay, but rather anticipates humanity's sentiments after the last of the historical revolutions. If man should be discontented 'after the end of history', even if such an end were not to come for several centuries, then he is discontented with *everything*, and it must be that everything as such is insufficient:

[7] *L'entretien infini*, pp. 303–4.
[8] *Logique de la philosophie* (Vrin, 1950).

> We assume man to be essentially satisfied; as universal
> man, he has nothing left to do, is without needs, and even
> though as an individual he still dies, he has neither
> beginning nor end, but is at rest in the becoming of his
> static totality. What awaits this ultimate man, capable
> once more and for the last time of not stopping at the
> sufficiency which he has reached, is a limit–experience. It
> is the desire of man without desire, the dissatisfaction of
> those who are satisfied 'in all things' ... The
> limit–experience is the experience of that which exists
> outside everything, when everything excludes anything
> outside itself; and of what remains to be reached, once
> everything has been reached, or to be known, once
> everything is known: the inaccessible itself, the unknown
> itself.[9]

If *everything* is not enough, and since there is *nothing* outside
everything, then the situation is unintelligible. Or at least, it
cannot be accommodated within the dialectic, that is, within the
thinking of *dialectical identity* which prides itself on having
included *everything*, by virtue of the concept of identity, within its
concept of totality – everything, including the *nothing* itself (in the
form of negativity, i.e., for French Hegelians, human freedom).

As soon as there is reason and history, there are madmen. Thus
there was no *madness* before this decision in favour of reason and
history (in favour of a work). The division of reason and madness
constitutes the latter as unreason, as the opposite of reason,
thereby producing the object of psychiatric knowledge. In the last
analysis, the matter which Foucault deals with in his thesis is
indeed the history of psychiatry. But, as a disciple of neo-Kantian
epistemology, he does not omit to pose the initial question: how is
a learned discourse on madness possible? What is the condition of
its possibility? It is that the phenomenon of unreason should exist.
How is this phenomenon produced? The answer lies in the
division between reason and madness, of which the pyschiatrist
knows nothing. For psychiatry is a reasonable discourse upon
madness, and is unable to project itself beyond the division. This
is why a history of psychiatry would teach us nothing. It would

---

[9] *L'entretien infini*, pp. 304–5.

only reiterate the founding prejudice, and show how mental illness is the object of an ever more enlightened, ever more humane treatment; it could never retrace the itinerary by which madness became 'mental illness', with its own appropriate branch of medicine. The history of psychiatry will inevitably celebrate the successive victories of science over evil and disorder. But the reverse is true. It is not the progress of knowledge that discovers 'mental illness' where barbarous humanity had thought to be up against the diabolical and the demonic; it is rather the appearance of the mad person in his new guise of 'mental patient' that gives rise to a scientific discipline by means of which to treat him.

The archaeology, in opposition to any retrospective history of the progress of reason, begins with a methodical ignorance of what unreason is. It goes on to show how the production of that identity with oneself known as 'reason' involves the expulsion from the common space (and, in practice, the 'confinement' within designated spaces) of all that refuses submission to such identity, all that is negatively denoted as difference, incoherence, and unreason. Internment and hospitalisation come to have rational authority over this 'other than reason'. All 'dialectical' history is rejected here. For reason, madness is its negative, now as the *absence of reason* (deficiency), now as the *refusal* of reason (irruption of irrational forces). An 'expanded' reason, toughened by dialectical logic, or again by the structural method, would have made short work of 'accommodating' this negative. Foucault, on the contrary, maintains that reason, originating in a division between itself and its other, cannot return to this origin.

Such a non-dialectical philosophy of history evidently requires a re-examination of the most fundamental distinctions in our thought: being and non-being, the same and the other, the finite and the infinite, etc. Instead Foucault's later works take the form of historical research: the birth of modern medicine in the nineteenth century, the birth and death of the human sciences etc. Foucault's theory of history must be sought in his manner of detailing these births and deaths. There are two ways of reading his accounts, and his works have two kinds of reader. *La naissance de la clinique (Birth of the Clinic)* or *The Order of Things* may be read as history books, offering a survey and theory of the transformations undergone by medicine in the nineteenth century, or of the appearance of the 'human sciences'. But these books may also be read because they are written by Foucault, less to discover the history of medicine and anthropology than to grasp his approach to the writing of history – by way of the illustrations which his arguments provide – and hence the possibility of a new historical narrative, a non-dialectical apprehension of becoming. Foucault's position as regards this is far from clear. Is there, for instance, a 'classical age' stretching from the end of the sixteenth century to the end of the eighteenth, followed by a 'modern age' beginning with the nineteenth century and lasting until 1950? These are historical questions, and the only way of proving anything in such matters of 'periodisation' is to produce documents and to suggest constructions which override their competitors. It may also be asked in what way 'reason' is the result of any more fundamental occurrence than the historical course of things, accessible to an 'archaeology'. What could a history be, if it were not the history of meaning and reason? This time, no document can shed the faintest light, for such questions concern the very possibility of calling anything a 'document', and of producing it in an account that purports to be 'historical'. Thus there are two kinds of question. But Foucault's historical works elude discussion, in that the gist of their argument remains indeterminate. Are we moving from philosophy to history, or vice versa? Should historical exposition be seen as the terrain on which a hypothesis concerning the non-dialectical essence of history may be verified? Or, on the contrary, does this exposition find its ultimate justification in the philosophical thesis? Nobody can pinpoint the truth or the false-hood of these narratives. On the one hand, Foucault's approach is that of a positivist: the evolution of concepts and thought is traced in the various states of different disciplines, as if in so many documents. Recourse to texts, archives, documents and monu-ments is therefore indispensable. Yet, on the other hand, Foucault as a reader of Nietzsche does not believe in the positivist notion of *fact*. He is aware that all interpretation is polemical: to back one interpretation is to declare war on another. Indeed every inter-pretation of a fact purports to supply its *meaning*, but given that facts have no meaning in themselves, interpretations can only find one for them by making them speak, so that each interpretation of a fact is really always the interpretation of an earlier interpretation disguised as a plain, positive fact. The conviction that facts are meaningless defines the *nihilism* of Foucault's generation – nihilism in the sense that Nietzsche understands it when he proclaims the disarray of positivism: 'no facts, only interpretations'. The phrase is simply another version of the more celebrated 'nothing is true, everything is permissible'. As Foucault said at a Royaumont Colloquy:

> Interpretation can never be brought to an end, simply because there is nothing to interpret. There is nothing absolutely primary to be interpreted, since fundamentally, everything is already interpretation; every sign is, in itself, not the thing susceptible to interpretation but the interpretation of other signs.[10]

The conjunction of positivism and nihilism in the same intelligence produces a surprising mixture. Every one of Foucault's affirmations is ringed with a formidable critical apparatus (documents, quotations, intricate references), and yet it would be possible to construct alternative accounts using the same data – variations which Foucault himself is the first to sound. As certain historians have said, Foucault's work properly belongs to the genre of fiction ('Once upon a time . . .', 'If I were King . . .'). His histories are novels. This is an unpleasant conclusion for historians, and difficult for them to admit in so far as their own work presents the same external features as that of Foucault: a seductive construct whose play of erudite cross-reference lends it an air of verisimilitude.[11]

Marxism in Peril

For Sartre in 1961, Marxism was both the way and the truth, 'the unsurpassable philosophy of our time'. He none the less observed that, having become an official state doctrine, 'Marxism was at a standstill'.[12] Sartre therefore volunteered his services and suggested restoring the movement to what he called 'le Savoir', by the addition of a 'concrete anthropology' (the philosophy of praxis). During the same period, another refrain began to be heard in Paris: history is a myth.

[10] *Nietzsche* (Minuit, 1967), p. 189.
[11] On the question of the 'fiction' inherent in 'historical narrative', see Michel de Certeau, *L'écriture de l'histoire* (Gallimard, 1975).
[12] CRD, p. 25.

Such is the 'theoretical conjuncture' of what Louis Althusser himself describes as his 'intervention'.[13] Marxism was in difficulties on two sides.

1. In the rear, where it ran the risk of being drawn along in the decline of those philosophies (assembled by Althusser under the heading 'theoretical humanism') with which opinion tended to associate it.

2. In the front, where its theory of economic determinism (positing a relation of *cause and effect*, rather than one of isomorphism, between infrastructure and superstructure) came under fire from the structuralist positions.

Caught between the two, Althusser, a self-acknowledged communist philosopher, might well have described himself in the words that Stendhal gives to Lucien Leuwen: 'I am a cavalry general in a lost battle, who forgets his own interests and attempts to have his cavalry dismount in order to engage the enemy infantry.' It is a difficult manoeuvre that Althusser attempts in abandoning the treacherous ground of *praxis* and the 'dialectic', leaving the existential regiments to fight it out alone with the structuralist artillery, siding with the latter himself, taking advantage of the general surprise to consolidate his hold, and emerging finally as winner of the day. Such audacious tactics evidently entail certain sacrifices which his ranks must first be persuaded to accept: the entire Hegelian heritage must be repudiated, and likewise all kinship between Marxism and the dialectical philosophy of history. The charger of 'contradiction, driving force of history', on which only a while before the Marxist philosopher was seen to parade, becomes a jaded Rosinante, to be rid of in all haste.

However, the 'theoretical conjuncture' alone is not sufficient to situate Althusser's interventions. They should also be related to the 'political conjuncture', as he himself has insisted.[14] 'Political conjuncture', from any pen but Althusser's, would mean the situation in France, and more generally, the evolution of western societies, East–West relations, the crisis of the dollar, etc. Althusser mentions none of this. Nothing in his writings between 1960

---

[13] *Lénine et la philosophie*, (Maspero, 1969), pp. 49–50; *Lenin and Philosophy and Other Essays*, trans. Ben Brewster (London, New Left Books, 1977).

[14] PM, pp. 11–21; *Réponse à John Lewis* (Maspero, 1973), pp. 10–11, etc.

and 1967 anticipates the revolt of May 68, for instance.[15] His interpretation of 'political conjuncture' is restricted to two events: the condemnation of Stalinism at the Twentieth Congress of the Soviet Communist Party, and the split in the world Communist movement, between the Russian and Chinese Parties.

Although for Althusser the meaning of the theoretical conjuncture is political, the two terms could usefully be distinguished here. I will begin with the theoretical question.

Post-war 'existential Marxism' was presented as a philosophy of history. It provided a connection between the course of events (from human origins through to the end of history) and the subjective experience of individuals. It sought to endow Marxism with a phenomenological foundation ('being' as the 'presentation of a meaning to a consciousness'). The truth of Marxist theories of class struggle and the necessity of revolution lay in the experience of the individual, conscious of existing as exploited or exploiter and freely choosing to invest his life with the meaning of struggle for or against a society of universal recognition between consciousnesses. Now all this had the air of a myth. The lived meaning, as Lévi-Strauss explains, is never the correct one. Althusser's definition of *ideology* (in the pejorative sense of 'false representation') invokes this very discrepancy between experience and knowledge. Ideology, he says, is the expression of the lived relations of men to their conditions of existence, given that this expression of a (real) relationship is never synonymous with knowledge of it, and always includes an element of the imaginary. The truth of Marxism can no longer be guaranteed by the testimony of consciousness. Another basis has therefore to be found. So we arrive at what might be called the formula of the Althusserian intervention: it is not in a philosophy of freedom, or *praxis*, that the foundation of Marxism must be sought, but rather in an *epistemology* whose central thesis would be the opposition of consciousness and concept (and as a result the impossibility of all phenomenology).

Althusser's first move in this tight game is to divide Marxism

[15] A detailed explanation of the successive political positions held by the small core which formed around Althusser at the Ecole Normale may be found in the essay by Jacques Rancière, *La leçon d'Althusser* (Gallimard, 1974). Rancière, who had been an adherent at the outset, now denounces Althusserianism as a doctrine for mandarin academics.

into the science of history, or *historical materialism* (HM) on the one hand, and on the other, the philosophy which founds this science, or *dialectical materialism* (DM). The division has two advantages.[16] First, everything here is in order as regards the French school of epistemology, whose support Althusser wishes to enlist. According to this school, it is for science to state that which is, i.e. to know, whereas philosophy must address itself, not to being, but to scientific discourse. Secondly, it dissociates Marxism from the 'philosophy of history'. The post-war generation attached great importance to Marx's early writings which, with their Hegelian vocabulary ('alienation', 'labour', 'negativity'), readily afforded a phenomenological interpretation. The scientific claims of *Capital*, however, were condemned. The notion of an 'objective dialectic', asserting that relations between men need be approached no differently than relations between things, was said to be meaningless.

HM is the science founded by Marx and set forth in *Capital*. Althusser repeatedly insists upon the point that if *Capital* is of any interest, it can only be as an event in the history of science, comparable in importance to the foundation of mathematics by Thales, or that of physics by Galileo.[17] Here we will recognise the scenario lifted by neo-Kantianism from the preface of the second edition of the *Critique of Pure Reason*: at the origin of all science, there is a revolution in method which consists in interrogating the object rather than being directed by it. Or in neo-Kantian terms, science begins where the evidence of the senses and the primary truths of consciousness are no longer trusted; science 'constructs' or 'produces' its object. This 'revolution in method' is now known as the 'epistemological break' (a term borrowed from Bachelard), and the 'empiricism' with which it must break corresponds henceforth to 'ideology'. The object of philosophy is reason. But since reason evolves in history, it can only be known by a study of method in the sciences which develop over the course of that history (as we know, this was the programme of Comte's *Cours de philosophie positive*). For Althusser, DM should perform the office

---

[16] Not to mention a third advantage, namely the reproduction (ostensibly) of the distinction taught in Communist Parties by official Marxism, which is to be found for example in the title of Stalin's classic pamphlet (cf. PM, p. 25). HM and DM are customary abbreviations in Althusserian circles.

[17] *Lénine et la philosophie*, p. 24.

of relating what it is about Marx's method (his 'logic', or again his 'dialectic') that is scientific. Where is Marx's philosophy to be found? Nowhere, replies Althusser.[18] Marx's philosophy is the 'logic of *Capital*'. However, while it is true that Marx proposed to set forth this 'logic', 'in two or three pamphlets', he did not actually do so, nor, as Althusser observes, has anybody who came after him. Nobody has explained why *Capital* is a scientific book. However, though a theory of the science may be lacking, the scientific book has been written. *Capital* exists, and in it, Marxist philosophy may be found 'in practical form', which is to say that although it is not set forth as such, the scientific method can be seen in application there. Thus the task of the Marxist philosopher is to 'read *Capital*' with a view to discovering its logic.

The operation is meaningless unless we already accept that *Capital* is a scientific book, comparable to Euclid's *Elements* or Newton's *Principia*. How do we know it is? The question is all the more urgent for the fact that only a reading of the book will equip us with the criterion of what is scientific.

The answer, apparently, is to start out on the understanding that ideology is in league with idealism, whereas science is on the side of materialism. Now Marx's method in *Capital*, as the subtitle suggests, consists in a critique of classical political economy. The critical work performed by Marx upon the texts of English economists may be described as *productive* work in the literal sense of the word – a transformation of raw material culminating in a finished product. Marx produces *knowledge* (that is, we know the real as a result of his labour) by working on a raw material which is not something 'real', revealing itself in phenomenological experience, but an ideological discourse upon the real – the discourse of political economy. We may therefore say that a science is the knowledge of the *ideology* from which it springs (by means of the 'break'); and it *is* this knowledge as a result of its having *transformed* the ideological material.[19] To describe the instruments of work and the productive operations of science is precisely to develop the 'theory of knowledge' to which philosophy is here reduced. Anxious to avoid neo-Kantian terms, Althusser prefers to speak of the 'theory of practice'. If this knowledge is produced

---

[18] LC, I, pp. 35–6.
[19] LC, I, pp. 56–7.

by the application of (conceptual) tools to matter – tools which are as heterogeneous to this matter as the carpenter's saw to the wooden plank he is cutting – then Marx's method is no longer 'dialectical' in the idealist sense; knowledge is no longer the move to know oneself in something other than oneself. Q.E.D.

A first objection to this conception of the opposition between the idealism of ideologies and the materialism of scientists can be gleaned from the testimony of Marx himself, who wrote that his method in *Capital* was the 'direct opposite' of Hegel's. In Hegel, the dialectic is on its head; it must be stood back upon its feet. This phrase had always been understood in a 'dialectical' sense; the passage to the 'direct opposite' was a 'dialectical progression', an *Aufhebung* which, in refuting the error, preserved the truth that lay concealed within it. But Althusser condemns this interpretation. If the relationship of idealism and materialism were itself 'dialectical' in the Hegelian sense, there would finally be a 'dialectical identity' between the logic of Hegel and that of Marx. The relationship must be non–dialectical; alternatively it must be 'dialectical' in a new sense, one which would be radically foreign to Hegel.

Thus presented, Althusser's thesis on the Hegel–Marx relationship is quite simply untenable. If Marx speaks of a 'dialectic', there must be a connection between what he understands by the word and what he has read in Hegel. This common characteristic must recur in the dialectical relationship – in the Marxist, materialist sense – between the two dialectics, idealist and materialist. The dialectic in play between the two dialectics is thus the *sole* dialectic, and the transition from Hegel to Marx is well and truly a *dialectical* one, at least in Marx's view. But in all likelihood, Althusser has something else in mind here. In reality, he seems to tell us between the lines, Marxism is not at all dialectical, and Marx's method is radically new, but when Marx wishes to formulate this newness, for which no language as yet exists, he is obliged to use Hegelian terms. This creates the semblance of a common ground between idealist and materialistic logic. In brief, Althusser's enterprise implies that in the long term the word 'dialectic' should be discarded – a project which could not be disclosed until the ground had been prepared for its reception.[20]

[20] Hints of this intention to strike the word 'dialectic' out of the vocabulary can be found in certain contributions from the authors of LC (e.g. vol. I, p. 256 and vol II, p. 401).

Althusser has been charged, more generally, with ignoring certain of Marx's statements, neglecting to quote a page here, a letter there, failing to take the *Grundrisse* into account; in short, with mishandling the *corpus* in order to substantiate a historical untruth (Marx's rupture with Hegel). Althusser has been challenged on historical grounds, while he wished to confine himself to those of epistemology. Althusser's Marxism is a doctrine which should, in its own view, be susceptible of exposition *more geometrico*. If the name Marx designates the author of every sentence contained in the books signed 'Karl Marx', then it goes without saying that Marx is frequently Hegelian, and Althusser is the first to acknowledge it. He explains this in terms of the fatality whereby what is new must be said in the language of the old. None the less, if we decide to call Marx the founder of a science of history, and if this foundation of a new science requires a 'break', and if the pre-scientific ideology of history is embodied in Hegelianism, it follows that only the statements which effect the said 'break' will be considered as Marxist. Quotations prove nothing for the purposes of this discussion, since a statement may be 'Marxist' in the first sense but not in the second.

There is a more serious objection. By positing that DM is the epistemology of HM, Althusser sets in motion the celebrated vicious circle whereby neo-Kantian positivism palms the ontological issue. What is in question here is the validity of the equation between *being* and *representation*. First, the fact of science is assumed and the preconditions for this fact are sought. Given that there is science, in Newton's physics for example, how can it be explained that a man (Newton) is able to state the laws of nature? The answer is that this science concerns phenomena (being=representation, laws of nature=laws of representation). It is then claimed proven that knowledge of nature is indeed given us by the sciences, on the pretext that they fulfil the general conditions for knowledge of a thing – as if these conditions had not just been defined by the analysis of the 'fact of science' based on the example of those very sciences! Similarly Althusser derives an epistemology from *Capital*, and then corroborates historical materialism's claim to the status of science with the aid of this self-same epistemology. Thus he appears to have replaced the phenomenological foundation of Marxism (for what it is worth) purely and simply by begging the question. First we read *Capital* in order to learn from its example what a science is, then we congratulate ourselves upon finding that this same *Capital* conforms to the requirements of the epistemology we have just derived from it.

Althusser admits that there is something circular about his procedure.[21] But perhaps the circle is not a vicious one. Only Althusser's exaggerated caution in the exposition of his project makes it seem so. Everything leads us to suppose that his intention is as follows: by the fusion of DM with the epistemology of the French school, to endow HM with scientific form, using the ideological raw material supplied by vulgar Marxism. Clearly there can be no epistemology proper to Marxism (as the science of history) as distinct from the epistemology of the mathematical or physical sciences etc. It is therefore necessary that DM should be the theory of science as a whole. Not only is DM to set forth the conditions in which HM produces the knowledge of history, but it is also to explain how arithmetic produces the knowledge of numbers, physics that of energy, etc. Althusser would have achieved this objective – the substitution of foundation *in the concept* for foundation *in consciousness* or in *lived experience* – if he had been able to show that *Capital* satisfies the norms of general epistemology, the supreme jurisdiction. In Marxism thus reconstructed, the decisive and final authority on points of theory would no longer be political but scholarly. The last word should go to a scientific committee and not to the *bureau politique* of the P.C.F., for the first would understand why a proposition is scientific, while the second is highly likely to be steeped in ideology.

But would epistemologists confirm that HM, in its reformed Althusserian version, is a science comparable to chemistry or astronomy? Most probably some would and others would not. Epistemology was to have endorsed the scientific validity of HM, but if there are several epistemologies, the epistemological validity of DM (remaining to be constituted) must now be guaranteed in the face of rival theories of science (those of Popper or Habermas, for instance).

The correct epistemology will be one which allows us to understand the fact that scholarship supplies us with knowledge. Here Althusser rejects all *empirical* criteria. Marxism, as the science of

[21] PM, p. 31; LC, I, p. 40.

history, is not true or false according to whether such and such an event (a world crisis for example) takes place or not. Science must satisfy purely internal demands; it is defined by the way in which it orders its statements, and not by 'successes'. The question is therefore this: how is it that the products of the scholar's 'theoretical practice' (his science) are *knowledge*? How is it, in other words, that his work results in our knowledge of that which is (Althusser calls it 'the real object', without further explanation)? This ultimate question, which for the philosopher is also the primary one, is left unanswered at the moment of asking. [22] Is all this groundwork to remain suspended? Perhaps not, for the answer that is 'unable to be found' in the text of 1965 had already been provided in 1963, by an article in which Althusser sought to show that there was nothing Hegelian about the Marxist dialectic. [23] In it, he supplied the following definitions: sciences are *theoretical practices* which transform the ideological products of existing *empirical practices* (namely all the 'concrete' activities of man – work, play etc.) into 'knowledge' (i.e. into scientific truths). The dialectic (or philosophy) is *the general theory of practice in general*, and should be elaborated on the basis of epistemology, that is, of the theory of scientific practices. But why, it may be asked, should philosophy take human practice for its object (rather than *nature*, for example, as partisans of a 'dialectic of nature' maintain, human practice being no more than one area of nature)? Why should the theory of practice in general be constructed from the theory of certain specific practices, scientific ones? The answer to both these questions is provided in the following way: in general or dialectical theory

> the essence of theoretical practice in general is
> theoretically expressed, through it the essence of practice
> in general, and through it, the essence of the
> transformations, of the 'development' of things in
> general. [24]

Unfortunately, Althusser says no more. The reader who finds this transition from the knowledge of 'theoretical practice' to that of 'the development of things in general' obscure or debatable will comb Althusser's writings in vain for a more rigorous

[22] LC, I pp. 88–9.   [23] PM, pp. 169–70.   [24] PM, p. 170.

development of the question raised here, that of the foundation of truth. But although in these lines Althusser does not say how it appeared to him that the essence of things was expressed in the essence of theory, he none the less indicates very clearly to what extent the 'theoretical anti-humanism' and the 'break' between the science of Marx and the ideology of Hegel are frail constructions, collapsing like card-houses at the least breath of philosophy. For after so many 'ruptures', Althusser has still not gone beyond the *humanisation* of the identity between subject and object, that is, the point around which contemporary French philosophy has continued more or less unwittingly to turn. Doubtless it is no longer said that the concept conceives of itself, or that it discovers in its conception (or consciousness) of itself the identity of being and concept. But it is freely said that theory, in knowing the essence of theoretical practice (its own essence therefore), knows every practice. Such a 'practice in general' means less the activities indulged in by specimens of the human race on the surface of the earth than an equivalent of 'the unity of man and nature',[25] the noblest designation of the *totality* (the synthesis of the *in-itself* and the *for-itself*, as Sartre said in his Hegelian moments). As we can see, the Hegelian dialectic is alive and well.

Superstructures

In the eyes of a Marxist theoretician, the denunciation of Stalinism and the Chinese secession have one point in common: in both cases, the rule that superstructure (ideology, political and juridical forms) should be explained by infrastructure (relations of production) is seriously infringed. In 1956, the Twentieth Congress of the Soviet Communist Party condemned Stalinist dogmatism ('an ideological error') and the 'violations of socialist legality' ('a political error'). But if these errors were committed, how can it be explained that an aberrant superstructure should correspond to a flawless infrastructure? If the economy is socialist, why does the proletariat not predominate both in the State and within ideology? Again, in 1966, China embarked on the Great Proletarian Cultural Revolution. How is a progressive revolution conceivable within a state which is already socialist? Maoists argue that in

[25] LC, II p. 149.

the cultural field of customs and ideas, it is necessary to struggle against the threat of a restoration of the old regime. Here again, ideology would seem to be more than a faithful reflection of the economy. In order to solve these two puzzles, Althusser resorts to a certain kind of structuralism, more apparent than real.[26] We have seen that in proper structuralist procedure, the economic determinism professed by Marxists is unacceptable, since it affirms a direct causal link between the content of the discourse and the reality of its enunciation, neglecting the specific role of the *code*. Take any novel; for orthodox Marxism it will reproduce either the ideology of the ruling class or that of the oppressed class. For structuralism such a view is premature, to say the least, for the novel originates primarily in the code of novelistic discourse, and not in the author's social awareness. It is only secondly that as the analysis progresses, a structural correspondence may perhaps be established between the novelistic code as a whole (but not this or that particular novel) and the relation of subordination which, of all the relations possible in one group's power over another, defines the rule of the bourgeoise. Should this hypothesis of a relation between novelistic code and bourgeois domination be verified, then the 'progressive' novels would not be those whose content refers to the experiences of the workers ('popular literature', 'socialist realism'), but those which in one way or another transgress or endanger the code of the novel. The progressive writer will then be Joyce or Mallarmé, not Zola or Aragon.[27]

The Althusserian formula of 'structural causality' provides the required solution, allowing ideology to be credited with 'relative autonomy' while maintaining, against orthodox structuralism, a determination 'in the last instance' by economic factors. The public success of this subtle enveloping manoeuvre was devastating. Not only did Althusser's 'structural causality' avail itself of the key to structuralism's prestige – its technique of analysis – but it went further than structuralism by endowing the 'autonomy of the symbolic' (Lévi-Strauss) or the 'signifier' (Lacan), notions

---

[26] As he himself subsequently admitted, cf. *Eléments d'autocritique* (Hachette, 1974), ch. III; *Essays in Self-criticism*, trans. G. Lock (London, New Left Books, 1976).

[27] *Tel Quel* popularised these themes in the sixties. However, they leaped directly to the conclusion (that a literary avant-garde is *ipso-facto* the political avant-garde) without troubling themselves unduly over the isomorphism between the novel form and bourgeois modes of power.

now transformed into the 'relative autonomy of ideology', with the political dimension they lacked. Thanks to this causality, Stalinism and the Cultural Revolution could now be explained. It should be emphasised that the major exponents of structuralism had remained somewhat evasive on the terrain of political analysis – the terrain, in France, upon which the value of an idea for public opinion will 'in the last instance' be decided.

How can an identical cause account for different effects? The diversity of cultural, political and social modes protests against a uniform explanation in terms of the eternal 'contradiction' between the growth of 'productive forces' (PF) and the maintenance of existing 'relations of production' (RP). A certain 'play' in the explanation is necessary, and this is precisely what Althusser introduces by defining society as a 'structured complex whole'.[28] Citing texts of 'concrete analysis', not only by Marx but also by Lenin, Mao and even Comrade Stalin,[29] he has no difficulty in showing that the historical analysis *practised* by these authorities is not the one recommended by official doctrine. Reading *Capital* in this new light, we can say that every society is a sum of 'instances', ideological, political and economic.[30] Instead of supposing relations of direct or mechanical causality between these instances (if A, then B), we should envisage relations of 'structural' causality. What is meant by this? All instances co-exist, and they are irreducible one to another. The economic instance remains privileged; no longer inasmuch as it acts directly upon political relations which are in turn reflected in ideology – this theory is now condemned as an 'economistic' error – but inasmuch as it assigns to one instance of the 'whole' the role of dominant instance. For example, in a social formation with a certain economic base (the feudal mode of production), the dominant instance will be political. Political contradictions will dominate, but they will not explain everything, since the dominant contradiction is itself 'overdetermined' by the contradictions of the other instances. Causality is therefore structural in that it is structure – a term that for Althusser designates the way in which instances combine with one another – that decides 'in the last instance' which of them will dominate.

In 1963 Althusser maintained that the relative autonomy of superstructures

[28] PM, p. 211.   [29] PM, p. 96.   [30] PM, p. 238.

explains very simply, in theory, how the socialist *infrastructure* has been able to develop without essential damage during this period of errors affecting the superstructure. [31]

What do these words mean? They mean that the discrepancy between instances, between what takes place in the infrastructure and what occurs in the superstructure, authorises us to speak as much as we like about *repression* (the crimes of Stalin etc.) but never about *exploitation*. We find, then, that Althusser is able to sustain his thesis regarding the nature of the Soviet System (a socialist infrastructure supporting a non-socialist superstructure) only by contenting himself with a naïve and idealistic notion of power. This naïvety was to become apparent on the occasion of May 68. The point should be stressed, for it is the key to several episodes which will be dealt with later, and it explains the stagnation of Marxism, followed by its complete disappearance from the French scene, with the advent first of the 'philosophies of desire' (1970–5) and later of the New Philosophers (1977–8).

The Marxist analysis of the Stalinist system that everyone was looking for in 1960, Sartre with his 'practico-inert', Althusser with his 'overdetermination', had in fact been provided in 1949 by Cornelius Castoriadis* in his article, 'Relations of Production in the U.S.S.R.', published by the review, *Socialisme ou Barbarie*. [32] It is true that this analysis had been considered null and void by the leading lights of the intelligentsia, and particularly by the team at *Les Temps Modernes*. For although each voiced his desire to find a Marxist explanation of the notorious facts of repression in Russia, it was agreed in advance that such an explanation should under no circumstances challenge the title awarded to the U.S.S.R. of 'home of world socialism', nor the C.P.'s role of political leadership. Sartre's attitude in this respect is extremely edifying, and would merit a special study. [33] For these reasons, the conclusions of Castoriadis and the *Socialisme ou Barbarie* group were not circulated among the main body of the public until after 1968,

---

* Castoriadis is published in Britain by Solidarity, under the name Paul Cardau. (Trs.)

[31] PM, p. 248.

[32] *Socialisme ou Barbarie*, no. 2, May 1949 (republished by the author in *La société bureaucratique*, vol. I, 10/18, 1973, p. 205 ff.).

[33] Sartre's articles on this question, and in particular the polemic against Lefort, are assembled in vols. VI and VII of *Situations* (Gallimard, 1964, 1965).

when everyone expressed their astonishment that the most enlightened minds could have been blind for so long.

A Marxist analysis of any phenomenon consists in establishing its 'class nature' by means of an inquiry into its relationship with *production*. To analyse a society, then, the first step will be to ascertain its relations of production – that is, the relationship of the various layers of the population to *the means of production*. *Exploitation* exists where one social class appropriates these means of production for itself. Indeed, exploitation is defined neither by inequality of incomes, nor by the fact that workers produce more goods than are necessary for simple reproduction, but by the fact that the dominant class appropriates the *surplus value* (i.e. the difference between the *value added* to raw material by labour and the value of the labour power itself, measured by its wage). Having recapitulated these basic concepts, Castoriadis begins his inquiry. In Russia the mode of production is evidently not capitalist: the bourgeoisie has not been restored, private property has not been re-established. Nor can we speak of State capitalism, since a planned economy has replaced a competitive market economy. Thus the great majority of Marxists, even outside the P.C.F., could only conclude like Althusser in 1963 that the infrastructure was socialist. But then *in the name of what* was it possible to protest against Stalinist 'errors' (since the criterion of progress is 'in the last analysis' the growth of productive forces)? Castoriadis shows that by virtue of the very definitions which have just been mentioned, the Soviet mode of production should be considered, from a Marxist point of view, as a new mode of exploitation, a system which was unforeseen and 'infinitely closer' to fascism (that is, the reduction of workers to 'industrial slaves') than to competitive capitalism.[34] The following characteristic indicates that a regime is exploitative: surplus value is shared out between the productive costs of capital accumulation (machinery, industrialisation) and the 'unproductive consumption' of the exploiting class. The entire question thus hinges upon whether it is possible to detect *incomes arising from surplus value* in the U.S.S.R. If this is the case, then the existence of an exploiting class will have been demonstrated. Castoriadis next proposes a very simple reasoning, accessible to the plainest intelligence. If the totality of surplus value

---

[34] *La société bureaucratique*, I, p. 253.

(corresponding to the surplus labour of the producers) were used for accumulation, the difference in incomes should correspond to the difference in the value of the labour power. Now a labour power is worth what it costs to produce an equivalent labour power. In the hypothesis of a socialist economy – for which the maxim is, as we know, 'to each according to his labour' – the difference in salaries should not exceed a proportion of 1 to 2. Let us suppose that the least qualified worker (X) begins his working life at sixteen, and the most qualified (Y) at thirty. Let us also suppose that both retire at the age of sixty. X's annual wage should be

$$1 + 16/44 = 1 \cdot 4,$$

a sum which represents the cost of maintaining him for a year, plus the fraction of the costs of his education over sixteen years, repaid progressively during the forty-four years of his active life. Y's wage will be

$$1 + 30/30 = 2.$$

The calculation need not be any more detailed, given the enormous disproportion between the relationship set out here, which defines a *socialist* economy (never more than 1 to 2, since it would still be $1 \cdot 2$ to 2 if children worked from the age of ten) and the relationship that transpires from known figures. In 1949, Castoriadis quoted figures for the year 1936; the relationship was of 1 to 250 in the case of incomes at the extremes, and at least 1 to 10 if the calculation were based on averages (not taking into account any extra-salarial income, and payment in kind for the privileged). Castoriadis concludes that State ownership of the means of production has led to the emergence of an exploiting class (the bureaucracy), a development which Marxist doctrine had not foreseen.

Introduction to the Problem of Power

If the Soviet regime appears to be a particularly efficient system of exploitation, Marxists must examine it for symptoms of class struggle and signs of an impending revolt of the exploited proletariat against the ruling class. Several events which took place could be interpreted in this way, above all the Hungarian uprising of 1956. As for those organisations which, in capitalist societies, supported the Soviet Union (Communist Parties and trade unions), they should be seen, so this theory runs, as the kernel of a potential ruling class in the future. After the compromise of peaceful co-existence, these organisations, which had been candidates for power during the Cold War, confined themselves to the bureaucratic supervision of wage-earners' demands (bureaucratic in the sense that they took control of what the members of these organisations call *la base*, the rank and file – presumably the base of the bureaucratic pyramid...).

The critique of Marxism, followed by its disappearance – possibly only temporary – from the forum of debate, commenced in France after May 68, because the *legitimacy* of communist organisations came into question. Stunned, dismayed, scandalised, the activists of May, steeped for the most part in the *gauchiste*[35] illusion, were forced to recognise that the 'proletarian leadership' had not hesitated to condemn their movement and had done its utmost to avoid even the suspicion of its hoping to profit in any way from disorders for which it was not responsible. The débâcle of *authority* in all parts of France, its total absence for the space of a few weeks, aroused the same panic both at the ministries and at the headquarters of the so-called revolutionary organisations. On the other hand, the equally sudden restoration of authority in July 'as if nothing had happened' filled the dissenters with anger. It was realised that there had been a failure to reflect upon the nature of power. The poverty of run-of-the-mill political theory became flagrant. How could it have been believed that the communist organisations, immense power-producing machines, had no purpose other than to prepare for their own dismantling, along with the future 'withering away' of the State promised by Marx? A naïve conception of power identifies the *potentate* and his *subjects*. This prejudice has dominated the politics of intellectuals for more than thirty years. As if the famous *Caesar fecit pontem* were to be taken literally. Julius Caesar is imagined in shirt sleeves, hauling stones one by one, to construct the pillars of the bridge. The confusion of *represented* and *representing* is highly conspicuous in

---

[35] *Gauchisme:* a political programme, defended by certain far-left groups (Trotskyists, etc.), proposing to exert pressure on the P.C.F. *from outside*, and oblige it to 'return' to a revolutionary line (as distinct from the *'opposition de gauche'*, which believed in action *from within*).

certain of Althusser's expressions. Engels and Lenin are described as 'great working-class leaders',[36] and Lenin as a 'proletarian political leader'.[37] Engels was always thought to have run his father's textile firm; by what miracle has he suddenly become a worker? And what is meant by a 'proletarian leader'? In reality, such notions belong to the series of unaccountable twentieth-century freaks, of which Lyotard has drawn up a preliminary inventory:

> the Stakhanovist worker, the proletarian manager, the Red Marshal, the Left nuclear warhead, the unionised policeman, the communist labour camp, socialist realism.[38]

By a simple slide from genitive to adjective, the party that purports to be *of* the working class is held to be a *working-class* party, whose leader is therefore a *worker*. But a moment's reflection will show that the expression 'proletarian power' is a contradiction *in adjecto*. The proletarian is by definition bereft of all power.

Hence a second question, which takes us beyond the intellectual confines of Marxism. It is already a step to realise that 'workers' power' cannot be the power *of* workers, that it necessarily means power *over* workers – a power of which mass organisations offer a periodic demonstration by showing that they can mobilise their forces at any time they choose. If we remain within the limits of Marxist thinking, we will have to conclude that the battle-front of class struggle is drawn between the working class and its leaders, who in the East constitute the ruling class, and in the West are the 'allies' of management. However, the argument that the gap between represented and representing (between the 'rank and file' and the 'bureaucrats' at the top) could give rise to a confrontation between *two classes* is an extreme one, and cannot be maintained for very long. If, in the West, unions are a cog in the machinery of exploitation, why do wage-earners unionise? The reality is quite different: it is thanks to the unions, when they are skilfully run, that wage-earners receive a share of surplus value. It would be hard to tell whether this share (wage increases, social security)

---

[36] *Lénine et la philosophie*, p. 32.
[37] *Ibid.*, p. 56.
[38] *Disp. puls.*, p. 17.

corresponds to their own surplus labour or to that of other workers. Each now being both exploiter and exploited, the concept of exploitation no longer operates, and that of a revolt by the exploited against the mode of exploitation of labour loses all assignable meaning. Such are the ultimate consequences of the article written by Castoriadis in 1949.[39]

Divest of what had served it as political theory, the intelligentsia of the seventies fell to mulling dejectedly over its contradiction: the revolution would be that of the powerless against all forms of power! Yes, but how confront 'Power' from a position of powerlessness? The only solution to have been found to this problem is that of mystical renunciation. The Stoic sage, the Indian yogi or the Christian martyr have shown how to resist power without falling prey to its logic, or to the process which encourages an *identification with the adversary* in order to defy him. They have all pointed to the anarchist solution of the political problem, namely the renunciation of all politics and the search for human comradeship beyond the limits and constraints of a *polis*.[40]

In 1969, Althusser did away with Althusserianism, and restored the priority of the political over the theoretical instance. In his preface to a popular edition of *Capital*, he asked himself the following question: if *Capital* is 'quite simply one of the three great scientific discoveries of all human history',[41] how is it that men of science, in the vast majority, know nothing of it (and that what Marxist scholars there are, are often so for sentimental reasons only) whereas the *ignorant* have made it their bible? The answer is simple: the former are *blinded* by the dominant ideology, while the latter undergo the experience of exploitation:

---

[39] Cf *La société bureaucratique*, I, p. 44.

[40] The mystical solution, renunciation of the world and the flesh, was acknowledged although not practised by the representatives of what was known in 1976 as the 'new philosophy'. Most New Philosophers claim descent from the Maoist groups which had formed after 1968 with the impetus of the more radical elements from the sacred Althusserian ranks of 1965. One by one, they have told the tale of their political misadventures. Their doctrine, in its pure and overtly gnostic form, is to be found in *L'ange* (Grasset, 1976) by Guy Lardreau and Christian Jambet; and in a moralistic rather than religious form, more accessible to the public at large, in *La barbarie à visage humain* (Grasset, 1977) by Bernard-Henry Lévy.

[41] 'Avertissement aux lecteurs du Livre I du Capital', in Marx, *Le Capital*, livre I (Garnier-Flammarion, 1969), p. 7.

> In spite of the bourgeois and petty bourgeois ideology weighing terribly upon them, it is impossible for them *not to see* this exploitation, since it is the substance of their daily lives. [42]

Returning in this way to experience and the 'lived-through', Althusser abandons the attempt to endow Marxism with an epistemological foundation and reverts to the phenomenological foundation which previously had been thought satisfactory enough. In 1965, Althusser had denounced the confusion of the 'real object' (e.g. the circle) with the 'object of knowledge' (the idea of the circle, which is not itself circular). The rehabilitation of the identity between the two after 1970 brings the Althusserian undertaking to an official close.

[42] *Ibid.*, p. 25.

5

Difference

Hegel had said that difference is contradictory in itself. But the question now is to pave the way for a non-contradictory, non-dialectical consideration of difference, which would not envisage it as the simple contrary of identity, nor be obliged to see itself as 'dialectically' identical with identity. In tackling this difficulty, French philosophy – in the form of Gilles Deleuze and Jacques Derrida – at last approaches the crux of the matter. We come finally to that remarkable point of modern metaphysics which all preceding discourse had indicated like a flickering compass. This metaphysical point may be situated in two ways.

1. In the language of *logic* (or of *ontology*), the question is that of the 'dialectic'.

2. In the language of the *philosophy of history* (or of metaphysical *theology*), the question is that of 'the unity of man and nature', as Marx called it; the meaning of this unity is precisely the meaning of *identity*, as defined by the dialectic.

The order that I now propose to follow – first Derrida, then Deleuze – is arbitrary, but no more so than the reverse.

The Radicalisation of Phenomenology

At the beginning of the sixties, there was much talk concerning the 'end of philosophy'. It was thought that the western *ratio*, its resources exhausted, was nearing the end of its run. The phrase, 'end of philosophy', was taken from Heidegger, and put to a great variety of uses. Some (Marxists and readers of Sartre) meant by it that the time had come to move from theory to political action; others brought the same charges against philosophy as the

Romantics had levelled against the Classicists (that it had presented as universally valid that which was the expression or representation of a particular people or time). In a sense which is scarcely Heideggerian, the 'end of philosophy' more commonly amounted to the accusation that philosophy is *the ideology of the western ethnos*. The discourse which presents a *de facto* situation as being founded *de jure*, or a traditional privilege as a natural superiority, is an ideological one. Reason, to the extent to which it is presented as 'reason' (light illuminating all men in this world), is an instance of injustice and violence. It would not be irrelevant to note that this philosophical examination of conscience was contemporaneous with the disappearance of the European colonial empires (1962, the end of the Algerian war).

Derrida has no objection to a reductive formula such as 'philosophy is the ideology of the western ethnos', except for the fact that to say it is impossible. The formula is essentially meaningless, and also, therefore, incapable of producing the critical effects attributed to it. What permits us to speak of *ideology*, if not precisely the opposition of *de facto* and *de jure*? By 'ideology' is meant a particular or relative discourse, seeking to pass itself off as universal or absolute. Now the opposition between the contingent particularity (the example) and the universally valid (the essential) is a philosophical one. Derrida would probably call it the very opposition that founds philosophy: on one side the *a priori*, which has value, and on the other the empirical, which has none. Derrida does not contest the charges brought against philosophy at that time: its violence, disguised as 'pacification', its colonial, imperial essence. He simply observes that the prosecution's indictment is couched in the language of philosophy. Either it has fallen into flagrant self-contradiction or, as seems more likely, it is demanding a more universal philosophy as a protest against the one which it judges to be both impoverished and partial. At best, the critique of philosophy proposes a programme of broadened rationalism. 'Philosophy is an ideology'; whether the intention is anti-colonial (philosophy=western ideology), Marxist (=discourse of the ruling class), Freudian (=sexual symptom), anti-Freudian (=phallocratic ideology), the formulation of it is meaningless. Such a programme continues to assume that reason has a future ahead of it. In the wake of Bataille and Blanchot, Derrida suggests an alternative diagnosis: history is already over:

> We believe, quite simply and literally, in absolute
> knowledge as the *closure* if not the end of history ... As
> for what 'begins' then, 'beyond' absolute knowledge
> *unheard of* thoughts are required, sought for across the
> memory of old signs.[1]

From now on, whatever the improvements of fact that may be introduced into the encyclopaedic exposition of philosophy, reason is absolute since it knows that it is so *by right*. The order of reason is absolute, since

> it is only to itself that an appeal against it can be brought,
> only in itself that a protest against it can be made; on its
> own terrain, it leaves us no other recourse than to
> stratagem and strategy.[2]

It is finally impossible to speak against reason, good, meaning or truth. For all one can say about the true or the good is this: it is true that the true is true, it is good that the good is good. If we wish to maintain the contrary (it is not true that the true is true), we are merely challenging an appearance of the truth; if we were to say, paradoxically, 'It is bad that the good is good,' we would simply be justifying the existence of evil by the most classic theodicy:

> Only able, as soon as it appears, to operate at the *interior*
> of reason, the revolution against reason has only ever the
> limited scope of what is called – precisely in the language
> of the Ministry of the *Interior* – unrest.[3]

To speak in order to say nothing (whether we approve reason, which can forego our approval, or whether we address our criticisms to it in a highly reasonable manner) – this dilemma is Derrida's point of departure.

There is a third possibility, however – that of guile; of *stratagem* and *strategy*.[4] Here Derrida begins a very close contest against a formidable Master, whom we might think certain to win at a game with rules which he himself has fixed. Derrida opts to play a *double game* (in the sense that a 'double agent' serves two sides),

[1] VP, p. 115.
[2] ED, p. 59.
[3] ED, p. 59.
[4] See also *Marges*, p. 7.

feigning obedience to the tyrannical system of rules while simultaneously laying traps for it in the form of problems which it is at a loss to settle. The strategy of *deconstruction* is the ruse that makes it possible to speak at the very moment when there is, 'when all is said and done', nothing more to say since the absolute discourse has been achieved. Such is the stratagem which challenges the dilemma posed by philosophy.

These stratagems have none the less had to be calculated and constructed. Between the moment at which the dilemma obliges the 'speaking subject'[5] to speak for reason and order, and the moment when, trapped, the Master is put into check and can only garble his arbitrary essence – between these two moments, then, a *silent arrière-pensée* must have guided the strategist. In silence, the strategist has thought what he could and should not say, namely that the true is not *truly true* (but often *false*), that the lawful and the arbitrary are indistinguishable, etc. How did this *arrière-pensée* come to him? In what silent region was the insurgent able to hatch his plot against the Logos, while pretending to speak the language of the Master? The question of this mental reservation (in the casuistical sense) is decisive, in the first place because, as Derrida observes to Levinas,[6] the only way of pretending to speak Chinese when speaking to a Chinese citizen is to address him *in Chinese*. Consequently, in this order of enunciation, dissemblance is the dissemblance of dissemblance (to pretend, I actually do the thing; I have therefore only feigned pretence). In the second place, the question here is to pretend to speak the Master's language in order to kill him.[7] We should emphasise the difference. If the traitor pretends to assassinate the tyrant, then the crime has not taken place; but if he feigns the pretence, then he kills in earnest, and the actor was concealing an assassin all along.[8]

The mental reservation alone, then, distinguishes sincere speech from speech which dissembles. But this reticence must still be able to insinuate itself between the 'speaking subject' and his word; the *arrière-pensée* must still be able to secrete itself somewhere in his head outside all language, never to be uttered. Here is precisely Derrida's objection to Levinas. Since the language of

---

[5] ED, p. 84.   [6] ED, p. 133.   [7] ED, p. 133.

[8] In an article on Bataille, Derrida writes, 'When describing this sham, the inconceivable for philosophy, its blind spot, Bataille must, of course, pretend to speak in Hegelian language.' (ED, p. 378.)

philosophy is irremediably Hegelian, Levinas should not dispute the Hegelian totality except in silence:

> As soon as *he speaks* against Hegel, Levinas can only confirm him, has *already* confirmed him.[9]

So that a mental reservation may be possible, in which to foment the plot of deconstruction, it is therefore necessary that two conditions concur.

1. Since Derrida finally rejects the idea of a thinking that is silent, the unsayable is also unthinkable. This mental reserve, as site of calculation, must therefore be speakable. The *double game* is thus not only of the deconstructor's doing: in order for it to be played, the language of philosophy must itself already be full of duplicity (in both senses of the word – state of doubleness, or hypocrisy and lying). Indeed, ever since his first published text, the introduction to Husserl's *Origin of Geometry*, Derrida has done nothing but denounce the pretensions of philosophical language to univocity. He has not ceased to wage a campaign, certainly reprehensible in the eyes of tradition, in favour of equivocity.[10] The metaphysical tongue is double; its words may always be shown to have two irreducible meanings (although not indeed 'opposed'). It is also deceptive, for it dissimulates its duplicity by retaining only one meaning, the 'right meaning', thereby claiming that the good is only good, that the true is all true and that meaning is full of meaning, etc.

2. The second condition is that somewhere outside Metaphysics the strategist should find the *strength to resist* the pressure of the *Logos*, which as we shall see in a moment, poses the problem of a philosophical *empiricism*.

Philosophy commences with the opposition of *de facto* and *de jure*. At least, it is so for those whom Husserl initiated into philosophy with his 'eidetic reduction'. A fact can prove nothing with regard to essence, to the question of right. Confusion of the two is the philosophical fault *par excellence*, as Derrida somewhat tersely informs Lévi-Strauss.[11] The word 'fault' should be stressed, for it is not inadvertently that Derrida uses a term with moral connotations.[12] The *fault* is known as empiricism. The

[9] ED, p. 276.
[10] OG, pp. 104–7; cf. ED, p. 167.
[11] G, p. 172; cf. already ED, p. 189.
[12] ED, p. 178.

empiricist does not believe in the distinction between *truths of fact* and *truths of reason* (to use Leibniz's terms). The alleged 'truths of reason' are finally truths of fact, for the ultimate reason of a truth of reason is always a *primitive fact*. He maintains therefore that there is no pure reason. The founding of truths of reason resides, not in any capacity of reason for *a priori* knowledge, but in its relationship to this primitive and ultimate fact, i.e. in the *experience* that reason has of it. In other words, the founding principle is not an identity of the kind, 'I=I', but a *difference*, since it is the relationship to something else. Empiricism, for Derrida, is

> the *dream* of a thought which is purely *heterological* at the source. *Pure* thought of a *pure* difference... We say *dream*, because it fades with the coming of day, the dawn of language. [13]

But of what is heterology so gravely guilty? Here are traces of the Husserlian, and more generally, neo-Kantian heritage; heterology is guilty in the same way that Aristotle was found guilty by the neo-Kantians for having written, 'We must stop.' The very notion of a primitive fact is philosophically irresponsible, [14] for the empiricist cannot answer for his fact, that is, measure it against a still more primitive right. The empiricist, then, is revealed as a barbarian who imagines that strength creates right... The distinction between the *a priori* and the empirical must be maintained, for we must never stop our inquiry.

Thus Derrida prepares to commit, knowingly, the fault of empiricism. But this will have to be *irreproachably* done, or else the Master will win the game against a bad player, whereas Derrida means to be a double player – his intentions bad, but his moves impeccable. This is why he conserves a certain loyalty to phenomenology. The latter must be *traversed*, he says, if we are not to drop short on the *hithermost* side, into positivist naïvety. [15] Or again, it must be 'radicalised' in order to salvage its intention. This intention may be honoured by delivering phenomenology from that which 'still holds it within the confines of a metaphysics', the metaphysics of *presence*. [16] This is what we should now proceed to examine.

[13] ED, p. 224.   [14] *Marges*, p. 7.   [15] G, pp. 90 and 232.
[16] VP, p. 94.

'La différance'

In his Introduction to the *Origin of Geometry*, Derrida considers the possibility of a phenomenology of history. French phenomenologists, taking Merleau-Ponty's quotations from the 'late Husserl' on trust, did not doubt that such a doctrine existed, in more or less latent form, in the *inédits* at Louvain. There, in those pages, would be found the means of passing from immobile essences to becoming, and from subjective solitude to inter-subjective community. But the situation remained one of 'empty intention', as a phenomenologist would aptly say, and the phenomenology of history, solution to all doctrinal impasses, continued to be postponed. Derrida shows that this would always be the case – in other words, that it was impossible.

What would a phenomenology of history be? Like all phenomenology, it would reply to the question, how is a truth possible *for us*? If truth is genuinely truth, then it must be so not only *for us*, but for every being (critique of psychologism). If it were only *for us*, it would not be truth in the sense that the word has, precisely, for us. Real truth requires that it be absolute, independent of any particular 'point of view'. If truth-for-us is indeed truth, we must recognise that we are the absolute (or rather that 'I' am 'the absolute source'). The phenomenology *of history*, therefore, together with all phenomenology of whatever kind, seeks the *origin* of truth. But phenomenology, as long as it is 'static', locates this origin in an act which may be accomplished by consciousness at any moment. For it calls origin (of the truth of the judgment about the thing) the *intuition* of the thing as it is present 'in flesh and blood'. Such is, as we know, the Husserlian 'principle of principles'.[17] If origin is intuition, I may at any time return to this origin, just as I may go to the origin of all postcards depicting the Eiffel Tower by visiting the Champ de Mars. Yes, but if it were a question of postcards depicting the *inauguration ceremony* of the Eiffel Tower, I could never recapture 'in flesh and blood' the event of which all these postcards inform me. The characteristic feature of historical phenomenology is that 'the thing itself' is the *inaugural fact*, which by definition can only occur once. In any event, the fact takes place the first time – the

---

[17] Husserl, *Idées directrices pour une phénoménologie*, vol. i, § 24, (trans. P. Ricœur, Gallimard, pp. 78–9).

first time of which the documents speak. But supposing we lose these documents? The Eiffel Tower would then be a monument whose origins are unknown to us. How could we tell whether it *is* – i.e. *was*, for its builders – a war machine, a phallic symbol or a religious spire? *Being would no longer be identifiable with meaning*, for there would be being that was not *for ourselves*, namely the being of that enigmatic monument as it was when it stood, in all its meaning, before those who built it. But this possibility is inadmissible for phenomenologists. The phenomenology of history is founded upon the description of what Husserl calls the 'Living Present'. The past can never be cut off from the present (any more than can the future). If the past were not always *retained* in the present, if the future were not already *mooted* there, past and future would be nothing; that is to say, they would be altogether absent. It would be impossible for us to speak of a mysterious past, of time immemorial, if there were not for us the *present* ruins of the civilisation which has *vanished* for ever. But in order for the future to be 'announced' in the present, and for the past to be 'retained' there, this present must not be merely present. It must also be both a present that is *already past* and a present that is *still to come*. By virtue of this past that is *still present*, the past as such is for us a present which is *no longer* present, while the future has always been, and will always be, a present which *is not yet* present. It is at this point that *difference* appears, the difference or non-coincidence of the present with itself. It must be decided here what significance to accord such a difference dividing the present. Either it means that nothing is ever altogether absent, or that the present itself never really takes place.

Husserl's reply, as Derrida demonstrates perfectly, is once more located within the opposition of *de facto* and *de jure*. In fact, we can come across monuments (present) whose sense escapes us, and which are therefore the present traces of a past about which we know nothing. We cannot say what this past was when it was present, and sense the impending threat of a being that is nothing for ourselves. But by right, the return to origins is always possible. For instance, even if the meaning that the (for ourselves) meaningless trace has *for ourselves*, and the meaning that it had *for them* cannot be made to coincide, we know *a priori* that this past, when it was present, had all the properties of the present. This *other* is therefore a *same*.

What is meant by the *right* to rediscover origins? That history must be conceived as the 'pure history of meaning',[18] a tradition or trans-lation of meaning across time, but never a betrayal. By reason of this 'principle of principles', phenomenology must posit that the history of man is meaningful through and through, the sound and fury always reducible, even if at the price of as many mediations as we please, to the peaceful transmission of the heritage of meaning from generation to generation. The model for history thus seems to be provided by the tradition of Thales' theorem, in so far as this theorem has apparently the same meaning for us today as it had formerly for Thales. History is univocal *by right*, even if *in fact* the integral recollection of meaning is impossible. The identity of being (implying here the *having-been*) and meaning is never given here and now, but 'at infinity'. Once again we encounter the 'infinite tasks' and the interminable 'tele-ologies' dear to the neo-Kantians. By right, the phenomenology of history is a philosophy which shows the itinerary *of the absolute* (the *Ego*, source of meaning) towards a *telos* situated 'at infinity', now called 'God', now 'the Logos' by Husserl, and which he says is the Idea 'in the Kantian sense' of a perfect society.[19] In other words, the meaning of universal history would be its tendency towards a final and ideal state (which, as we should note, retreats as fast as we advance towards it) – a state of mankind reminiscent of some perpetual mathematicians' congress. Such an account of history could not be more in keeping with the onto-theology of modern times.

If the *true* is identical with the *true for myself*, I must then be the Cartesian God, creator of eternal truths, as Sartre would have it, and perhaps also Husserl;[20] otherwise, truth is no more than a 'value' or a 'point of view', a 'perspective'. So that the identification of being with meaning should not entail the relega-tion of the phenomenon to simple appearance, I have to be God. However, this divinity is postponed indefinitely. *We know in advance that fact and right will never coincide.* Nothing therefore entitles us to behave as if equivocity were a moment destined to be

---

[18] OG, p. 107.

[19] *By right* only, for *in fact* phenomenology fails to become such a philosophy, being unable to found it upon the intuition of this *telos* 'in flesh and blood'.

[20] See Derrida's note, OG, p. 28.

abolished in the final triumph of univocal meaning. There is an 'originary difference' between fact and right, or between being and meaning.[21] This originary difference was later baptised '*différance*' by Derrida – a word in which both senses of the verb '*différer*' are to be understood. Clearly, *différer* means 'not to be identical' (as for example when we say that the present *differs* from itself), but it also means 'to defer' (as for example when we say that the present is always a *deferred* present, that the wholly present present will always exist tomorrow). It is this *différance* which produces history, among other effects. There is history because, from the origin onwards, the present is, so to speak, always delayed with regard to itself.

Originary Delay

The concept of an 'originary delay' is paradoxical but necessary. If *from the origin onwards* (each time there is origin), from the 'first time' onwards, there were no *différance*, then the first time would not be the 'first time', for it would not be followed by a 'second time'; and if the 'first time' were the 'only time', it would not be at the origin of anything at all. In a way which is perhaps a little dialectical, but not at all improper, it must be said that the first is not the first if there is not a second to follow it. Consequently, the second is not that which merely arrives, like a latecomer, *after* the first, but that which permits the first to be the first. The first cannot be the first unaided, by its own properties alone: the second, with all the force of its delay, must come to the assistance of the first. It is through the second that the first is the first. The 'second time' thus has priority of a kind over the 'first time': it is present from the first time onwards as the prerequisite of the first's priority without itself being a more primitive 'first time', of course; it follows that the 'first time' is in reality the 'third time'.

Origin must therefore be conceived as a dress rehearsal (*la répétition d'une première*), in the theatrical sense of these words: the reproduction of the first public performance, yet prior to this performance. Thus 'it is non-origin that is originary'.[22] At the origin, or if we prefer, *in principio*, there no longer subsists that tranquil identity in which the primitive is only primitive. If there

[21] OG, p. 171.   [22] ED, p. 303.

had only been simple identity at the origin, nothing would have come of it.

'In the beginning, the rehearsal (*répétition*)'. 'In the beginning, the performance (*re-présentation*)'. [23] Accordingly, there is not even *representation*, since the *presentation* (of which this representation is a reminder) never took place. The original is always a copy. Here is something akin to a 'principle of non-principles' whereby Derrida deconstructs the Husserlian 'principle of principles', which rests upon the possibility of always distinguishing the *original* (intuition, known as 'originary donor' of the thing itself in flesh and blood) from the *derived* (intentions of consciousness not fulfilled by intuition). An alternative version of the same 'principle of non-principles' would be to say, 'In the beginning, the sign' – the sign, not the thing (referent) of which this sign is supposed to be the sign. This *semiological* version has been particularly developed by Derrida, for a variety of reasons, not the least of which is, no doubt, that it wrecks all the pretensions of semiology at a period when the latter was all-prevailing, by eliminating the possibility of separating 'sign' and 'referent'. There are two means of access to this semiological version. One is the direct radicalisation of phenomenology. By showing, in opposition to Husserl, that consciousness is never anterior to language, it may be concluded that language cannot be taken as the 'expression' (representation) of a silent 'lived-through' (originary presentation). This is the progression in *La Voix et le Phénomène*. [24] Alternatively, access to the priority of the sign is gained by means of an inquiry into writing. There exists an entire tradition subordinating the written to the spoken word. One may write, for example, a letter to an absent person, or a will to be read after one's death. Writing is considered as a means of signification in the absence of the speaker or the listener, whereas in the presence of the listener one would simply speak. The definition of writing is thus as 'sign of a sign'. The graphic sign is the sign of the oral sign – it stands in for it, replaces it in its absence – whereas the oral sign is the sign of the thing. Writing fulfils a supplementary function:

> Writing is the supplement par excellence, since it marks the point where the supplement proposes itself as

[23] VP, pp. 50 and 64.
[24] See *Marges*, pp. 16–17 for an outline of the argument.

supplement of supplement, sign of sign, taking the place
of a speech already significant.[25]

But if it could be shown, as Derrida attempts in his essay, *De la
grammatologie*, that

> 1. the subordination of writing to speech is a prejudice,
> which not even the special case of so-called phonetic
> writing substantiates (although it is the case most
> favourable to this hypothesis); and that
> 2. the definition of the graphic sign is really the definition
> of any sign (that every sign is a *signifier* whose *signified* is
> another *signifier*, never 'the thing itself', visible, present
> before us 'in flesh and blood'),

then the Derridian 'principle of non-principles' will have overrid-
den the Husserlian 'principle of principles'.

This brings us to a theory with a somewhat dialectical air:

> The same is the same only in being affected by the
> other.[26]

Hence our query: is the beyond of the 'logic of identity'[27] a
dialectical beyond, or a beyond-the-dialectic? But it is also the
question that Derrida asks himself: is not the beyond-the-dialectic
inevitably a dialectical beyond?

Derrida acknowledges an affinity between what he calls the
'logic of the supplement' – at the origin, there is no originary, but
only a 'supplement' in the place of an ever-defective originary –
and the dialectic.[28] For does not this logic consist in subjecting (to
use Kantian terminology) the *unconditioned* to a *condition*, that of its
difference from the conditioned? Does it not demand that
difference be instated within identity, the relative within the
absolute, becoming within the eternal, and the 'work of the
negative' within the plenitude of the infinite, etc.? In this respect,
the logic of the supplement is instructive, for the supplement (any
supplement) is all too readily likened to a surplus, a supernumer-
ary appendixed to the integral whole. As if, in other words,
there were one already complete whole and, *outside* of it, the

[25] G, p. 398.   [26] VP, p. 95.   [27] ED, p. 302; G, p. 90.
[28] *Marges*, p. 15.

supplement. But if this were the case, the supplement would be
nothing: everything is presumably already included within the
whole. If the supplement is something rather than nothing, it
must expose the *defect* of the whole, for any whole that is able to
accommodate the addition of a supplement testifies thereby to the
lack of something *within* itself. The supplement outside stands for
the missing part inside the whole. It is because the whole does not
succeed in *being everything* that a supplement from without must
be added, in order to compensate its defective totality. This is why
the 'logic of the supplement'

> would have it that the outside be inside, that the other and
> the lack come to add themselves as a plus that replaces a
> minus, that what adds itself to something takes the place
> of a default in the thing, that the default, as the outside of
> the inside, should already be within the inside, etc. [29]

In a more general way still, the present is present only on
condition that it allude to the absent in order to be distinguishable
from it (an absent which is the past or the future). According to
Derrida, metaphysics would be the gesture of erasing this distinguishing mark, this trace of the absent, thanks to which the
present is the present. We may now observe that by *trace* we
normally mean the present sign of an absent thing, the sign left by
the absent thing, after it has passed, on the scene of its former
presence; but if every present bears the trace of an absent which
circumscribes it (and by which, in this sense, it is constituted,
produced and given to be what it is), then paradoxically an 'originary trace' must be conceived of; that is, a *present trace* of a *past
which never took place* – an 'absolute past'. [30]

At what distance does Derrida stand from Hegel? In what way
is *différance* not reducible to Hegel's dialectic of identity? This
question, as we can see, reproduces the one above: if it is true
that the language of metaphysics is Hegelian, from where does
Derrida derive his notion of a beyond–absolute–knowledge?

Derrida himself mentions a 'displacement, both minuscule and
radical'. [31] He also admits that the debate with Hegel is infinite,

---

[29] G, p. 308.
[30] G, p. 97. (See also 'Freud et la scène de l'écriture', in ED, pp. 293 ff;
reference here to Merleau-Ponty's 'original past').
[31] *Marges*, p. 15.

interminable.[32] The game he is playing against the Master-philosopher will last for ever. But how might deconstruction ever win at a game in which any victories over the Master are at once chalked up as defeats for the disciple (any victory at the *game of the Master* belonging to the *Master of the game*)?

Derrida speaks of a debate

> between philosophy, which is always a philosophy of presence, and a meditation on non-presence – which is not perforce its contrary, or necessarily a meditation on a negative absence, or a theory of non-presence *qua* unconsciousness.[33]

This meditation, or *thinking*, of non-presence (neither negative theology, nor a philosophy of 'will' anterior to 'representation') is, at least, *another* thinking. It is therefore legitimate to ask how it has arisen here to take issue with the whole of philosophy. Derrida asserts that philosophy *always is*. He does not assert that it *always has been* (which might refer to a historical, i.e. an empirical, inquiry). The *always* also holds good for works of philosophy that we have not read, for those not yet written, etc. But how are we to know this? Here Derrida replies, as phenomenologist, that it is a matter of eidetic necessity: philosophy will always be a thinking of presence, it cannot be otherwise. Thinking is as impossible outside the precedence given to the *present* over the *absent* (present-past, present-future) as colour is without surface, or the valley without the mountains:

> How could being and time have been thought *in any other way* than on the basis of the present, in the form of the present, namely a certain *now in general* that no *experience*, by definition, can ever relinquish? The experience of thought and the thought of experience have to do with presence and nothing else.[34]

No experience will ever enable us to think outside the privilege of the present, for experience is always the proof, lived out in the present, of a presence (even if it be the presence *of an absence*, as when one speaks of the experience of exile or death). This,

[32] ED, p. 371.   [33] VP, p. 70.   [34] *Marges*, p. 41.

incidentally, is why Derrida ultimately rejects the 'philosophical empiricism' which on occasion he evokes.

But must it be said that no thinking may challenge the primacy of the present? Or is it that no *philosophical* thinking may do so? Since Derrida, in the last but one quotation above, opposes 'philosophy' and a 'meditation on non-presence', there must be a thinking which exists outside the privilege of the present, and therefore an *experience* of this other *thinking*, a thinking of this other experience. Why, in that case, does Derrida eschew empiricism? It is because he never appeals to a *particular* experience that might weaken a *general* proposition. For him there is no question of 'refuting' identity by invoking such and such a case of '*différance*'. To oppose by way of such syllogism in *Baroco* ('All philosophy thinks presence', 'A certain thinking thinks absence', etc.) is still, Derrida would say, to denounce the false identity of that which presents 'identity' as its avowed identity. By showing how in a particular case the alleged identity conceals a difference, one is working in the interests of a superior, a higher identity, and concluding that it belongs somewhere other than where tradition had thought to find it. Derrida places himself as it were in the hands of a *general* experience. It is the experience of the *general text* that requires this. Every text is a double text, there are always two texts in one.

> Two texts, two hands, two kinds of looking, two kinds of listening. At once together and separate.[35]

Only the first of these 'two texts in one' is preserved by classical interpretation; it is written under the aegis of presence, favouring meaning, reason and truth. Here all negation is a superior affirmation. If I denounce this or that unreason within reason, I am denying only the negative of reason, a defect of reason within reason. The second text – other and yet the same – is that which the classical reading never deciphers. The first text, however, the one which it is prepared to read, contains fissures or traces which give indications of the second.[36] Now comes the vital point: between the two texts no synthesis is possible, no fusing into one, for the second is not the *opposite* of the first (which might be reconciled with it by a 'surmounting' of their 'differences'), but

[35] *Marges*, p. 75.
[36] *Marges*, pp. 76–7.

rather its *counterpart, slightly phased*. A reading of the general text therefore requires a *double science*,[37] rendering apparent the duplicity of any text.

Now we hold the answer to the question asked earlier. The 'meditation on non-presence' with which metaphysics debates is not, for the latter, another thinking than itself, as a foreign tradition, oriental wisdom or a return to myth etc. would be. It *is* itself as other. Every metaphysics, being double, is its own *simulacrum*. Between the text by Plato and itself, or the text by Hegel and itself, there passes a 'scarcely perceptible veil',[38] separating Platonism from itself, Hegelianism from itself. A slight displacement, a slight play in the reading of the text, is sufficient to collapse the first into the second, the *wisdom* of the first into the *comedy* of the second. Metaphysics, as convention has us picture it, split the world into two: the sensible and the intelligible, the body and the mind, etc. Philosophical empiricism, in a protest no less classic, overthrew this 'Platonism', and maintained that the intelligible arises from the sensible, that thought is a faculty of the body, etc. Derrida's double science, by an unprecedented operation, splits the metaphysical text itself into two. It is the text's duplicity which enables the *manifest* text to 'exceed' or 'transgress' in the direction of the *latent* text (to use, by approximation, an analogy from Freudian dream theory). In a way the transgression is thus literally *justified* (which is strange indeed for a transgression).

The one crime that is authorised, not to say encouraged, by ethics is tyrannicide. Is Derridian deconstruction a tyrannicide (a serious action justified by superior obligations and higher *reasons*) or is it a game? It is 'both one and the other', and 'neither one nor the other'. It is impossible to decide. In a given formal system, a proposition which is neither true nor false with regard to this system of axioms is *undecidable*. By analogy, Derrida speaks of undecidable words, terms whose double meaning cannot be mastered. It is the stress laid on these words, these excessive points in the metaphysical text, that draws forth the second text, the simulacrum of the first. The *identity* (in the sense that to distinguish, or to tell them apart is impossible) of good and evil, of

[37] See 'La double séance' in *La dissémination* (Seuil, 1972).
[38] *Ibid.*, p. 235.

presence and absence, of life and death emerges in the word
'Pharmakon' in Plato,[39] the word *'supplément'* in Rousseau,[40] and
the word *'hymen'* in Mallarmé[41] etc. What is more, Mallarmé's
hymen is indistinguishable in its turn from Hegelian *identity*, of
which it is the simulacrum. For *hymen* denotes at once marriage
and the vaginal membrane of the virgin woman. Thus there is
hymen (virginity) where there is no hymen (copulation), and
there is no longer hymen (virginity) when there is hymen (marriage). The hymen is both difference (between the interior and
exterior of the virgin, between desire and its consummation) and
the abolition of difference. It is the abolition of the 'difference
between difference and non-difference'.[42] Now the identity of
difference and non-difference is indistinguishable from the identity (posited by Hegel) of identity and non-identity. Nobody can
say whether dialectical identity and difference are the same thing
or not. No Master can decide any longer. In this game at which
'whoever loses is the winner',[43] the player who calls 'identity' will
immediately find it changed into difference; and if he calls
'difference', it will be metamorphosed into identity. So much so
that in the end Hegel's victory is also indistinguishable from his
defeat. The outcome of the game is undecidable. His victory is his
defeat, but his defeat is his victory. The game will be interminable.

The Search for a Transcendental Empiricism

Gilles Deleuze is above all a post-Kantian. His thought is subsequent to Kant's *Transcendental Dialectic*, in which the ideas of the
soul, of the world and of God are criticised. No experience can
justify us in affirming a single substantial self, a totality of things
and a first cause of this totality. It is sometimes held that the
philosophers generally described as post-Kantian (from Fichte to
Hegel) were prompt to restore Metaphysics, momentarily shaken
by the Kantian critique. Deleuze agrees with this view, and would
call the restoration 'the dialectic'. In the hands of the neo-
Hegelians (Feuerbach, Marx) post-Kantian dialectics culminated,
as we have seen, in the divinisation of man, and his reappropria-

---

[39] See 'La pharmacie de Platon' (republished in *La dissémination*).
[40] See the second part of G.   [41] See 'La double séance'.
[42] *La dissémination*, p. 237.   [43] *Marges*, p. 21.

tion for himself of the riches hitherto attributed to God. Deleuze objects:

> By recuperating religion, do we cease to be religious man? By turning theology into an anthropology, by putting man in the place of God, do we suppress the essential, that is, the place?[44]

Deleuze readily insists upon the critical vocation of philosophy:

> Philosophy is at its most positive as critique: an enterprise of demystification.[45]

But authentically critical philosophers are scarce. The major works of philosophy serve the cause of order, appointing places, arranging things by rank and displaying a predilection for distributing properties among supposita and attributes among subjects. In order to set up a hierarchy, they invoke an ahypothetical First Principle: that the rank of each is a function of the distance separating it from this principle. Thus every philosophy, in its own way, posits the precedence of the *One* over the *Many*. Rare are the philosophies that dispense attributes in an *anarchic* fashion (in the absence of any ahypothetical *arche*) – a distribution which Deleuze calls 'nomadic',[46] in which it is no longer a matter of sharing out the sum of being among things (of conferring upon each an identity for its exclusive dominion), but rather of describing the way in which things are dispersed across 'the expanse of a univocal and undivided being',[47] just as a nomadic tribe spreads itself over a territory without dividing it among individuals, each member taking what he *can*, and touching a limit only at the point where he can expand no further. No supreme principle, no formal basis, no central instance governs this 'distribution of essence and even of "delirium" '.[48]

Clearly, even if philosophy is essentially demystificatory, philosophers often fail to produce authentic critiques; they defend order, authority, institutions, 'decency', everything in which the ordinary person believes. Genuinely critical philosophy is

---

[44] NPh, p. 101.   [45] NPh, p. 121.   [46] DR, p. 54.
[47] *Ibid.* To be understood no doubt as the extension of the concept, univocal in the manner of all concepts, of being.
[48] *Ibid.*

rare, and corresponds, according to Deleuze, to the tradition known as 'naturalist' (in the sense of a hostility towards any 'supernatural'): Lucretius, Spinoza and Nietzsche are its most influential figures.

Sedentary distribution is the thinking of the 'classical' world (romantic revolt also belongs to this world). Deleuze calls such a thinking the 'philosophy of representation'. The authority which it obeys is the principle of identity, whose mark is found in the iterative prefix RE- of the word 'representation'.[49] Every present must be re-presented, in order that it may be re-discovered as the same; it follows that in this philosophy the unknown is only ever a not-yet-recognised known, that to learn is to remember, that to encounter is to meet again, that to leave is to return, etc. What eludes this rationalism, then, is difference as such. The difference between *discovery* and *rediscovery* is the gap which separates an experience from its reiteration – whence the problem of *repetition*. The more perfect the repetition (as in the case of twins, or mass-produced objects), the less a rationalist philosopher is able to tell where the difference lies. This is why phenomena of repetition furnish a privileged approach to the most authentic understanding of difference; they afford examples of incontestable, while apparently inconceivable, difference. Repetition should therefore cease to be defined as the return of the same through the reiteration of the identical; on the contrary, it is the *production* (in both senses of the word: to bring into existence, to show) of difference.

Deleuze denounces the confusion of the 'concept of difference' with a 'simply conceptual difference'.[50] Conceptual difference is a difference at the heart of identity; a specific difference within a generic identity, for instance. But the concept of difference should make it possible to think not only the difference within identity, but also the difference between identity and non-identity. We can understand why difference may then be defined as 'the being of the sensible'.[51] The concept, as Kant says, is the representation of what is identical in several representations, which may in their turn be concepts themselves (general representations) or particular representations (intuitions). The most authentic difference is not the one that may be found to exist between two concepts (i.e.

---

[49] DR, p. 79.   [50] DR, p. 41.   [51] DR, p. 80.

between two identities), but the one which obliges thought to introduce difference into its identities, particularity into its general representations and precision into its concepts. The real difference is that which exists between concept and intuition, between the intelligible and the sensible, between the logical and the aesthetic. In so far as it contains a theory of the sensible understood as diversity (the 'diverse *a priori*', the object of pure intuitions), Kant's *Transcendental Aesthetics* proposes a philosophy of difference such as Deleuze demands. Kant did not go far enough, however. He gave an account of *a priori* diversity, i.e. only that which is common to all intuitions (temporal form). He isolated a non-conceptual *identity*, but stopped short of a non-conceptual *difference*. The *a priori* theory of the sensible applies by definition to all possible experience: all experience, whatever it may be, unfolds in a *here* and a *now*. But the *Transcendental Aesthetics* does not provide an account of the *real* experience inasmuch as this differs from the merely *possible* experience.[52] It says nothing of the difference that exists between what we know of the phenomenon in advance, even before being confronted with the object, and what we are to learn of it *a posteriori*, what we could in no circumstances have foreseen, anticipated or judged *a priori*. It speaks of the knowledge that we must always possess in advance in order to undergo any experience, and which we *re-discover* in the course of this experience. It does not speak of the difference between the re-presentation given in advance, then rediscovered, and the presentation proper. The empirical element of any experience is quite clearly the *a posteriori*, or what is called 'the given',[53] and herein no doubt lies the profundity of the empiricist inquiry. The theory of experience is thus incomplete if it has only dealt with the *a priori* conditions of experience. Philosophy, for Deleuze, is either dialectical or empiricist, according to whether the difference between concept and intuition (in the Kantian sense of a relation to the particular entity) is taken to be a conceptual or a non-conceptual difference. The Deleuzian expression 'concept of difference' is admittedly problematic, for if there is a concept of difference between concept and intuition, then

---

[52] DR, pp. 80 and 94; LS, pp. 300–2; *Le bergsonisme* (P.U.F., 1966), p. 13.

[53] 'Difference is not diversity; diversity is given. But it is by means of difference that the given is given.' (DR, p. 286)

there must be a purely logical passage from the intelligible to the sensible, or from the universal to the particular.[54]

Critique of the Dialectic

It is Nietzsche rather than Kant who accomplishes the project for a critical philosophy; indeed, Kant ventures neither a critique of truth (science) nor of the good (morality). His critique is confined to false science (dogmatic metaphysics) and false morality (heteronomy). Nietzsche, who is both Kant's heir and his adversary, directs his own critique at *true science* and *true morality*. He demonstrates 'with a hammer' that science as such – the desire for truth – originates in morality, in the 'ascetic ideal', and that morality as such is the result of resentment against life.

Liberation of the will is the significance of the critical idea. All truths are to be summoned before the tribunal of philosophical reason, for this reason is legislative and sovereign.

> The first thing we learn from the Copernican revolution is that we are giving the orders.[55]

Such is the lesson of Kantianism in Deleuze's view. In his study of Nietzsche (1962), Deleuze gives the name 'philosophy of being' to the old, pre-Kantian metaphysics, and 'philosophy of will' to the metaphysics born of the accomplished critique. As a result, the radicalisation of the critique occurs in the term 'value', evident from the first page of the book:

> Nietzsche's most general project is to introduce the concepts of meaning and value into philosophy ... As envisaged and instated by him, the philosophy of values is the true realisation of the critique, and the only way in which a total critique may be realised.

The critique is an examination of values, by which we should understand the principles that are applied in 'value judgments'. It

---

[54] The surprising fact that Deleuze speaks of the *concept* of difference, when for him the real difference lies between concept and non-concept, is not unrelated to his insistence upon speaking of a *concept* of being (and consequently upon the notion that 'being' is univocal). For he asserts that 'Being is Difference' (DR, p. 57).

[55] *La philosophie critique de Kant* (P.U.F., 1963), p. 19.

is an inquiry into the grounds for such values, into whatever invests them with the value they have for us. At this point, the philosophy of values becomes a genealogy, or a search for antecedents, conducted with a view to establishing the nobility or baseness of a lineage and its offshoots. Such an investigation into both the base and the noble origins of values is indispensable, for it must be understood that there are not and could never be universal values, common to all. What might common values be? They would have to hold good, either in themselves (rather than by virtue of their origin) or through ourselves (i.e. instituted by a kind of social.contract), either as values *in themselves* or as values *for us all*.

But the concept of a value *in itself*, as Nietzsche says, is as contradictory as that of a meaning *in itself*. Just as the meaning of a text is relative to a certain reading, so the value of what holds good is relative to a certain evaluation, that is, to the orientation of the will towards a certain goal. Values, then, cannot be held *objectively* in common.

Nor can they be held *subjectively* in common. Taken in earnest, subjectivity implies the divergence of consciousnesses, and between them the impossibility of a *consensus*. The various philosophies of subjectivity that have succeeded one another since Kant have sought to salvage the unity of the world and the universality of values (the beautiful, the good, the true) by authorising themselves to pass from particular consciousness, as on the first page of the *Phenomenology of Mind* (*me*, *here* and *now*, in front of *this*), to universal consciousness, the Hegelian '*I* which is a *we*'; or again, from phenomenological *consciousness* to logical *concept*. If there were a universal subject, it would posit values that were similarly universal, though subjective, since they would be common to all particular subjects participating in this universality. We say that *everybody* accepts the value of truth, that *nobody* prefers evil to good, etc. Every variety of rationalism postulates a *common sense*, a *sensus communis*, a reason identical for all human beings. But this 'everybody' does not strictly accommodate all particular cases. It holds at best for the *majority* and will always leave a *minority* aside. It does not propose a real transcendental condition (or subjective condition of the relation to an object, of whatever kind), but only an average, conformist, gregarious picture. When 'everybody' agrees upon such and such an axiom, the claim is of course that all persons are being *represented*. The claim, however, is not legitimate. The *particular* is not 'everybody', and will never countenance being treated as 'anybody'. A difference emerges here between the particular considered as a particular case, an example of the universal (Rover is an example of the species 'Dog', Socrates of the species 'Man'), and the particular considered in its particularity (Socrates inasmuch as only he is Socrates). This difference is *difference as such*, it is the being of the sensible; it lies between the concept (Man) and the intuition (Socrates). Earlier, I spoke of its metaphysical significance.[56] It also has a political significance. Mankind is divided into two portions: on one side, the mass of those who consent to be no more than replicas of a model, instances of a law, and on the other, the minority of 'eccentric' cases – or as one also says, 'particular' cases (in the sense of *uncommon*) – invariably excluded in any proclamation of unanimity. The first are the *Slaves* and the second the *Masters*. A philosophical genealogy will thus lay stress upon the difference separating values of servile origin (morality, religion) from those of noble origin (art).

Here is further confirmation that, since Kojève, the *Master–Slave relationship* has been a constant in French thought. The fact may come as a surprise, for after all the slavery referred to so ubiquitously is the version of antiquity, and not the slavery abolished during the nineteenth century. In reality the 'Master–Slave' commonplace represents an inquiry into historical progress, into the putative superiority of the moderns (Christian) over the ancients (pagan); it is also an inquiry into the origins of that progress. Is the civilisation which we enjoy today the fruit of the Slaves' *labour*, with the Masters envisaged in the role of parasites? Or is it the creation of a minority of superior persons? In post-Kojèvian discourse we witness some curious exchanges. Sometimes the 'dialectic of mastery and slavery' takes on Marxist connotations: the Master is exploitative, he enjoys his privileges without working (and his only justification before the tribunal of universal history is that he forces his slave to work

---

[56] We will observe that Deleuzian difference exists less between the *representation* and the *thing* than between two faculties of representation itself: the understanding, faculty of concepts, and the sensibility, faculty of intuitions. This decidedly post-Kantian 'philosophy of difference' is essentially a 'doctrine of the faculties' (read, faculties *of the subject*).

under pain of death). Elsewhere it has a Nietzschean flavour: the modern bourgeois is considered a despicable being because he is no more than an emancipated slave, a freedman who has interiorised the Master.[57]

The next step consists in differentiating between that which originates from the Slave, and that which originates from the Master. To this end a criterion must be found, which is obviously no longer provided by political status. In his essay of 1962, *Nietzsche et la philosophie*, Deleuze undertakes the quest for a 'differential' criterion.

1. *Strength and weakness*. Can such a criterion be found in the facts? Are superior values those of the ruling class, and servile values those of the oppressed class? Assuredly not, for although the sovereignty that defines the Master derives from his *strength*, while servitude derives from a *weakness* of will, we are not to confuse the strong with the rulers of the day, or those who dominate in practice. This for two reasons: first, that facts only say what they are required to say ('no facts, only interpretations'), and secondly, that *in fact* it is the weak who dominate – 'The strong are always having to be defended against the weak.'[58] The gregarious company of the weak overrides the strong. Victory in itself proves nothing.

2. *Active and reactive strength*. The criterion must be sought elsewhere. Deleuze says that the weakest is not the least strong, for:

> The least strong is as strong as the strong if he goes to the limit, because the cunning, the subtlety, the wit and even the charm by means of which he compensates his lesser strength belong precisely to this strength; his, then, is *not* a lesser strength.[59]

The difference will lie between two qualities of strength; a strength may be active (noble) or reactive (base). Reactive strength does not go to the limit, it lacks daring, it remains 'separated from its potential'.

But how could strength not go 'to the limit of its potential'? If it

---

[57] Kojève said, for example, 'The Bourgeois is neither Slave nor Master; he is – being the Slave of Capital – his *own* Slave.' (*Intr. Hegel*. p. 194)
[58] Quoted in NPh, p. 65.
[59] NPh, p. 69.

fails to do so, this is because it is impeded by an obstacle. If it fails to overthrow this obstacle, this is because it is not strong enough to do so. Thus the strength of the weak is, after all, a lesser strength which stops when it can no longer advance: that is to say, sooner than the strength of the strong. But then we return to criterion no. 1, which had been dismissed: the weakest is quite simply the least strong (as in any brutal apologia for force, or the crude politics of the 'fait accompli').

3. *Affirmation and negation.* Once more the criterion must be sought elsewhere. The weak are not characterised by the *weakness* of their desire for *strength*, like abortions of the will or ontological worms exercising their lamentable *conatus*. They are characterised by the *strength* of their desire for *weakness*. The weak may thus be the strongest from the point of view of efficacy, but would none the less continue to be weak by virtue of the negative orientation of their will, turned entirely towards self-annihilation:

> Whatever the ambivalence of meaning and values, we
> may not conclude that a reactive strength can become
> active by going to the limit of its potential. For 'to go to
> the limit', 'the final consequences', has one of two
> meanings, according to whether we affirm or negate,
> whether we affirm our own difference or negate that
> which differs. [60]

The affirmative or negative quality of the will is now the criterion. Truth, for example, is worth what the will to truth is worth. Truth is superior to illusion only if the will to truth is more affirmative than the will to illusion. Genealogy thus leads to what Deleuze calls the 'dramatisation method'. [61] Whereas the philosophy of being had asked, for example, 'What is the good?', the philosophy of will now asks, 'Who wills the good?' In other words, does the will to good (goodwill) will the growth or the diminution of will?

At this point Deleuze refers us to the *Genealogy of Morals*. The respective positions of Master and Slave are presented by Nietzsche as follows: the Master says, 'I am good, therefore you are bad'. The Slave says, 'You are bad, therefore I am good'. The Master's judgment proceeds from his pleasure. The Master is one

---

[60] NPh, p. 77.   [61] NPh, p. 88.

who delights in being who he is, affirming his happiness and goodness without any need to compare himself to others, or attend to their opinion. It is precisely such absence of deliberation that constitutes sovereignty. The Hegelian Master is, in this respect, a Slave; or rather, he corresponds to the Slave's image of the Master, since he experiences the need to be *recognised* by others.[62] As for the Slave, his judgment is the reverse of the Master's. In the first place, his starting-point is not himself, but others; he lacks the strength to affirm himself alone, and so begins by negating the other. Too weak to create values of his own, he overthrows those posited in sovereign fashion by the Master. The Master's values are wicked, *therefore* the opposite values (work, democracy, philanthropy) are good. Secondly, the Slave creates morality. He transforms the Master's *good* and *evil*, which had expressed states or degrees of power, one sublime and the other miserable, into *kindness* and *malice*. The point is illustrated by Nietzsche's fable. The bird of prey that devours the lamb does so because it is in its nature as bird of prey to devour lambs, and not in order to negate the not-I, which in this case is the lamb. Slaves therefore are like sheep that ascribe the predatory behaviour of their enemies to a malicious will, an intent to do them harm; they demand that the eagle behave as a lamb. Such is the revolt of the Slaves in morality, as a result of which they succeed in persuading the Masters of their guilt. Whoever is *able* to devour the other (or give him a shearing) and yet refrains, is good. Strength is thus 'separated from its potential', turned against itself and drawn into a 'becoming-reactive'.

4. *Affirmation of the affirmation and negation of the negation.* But then we find that the difference between the *yes* and the *no* of the will is insufficient to provide the criterion we are looking for, since there is affirmation and negation in the Master just as there is in the Slave. What changes is the order of their presentation. Resentment and reactivity draw affirmation from negation, and if morality is always the morality of resentment, this is because it is the affirmation of an ideal, of a good, of a beyond, where the just are rewarded and the wicked chastised. Such an affirmation originates in negation, or a rejection of life inasmuch as it is cruel and unjust. The *dialectic* must then be described as the 'ideology of

[62] NPh, p. 11.

resentment',[63] since it posits that the negation of a negation amounts to an affirmation.

The philosophy in which sovereign will is expressed would be a philosophy of the *yes*. But, as Deleuze insists, it is out of the question to say yes to everything that is. On the contrary, 'the yes which is incapable of saying no' is the nihilist's affirmation, 'because he says yes to all that which is no'.[64] We are now at a loss. Is there or is there not a *negative*? Or is the negative only an illusion, the Slave's interpretation of the Master's affirmative difference, of the Master's affirmation of his difference? If the negative is not anything, it cannot be addressed with a *yes* any more than with a *no*. Affirmation, then, would entail no negation, contrary to Deleuze's insistence. If on the other hand, affirmation can only be genuinely affirmative provided that it affirm exclusively whatever is *yes*, then the negative is not *nothing* – but how can superiority lie with whoever refuses *that which is*?

Here the genealogist must refine his criteria further; the difference to be established is becoming increasingly subtle. *Active* affirmation would not be purely affirmative if, in affirming only affirmation, it did not produce a 'shadow of negation'.[65] *Reactive* negations, for their part, manifest themselves by means of affirmations, but these are no more than 'spectre(s) of affirmation'.[66] Active strength must negate the negative in order to affirm the affirmative. Reactive strength is an incessant negation, even when it has the air of affirming or creating independent values. How are we to distinguish the *affirmative* negation proper to the first from the *negative* negation proper to the second? And the affirmation which affirms from the affirmation which negates?

5. *Eternal recurrence*. Deleuze responds to this difficulty with an interpretation of Nietzsche's eternal recurrence, a doctrine which he describes as 'almost initiatory'.[67] Ordinarily we give a cyclical sense to the hypothesis of eternal recurrence: similar states will reappear in the world indefinitely, the same events will be reproduced. We are incorrect however, for, as Deleuze explains, eternal recurrence eliminates the weak, leaving only the strong to return. Whatever is thrown into despair by the prospect of having to

---

[63] NPh, pp. 139 and 217.   [64] NPh, p. 213.   [65] DR, p. 76.
[66] NPh, p. 206.   [67] NPh, p. 78.

recur indefinitely is suppressed by 'eternal recurrence', never to appear again. Only the strong return, those who 'affirm their difference'. They come back, but differently, while all those who 'negate that which differs' are annihilated. There is thus a kind of *auto-destruction of the negative*,[68] an expression which inconveniently evokes the 'negation of the negation' condemned earlier, but which is supposed to intend the opposite, namely that the *no* opposed to the *no* proceeds from the *yes*; it does not (as in the dialectic) produce the *yes*.

Now we hold the criterion. It is the relation of priority between the yes and the no.

> If we consider affirmation and negation as qualities of will
> to power, we will see that they have no univocal
> relationship. Negation *opposes* affirmation, whereas
> affirmation *differs* from negation. We cannot think of
> affirmation, for its part, as 'opposing' negation, for this
> would be to introduce the negative into it.[69]

The difference we are looking for is that which exists between *difference* and *opposition*. The Slave interprets all differences as oppositions. The Master perceives no opposition where there is difference. In his difference he derives a satisfaction which he does not feel to be threatened by the opinion or the existence of other men who are not like him. But the Slave is fundamentally dependent; he is in competition with others from the outset.

The criterion is very clear: on the one hand, the nobility of an independent soul, and on the other, the baseness of a jealous and invidious mind. Is this criterion applicable however? Manifestly not.

From the point of view of affirmation, negation is not its opposite. No is not opposed to yes; rather it indicates a difference. In other words, difference is only apparently negative: 'A is not B' does not mean that 'A is non-B', that A's being is B's non-being, that A prospers by the demise of B. Such a differential judgment merely signifies that A is *something other* than B, or alternatively that 'non-B' (A) is not negative, but rather indefinite or indeterminate, as Kant would say. Negation is indetermination, not determination. Spinoza's *omnis determinatio negatio* must therefore be

---

[68] NPh, p. 79.   [69] NPh, p. 216.

rejected.[70] To distinguish two terms is not to introduce opposition between them.

If, from the point of view of affirmation, the relation between affirmation and negation is (non-negative) difference, and not opposition, it follows that the Master will never perceive negation as negative. When he negates the Slave, his negation does not *oppose* the other's affirmation; it issues from his own affirmation, which is different from that of the other. This affirmative negation is nothing less than the affirmation of the difference between two affirmations (that of the Master and that of the Slave). By the same token, however, the Master cannot perceive in the Slave's negation any *opposition* to his own affirmation. If he suspected that the Slave opposed him, the Master would lose the very basis of his superiority, and would enter into rivalry with his inferior. The Master is no longer master once he is aware of the Slave as slave. Under no circumstances must the Master know that the Slave is pure negation; he must imagine that servile negations are other affirmations.

Conversely, the baseness of the Slave prevents him from perceiving the Master's nobility. The Slave cannot know that the Master's negations are affirmations. From the point of view of negation, affirmation is an *opposition*. Realising that the wolf is going to devour it, the lamb cannot be aware that this negation of its own person has an *affirmative* nature. The lamb perceives only the negative consequences for itself. In the same way, the Slave is blind to what makes active negation *another* affirmation; in it he sees only destruction, which he must resist with all his strength in order to be. Thus he imagines that his own negation (of the Master), far from being the principle of his (servile) affirmations, is the consequence of (the Master's) negation of him. Flaunting his active negation, then, while claiming to derive it from his own self-affirmation and to oppose it only to what is negative in the other, this so-called Master is indistinguishable from the Slave; the reasoning in both cases is exactly the same.

The criterion proposed by Deleuze demands that the relation of Master to Slave should not be superimposable upon that of Slave to Master. In one, it is a relation of difference, in the other a relation of opposition. But if this is so, then the criterion is quite

---

[70] DR, p. 74.

useless, for there can be *no relationship* between Master and Slave. The Master will live only among Masters, and the Slave will only ever encounter Slaves. The worlds of Master and Slave being separate, the Master will never be obliged to question his difference from the Slave, nor the Slave his opposition to the Master. The Master must not even be capable of recognising a Slave, like Aristotle's God who is ignorant of matter, which itself is only definable by its desire to be what it is not – form. But the Slave is present in the world and in the thought of the Deleuzian Master, all too present in fact. The Master spends the bulk of his time 'affirming his difference', distinguishing himself from the Slave. In the same way, affirmative philosophy is defined by negative undertakings, such as the attack against high priests or the demystification of the people.

Again, we may say that, from the standpoint of affirmation, the non-identity of difference and opposition is not an opposition, but a difference, whilst from the standpoint of negation, the same non-identity is an opposition. The non-identity of these two interpretations can itself be interpreted both as difference and as opposition. But if this is so, affirmation will perceive *no opposition*, *only a difference* between its own perspective and that of negation; there will in the last instance be *no difference* for it between difference and opposition, the latter being only a difference. Nor will negation perceive *any difference* between the point of view of affirmation and its own, as regards the relation existing between both those points of view. The non-identity of difference and opposition will appear to both as an *identity*.

Generally speaking, the origin of the difficulty seems to be as follows: how is it possible to talk of an *incomparable* being (a singular or sovereign being) in a philosophy of *values*, i.e. of comparison? To evaluate means to compare: *this is worth more than that*. In a philosophy of values, the only question will be that of the competitiveness of evaluations, the clash of interpretations, the rivalry of world views. Nihilism, contested by Deleuze, concludes from the spectacle of the inter-destruction of all values that 'everything is worth everything else', 'it is all one', 'it all comes down to the same'. Everything is indeed worth everything else; there are only opinions, attitudes, interpretations and perspectives. No one can cite a truth as the source of his authority, since truth itself is a value competing with other values. But this nihilist

conclusion is dangerous for the will, and corresponds to a depressive condition in that faculty. If everything is worth everything
else, why this rather than that? When everything is un-
differentiated, the will can no longer fix itself upon any undertaking as it could when it thought that the truth was really the
truth. But how can *difference* be reintroduced into a world
menaced by indifference, without simultaneously going back on
the lesson of the Copernican revolution that 'we are giving the
orders'? Deleuze proposes a criterion drawn from competitiveness itself: certain evaluations are noble, others base. The noble
evaluation derives from itself, out of the richness of its being,
whilst the base evaluation derives from its own indigence relative
to the superiority it recognises and covets in another. But this
difference is meaningful only if it is possible to conceive of an
evaluation of a noble kind which would not be comparative. 'I am
good, *therefore* you are bad'; the Master does not derive this
affirmation of his superiority from a comparison with the Slave,
for he is never in competition with him. But if a relationship to the
other is not present in this sovereign affirmation of self, then
Deleuze ought not to say that 'the Master affirms his difference',
but rather 'he affirms his *identity*'. Deleuze's Master, however,
must on no account affirm his identity, or difference (between
himself and the other) would succeed identity (between himself
and himself); would, in other words, be subordinated to it. We
would then find ourselves with a hierarchy rather than an anar-
chy, with a sedentary distribution of the Platonic kind rather than
a nomadic distribution of the Deleuzian kind.

It is precisely because Deleuze's Master does not define himself
in terms of identity, but in terms of a relation of difference, that he
is drawn by the Slaves into a 'becoming-reactive'. The philosophy
of history which emerges from this version of the 'Master and
Slave' becomes confused, finally, with the Hegelian account,
except in so far as everything which Hegel thought of as progress
is now read as a symptom of decline:

> The active man is that young, strong, handsome man
> whose face however betrays the discreet signs of an illness
> to which he has not yet succumbed, a contagion which
> will only affect him tomorrow. The strong must be
> defended against the weak, but we know the desperate

character of this enterprise. The strong can oppose the weak, but not the becoming-weak which is inside them.[71]

The day that the Master with all his self-assurance meets, not another Master (i.e. another affirmation destined to negate him) but a Slave, he will learn the difference between a Master and a Slave, between a difference and an opposition. Thenceforth he will see that what he negates in the Slave is not another affirmation, but the actual negation of his own affirmation. He refuses the Slave's negation of him, but the discovery weakens him immediately. The time is coming when the Master, having discovered his own likeness in the Slave, will emancipate him. Indeed, how can it be distinguished, after a number of encounters between affirmation and negation, whether the *no* that one of the adversaries has just uttered precedes the *yes*, or follows it?

[71] NPh, p. 192.

6

The end of time

The recent orientation of the debate in France is a delayed effect of the experience of May 68, a month in which the French educated classes had the surprise of their lives. The revolution which had been spoken of for so long was triggered off without warning. Yet perhaps this revolution was not a revolution after all ... For more than twenty years, intellectuals had made great efforts to instruct themselves in historical materialism, hoping to break away from the 'petty bourgeois ideology' of their origins. Now they discovered in this theory of history, in this political mode of thought, the obstacle that separated them from history at the very moment when history was knocking on the door.

Authority

During May and June of that year, a thorough acquaintance with power was made, in the sense that everybody saw in the course of the famous 'events' the two contradictory features of authority: an extreme fragility combined with an unlimited capacity for resisting subversion. *The fragility of authority*: student unrest was enough to provoke general turmoil and to paralyse an entire nation. It became apparent that the authorities could successfully oppose a *coup d'état* such as the *putsch* of Algiers in 1961, but not a carnival.[1] Authority ensures that it is obeyed only if everyone is

---

[1] We will shortly see that to speak of 'unrest' or 'carnival' is not to judge these events insignificant, or lacking in real political impact. Political anthropology has shown that the function of saturnalia and carnival is to mime disorder, the better to enjoy the advantages of order (cf. Georges Balandier, *Anthropologie politique*, P.U.F., 1967; trans. as *Political Anthropology*, London, 1970).

convinced that it is *the authority*. Although power can be endlessly defined as the deployment of a panoply of means for control and coercion, it remains true that the authority of this power, its capacity to employ such means, resides in its legitimacy, that is, in public opinion. But there is also *the invincibility of power*: it seems that the prolonged absence of a recognised authority is intolerable to the social body. When powers appear to vacillate, the reconstitution of authority soon follows, with the legitimisation of one or another claimant (a legitimisation that disciples of Weber would call 'charismatic'). In May 68 the French acted out an abridged version of the principal modern revolutions, with props borrowed from the Parisian insurrections of the nineteenth century (barricades, 1848-style feats of oratory). In Act One, the old regime is denounced and invited to withdraw; in Act Two, 'everything is possible'; in Act Three, enthusiasm wanes and a new order appears, more rigorous than the last (and so it is said that 'the revolution is betrayed'). For philosophy, the merry month of May 68 raised the following two questions. Why is authority sometimes accepted, and sometimes rejected? Why do revolutions always end with the restoration of order? Marxism, which had been the basis of the intelligentsia's political thinking, had nothing to reply to these questions, since it refused to acknowledge the event that had given rise to them. To Althusser, for instance, May 68 meant 'the most powerful workers' strike in world history (ten million strikers in one month) ... A strike which was "preceded" and "accompanied" by a profound ideological revolt in the student and petty bourgeois intellectual milieux of France'.[2] 'Preceded', 'accompanied' – the inverted commas on either side of these two adjectives betray the sleight of hand whereby Althusser causes the unknown element of 'profound ideological revolt' which he resolutely ignores, to vanish behind the domesticity of a 'workers' strike'. Althusser attempts to persuade his readers that what conflict there was took place between government, representing the ruling class, and working-class organisations, representing 'the rank and file'. Unluckily though, his readers in 1973 could recall that this was not the case; five years earlier they were able to observe that the critical zone of turbulence was elsewhere, in educational

[2] *Réponse à John Lewis*, pp. 9–10.

establishments. The classic conflict, the only one which Althusser was prepared to admit, was simply the rebound, doubtless 'over-determined', of the conflict between the authorities and the community. The first victim of the upheaval was the man professing to knowledge, the *teacher*, for whom his field of competence is a justification of authority, and whose language is a *monologue* inasmuch as it leaves only one possibility open to the listener, that of *dialogue* – that is, of indicating that he has understood, and even of asking the occasional question, provided it is *relevant*. In such a world of dialogue, there is nothing that cannot be questioned, on condition that the correct forms are observed, that expressions are 'well phrased', in the language of learning. In this way, form eludes all criticism, as does the relation of authority which it sustains. The great wealth of the ferment of May 68 is not to be found in the 'ideas' propounded at the time (simply relics borrowed from the insurrectional legend which is the French Republic's referential myth); the interest of May 68 lies rather in the *impertinence* of its dissent, in the *unseemly* character of its criticisms. It was form, above all, that was seriously shaken.

On what grounds may knowledge usefully be challenged? Only these: that it does not know enough, that it is ignorant in this or that respect. Knowledge may only be countered, then, with knowledge. Once again we find the dialectical paradox stated in a variety of ways by Bataille, Blanchot, Foucault, Derrida, Deleuze and Lyotard. It is senseless to oppose reason, which, as a form of thinking subject to the principle of identity, holds sway over the logic of opposition. This is why reason will only ever be opposed by reasons, truth by truths, meaning by meanings, a Socrates by a Socrates and a Hegel by a Hegel. This paradox also obtains in the political domain. Only another power can oppose a power: here is the key to the alleged 'betrayal' of revolutions. How could the powerless possibly confront the powerful? The *dialectic* no doubt taught that proletarian powerlessness – negativity – was the greatest of all powers. It subsequently transpired that negativity could only assume power by availing itself of vast organisations, which were (as Sartre deplored) undeniably positive, constructed now on the model of the administration (social democracy), now on that of the army (P.C.F.). The negative was merely the negative of the positive, the same thing inverted, the likeness set against the likeness. The critique of the *logos* could be transposed into a critique of power. In 1973, Lyotard wrote:

> Reason and power are one and the same. You can dress up the first with prognosis or the dialectic, but you will still have the other dished up intact: prisons, prohibitions, selection processes, the public good.[3]

Foucault's work after 1968 illustrates the new orientation. The author of *Les mots et les choses* found new material here for his epistemological preoccupations. As his object, he took the recent history of institutions in which the frontier separating normality and pathology is defined: slow pupils are failed in school examinations, the sick are put in hospital, criminals in prison, etc. Foucault tries to show how these institutions, sites established by power, where numerous kinds of power are exercised, are the 'conditions of possibility' for their corresponding disciplines: teaching, medicine, psychiatry, criminology, etc.[4]

The crucial point, however, lies surely in the other question: how is it that power is respected? Why is it sometimes not respected? Hitherto satisfactory, the explanation in terms of self-interest, that the masses revolt when they are starving, now seems rather inadequate. The entire history of the twentieth century supplies the counter-example that weakens 'dialectical' theory, according to which the 'contradiction of productive forces and relations of production' produces an 'objectively' revolutionary situation. This in its turn becomes 'subjectively' revolutionary once the proletarianised masses realise that they have nothing to lose by a change in the mode of production. Such a begetting of subjective revolutionary passion by objective conditions was unconvincing, and already Althusser had had to invoke the principle of 'overdetermination'. So, in the seventies, an attempt was made to rehabilitate the referential political theory (Marxism) with an injection of *desire* and *jouissance*. Marx had to be completed with Freud, a new programme replacing that of the intelligentsia in 1945 – the completing of Marx with Kierkegaard. Again, the 'objective' doctrine required enriching with a 'subjective' complement. Productive forces, it was agreed, are the reality,

---

[3] *Dérive*, p. 13.
[4] See especially *Surveiller et punir* (Gallimard, 1975); *Discipline and Punish*, trans. A. Sheridan (London, Allen Lane, 1977).

but they cannot in themselves give rise to revolutionary fervour. In 1971 Roland Barthes made the following statement (in which 'we' should be understood as 'we intellectuals'):

> How can the two great *epistemes* of modernity, the materialist dialectic and the Freudian dialectic, be brought together so as to fuse and produce a new order of human relations . . .? This is the problem we have posed ourselves.[5]

The most accurate index of this general demand by the public is the sales success of Herbert Marcuse's books from June 1968 until the following year. However, Marcuse's brew of Freudo-Marxism was too thin for the appetite of the French reader, on two counts. Philosophically, the return to Hegelian Marxism appeared regressive; but above all, Marcuse's revised Freudianism was unacceptable to anyone who had learned from Lacan that desire is in no way a natural drive which society – and not reality itself – impedes. The likening of repression to social repression, the very principle of 'Freudo-Marxism', appeared as a reissue of eighteenth-century inanities: nature is good, the savage noble, society evil. According to Lacan, repression precedes and accounts for all forms of social oppression. Desire, he says, has its beginnings in the impossible, and is condemned to find its satisfaction only in dreams. Such is the lesson of psychoanalysis, from which an ethics might have been developed, he adds, 'if our age were not so prodigiously tormented with idyllic imperatives'.[6] It is understandable, therefore, that Lacan could have declared to the students heckling him at the (then 'red') faculty of Vincennes in December 1969: 'I am an anti-progressivist' and 'What you as a revolutionary aspire to is a Master. You will have one.'[7] Lacan showed that in this respect he was closer to Plato, who evokes the tyranny of democratic excess, than to revolutionary romanticism.[8]

[5] *Tel Quel*, no. 47, Autumn 1971, p. 16.
[6] Lacan, 'Du "Trieb" de Freud et du psychanalyste', *Ecrits* (Seuil, 1966).
[7] From the transcript published in *Le Magazine Littéraire*, no. 121, Feb. 1977, pp. 24–5.
[8] It is here that we find an explanation of the sterility to which the proponents of a more French formula of Freudo-Marxism have been condemned, although the odds appeared to be in their favour, i.e. 'Lacano-Althusserianism', as it was set forth in *Cahiers pour l'analyse* (1966–8) and *Tel Quel* during its crypto-communist phase (1966–70) and again during its Maoist phase (1971–7).

The alliance of Marx and Freud, that is, of politics and desire, had one prerequisite condition, then: a critique of Lacanianism. It is because it fulfilled this condition that the *Anti-Oedipus* (AŒ), written by Deleuze, in collaboration with Felix Guattari, a psychoanalyst from the Lacanian school, received such immense public acclaim.[9] The book proposes a political analysis of desire. Desire may take one of two courses: it may affirm itself, or it may fix upon power and established order as its object. By virtue of an analysis in terms of desire, it should be possible to reply to what Deleuze called 'the fundamental problem of political philosophy', posed according to him by Spinoza: why do men struggle *for their servitude* as if it were their salvation? Why does the Slave consent to his slavery, the exploited to his exploitation? The answer lies in the servile desire of the Slave, and the desire of the exploited to be oppressed. The masses supported Napoleon, Mussolini, Hitler, Stalin, Mao, not because they were prey to an illusion or because they believed that their interests were best defended by such dictators:

> No, the masses were not deceived; they desired fascism at such and such a point, in such and such a set of circumstances and it is this perversion of gregarious desire that requires explaining.[10]

The Fin-de-Siècle Disorder

If in 1972 Deleuze succeeded with the Freudo-Marxist synthesis where everyone else had tried in vain, it was because he adopted an irreverent style which meant, in the end, that his synthesis was neither Marxist nor Freudian. Deleuze realised that in order for anything to emerge, Marxism and Freudianism would require a little jostling. The vocabulary of the *Anti-Oedipus* is sometimes Marxist, sometimes Freudian, but the critical strand is Nietzschean, from start to finish.

For a Marxist, the words of which human discourses are made up may never have the final say. These discourses must be located within the relations of production in such a way that their 'class

---

[9] See the review *Critique*, no. 306, Nov. 1972, for the articles by René Girard and Jean-François Lyotard.
[10] AŒ, p. 37.

position' becomes discernible. The decisive opposition is thus between *production* and *ideology*. For a Freudian, consciousness is an unreliable witness, and may not usefully be questioned as to the sense of an individual's words or gestures, for the play of conscious representations is controlled from without, by unconscious desire. *Consciousness* and *desire*, then, are opposed. If we now proceed to translate these two 'critiques of consciousness' into the language of Schopenhauer and Nietzsche, we will obtain a 'general economy' in which the *political* economy of Marx and the *libidinal* economy of Freud are reconciled.

Will	Representation
Production Desire	Ideology Consciousness

The necessary solution was to shuttle desire *into the infrastructure*, or to see it as *productive*.

'Desire is part of the infrastructure.'[11] For the Marxist (who classifies desires under the heading of ideological representation), this solution is absurd, and it is an aberration for the Freudian (to whom desire is 'productive' only of dreams and phantasms). But it is no longer exactly a question of Marxist infrastructure or Freudian libido. This productive desire is none other than the Nietzschean *will-to-power*. Thanks to word-play, the 'active strength' described in the book on Nietzsche of 1962 may now be called 'revolutionary desire'. How could a Marxist reject this, when for him it is the 'productive forces' which in the last instance revolutionise the mode of production? If desire, being active, is productive, it must certainly be revolutionary. We will recall that active strength is countered by 'reactive strength'. The high priesthood, with its mystificatory fictions, has succeeded in turning active strength against itself, and thereby in producing bad conscience, that is, the sentiment of guilt which attaches to any active manifestation of the will. Reactive strength is now understood to be the desire for repression.

> To repress desire, not only for others but for oneself, to act the cop to others and to oneself, that's what brings the hard-on – which is not ideology, but economics.[12]

[11] AŒ, p. 124.   [12] AŒ, p. 415.

How could a Freudian (who believes, for instance, that whoever abstains from all sexual relations is merely the more faithful
to his first, incestuous love) refuse the idea that the man who
renounces something thereby derives gratification? Once more, it
is by means of mystification that desire is turned against itself; at
the head of the priesthood there now stands the psychoanalyst,
working to convince desire of its Oedipal guilt.

Such are the premises of the *Anti-Oedipus*. Its object is to analyse
the disorder of the period. In *Nietzsche et la philosophie*, universal
history was presented as the passage from prehistory to post-
history. Between the two extremes, a process of cultural training
was to have transformed the crude primitive as he originally was
into a 'sovereign and legislating individual',[13] a subject capable of
pronouncing the Kantian 'we are giving the orders'. Unfortunately, history had missed its mark. Instead of producing a
superior form of man, ever more active and autonomous, it had
thrown up the man of resentment. Contemporary man was sick,
and the sickness was known as 'nihilism'. *The last man*, 'having
annihilated every trace of what is not himself',[14] and having taken
the place of God,[15] found himself alone and miserable. This man,
in turn, had to be annihilated. The moment had come to pass from
the *nothingness of will* (nihilist sickness) to an active *will to nothingness*; from unfinished, passive and therefore morbid nihilism to
active nihilism. The *Anti-Oedipus*, in its new language, expounds
the same philosophy of history. The disorder affecting our period
is that of the fin de siècle: *schizophrenia*. Here again, the remedy is
to overcome the passive schizophrenia treated in hospitals with an
active schizophrenia:

> As a process, schizophrenia is desiring-production, but in
> its final form; as the limit of social production determined
> under the conditions of capitalism. It is our own 'sickness'
> as modern men. The end of history has no other
> meaning.[16]

In the anti-Hegelian works of Deleuze, and the Kojèvian works
of Bataille and Blanchot, exactly the same diagnosis is to be found.
The present 'discontent within civilisation', as Freudians say, is a

---

[13] NPh, p. 157. [14] NPh, p. 188. [15] NPh, p. 200.
[16] AŒ, p. 155.

symptom whose meaning is disclosed in the perspective of a discourse upon universal history, and not, as for Freud and his disciples, in one of familial psychology.

According to the *Anti-Oedipus*, universal history is a process of 'deterritorialisation'. 'Deterritorialisation' defines the essential movement of capitalism. Capitalism emerges at the end of history, and is the 'universal truth' of history.[17] But what exactly is 'deterritorialisation'? It is the transition from a *coding* to a *decoding*. Here the term 'coding' does not refer to a linguistic operation (construction of a message) but to the way that society regulates production (which, as we will recall, intends both the Marxist 'social production' and the 'desiring-production', or 'productive desire' introduced by Deleuze). The primitive tribe and the capitalist society mark the two extreme points of history. In the first, everything is coded: each gesture, each circumstance of life, each part of the body is governed by rules. Every instant of life is therefore social. Capitalist society, on the other hand, invents the private individual, owner of his/her body and organs, freely disposing of his/her labour power. Capitalism originates therefore in a generalised decoding (which corresponds, as we can see, to what Marxists call primitive accumulation: on the one hand, the decoding of the flow of producers, i.e. the proletarianisation of the peasantry torn from its *land*, its *soil*, its *place of origin*; on the other, the amassing of financial or commercial fortunes, no longer *of the land*, by a decoding of the flow of wealth). In this all-inclusive movement of decoding, ancient ritual, ceremony, every form which was once respected or held *sacred* must disappear. Capitalism is defined as a 'cynical'[18] system which, in order to function, needs no appeal to the sacred, to belief.

We are confronted here with the same aberration as before. The product of cultural training was to have been the sovereign individual, but is in fact the man of negativity. In the same way, capitalism, as defined by the cynicism of decoding, was to have brought liberation, since it destroyed all the beliefs and prohibitions which had enthralled humanity; but the reality of capitalism, according to Deleuze, is the greatest repression of desiring-production ever witnessed in history. By destroying all *ties*, capitalism should have created the conditions for the blissful

---

[17] ACE, p. 180.   [18] ACE, p. 267.

nomadism of a detached and *absolute* individual, as a consequence of 'deterritorialisation'. However, in this liberation of all flux, it has produced a world of nightmare and anxiety. Why should history have failed? The reason is that 'deterritorialisation' is accompanied by a perpetual 'reterritorialisation'. Capitalism postpones the limit towards which it tends (nomadism) by restoring artificial 'territorialities' (beliefs, forms).

> Everything returns or reappears – states, fatherlands, families.[19]

One of these territories, and the target of the *Anti-Oedipus* (doubtless pending a sequel in which others will come under attack), is the family. Thus the psychoanalyst is the modern priest. His function is

> to ensure that beliefs survive, even after they have been repudiated! And to instil a belief in something into those who no longer believe in anything![20]

If, following Deleuze, we propose an exclusively positive desire, then the *neurotic* has the air of a conformist, suffering from the self-imposed renunciation he undergoes in order to adapt to the demands of social existence. He corresponds to the *Slave*, to 'reactive strength' that will not go 'to the limit of its potential'. The neurotic is the normal man, with the proviso that the normal man is *normalised* by society. Normalisation consists in imposing a familial grid upon the child's desire. The child must have an *ego*, an *identity*; this identity is constructed during the ordeal of the child's rivalry with the parent of the same sex, for the parent of the opposite sex. The normal man's identity is thus founded upon the *fictitious* original guilt arising from this incestuous and patricidal (or matricidal) ego.

What about the *psychotic*? Here again, Deleuze takes issue with the Lacanian definition of desire in terms of lack ('lack in being', says Lacan). In Lacanian doctrine, the psychotic *is* the object which his mother lacks (the phallus), and so he himself may not manifest a *lack* of anything (may not desire in his turn). In this relation of the psychotic to his mother, the 'foreclosure' – a word which translates Freud's *Verwerfung* (rejection) – *of that which signifies lack* (namely, the father's phallus, the fact that the phallus desired by the mother should be the father's whilst her perversity is to seek it in the child) induces the return of this *signifier of lack*[21] into the real, by a terrifying experience (hallucination) in which the psychotic sees himself as *really* castrated, for want of having been castrated *symbolically* (of having been referred, by the word of the mother, to the fact of the father). In so far as it can be set out so briefly, this is the Lacanian view of psychosis. It is tantamount to saying that people go mad *for want of lacking*, and that 'the signifier' (language) introduces this 'lack' among human beings, this 'game' which is necessary to any stable relationship, to any exchange with others. Deleuze rejects the idea wholesale:

> Lack, Law and the Signifier are the names of the three
> errors concerning desire ... Transgression, guilt,
> castration – are these determinations of the unconscious,
> or *are they the way in which a priest sees things?*[22]

On the same page, he says that the unconscious is Rousseauist, for desire is 'natural man'. In the end, the fundamental conflict is between the 'natural man' or 'desirer' and society. Desire is repressed, even under capitalism which proclaims that 'everything is permitted' (understood: *to whoever can pay*), because it is incompatible with social existence. Thus it only becomes socially acceptable once it is disfigured, distorted and transformed, for example, into Oedipal desire:

> ... And no society can tolerate a position of desire
> without jeopardising its structures of exploitation,
> subjection and hierarchisation.[23]

The limits of Deleuze's Marxism are obvious. He politely consigns class struggle to the museum. There is only one class, that of the Slaves, in which some dominate the others; only one or two classless 'desirers' may escape from this servile condition.[24]

Deleuze's conception culminates in utter idealism. The man who at the end of history *should have been* active is in fact reactive. The opposition of fact and right is scarcely empirical, yet we encounter it in the *Anti-Oedipus* with the distinction between

---

[21] The phallus of the father is the 'signifier of lack': it is what the mother *hasn't*, and the son *isn't* (nor the daughter).

[22] AŒ, pp. 132–3.   [23] AŒ, p. 138.   [24] AŒ, p. 303.

schizophrenia as a *process* and as an *entity*. As Deleuze recognises, schizophrenics are in fact unhappy people who oscillate between paranoiac activity and painful prostration (catatonia, autism). This, as he says, proves nothing

> but the failure, induced by social oppression, of a venture in which the great artist, for example, succeeds. The latter crosses the barrier that separates the normal man from desiring-production. [25]

The mad person, whose strength is prevented from going 'to the limit', has failed. Might not the artist's be the authentic experience of active strength, of what Deleuze now calls 'true desire'? Not at all, for *in fact* the artist too is broken against the barrier. And the difference between active and reactive is not finally manifest in these two types of human being, but within one and the same individual, between the two poles of his desire. At times desire tends towards the revolutionary pole (described by Deleuze as 'schizoid') where it is the desire to 'flee the social', [26] i.e. the gregarious identifications offered by the group (fatherland, money, football). At others, desire switches to the repressive, 'paranoiac' pole, investing in power, institutions and honours (a place at the Académie Française etc.). The desire of each individual oscillates between these two poles. There can be no facile opposition, then, of the paranoiac herd to the minority of revolutionary artists, for in every group (even a revolutionary one) and every individual (even an artist), 'true desires' are to be found alongside 'desires for repression'. Schizophrenic delirium and paranoiac delirium are inseparable, for

> in all delirium both poles may be seen to co-exist, and fragments of schizoid revolutionary investment to coincide with blocks of paranoiac reactionary investment. The oscillation between these two poles is even constitutive of delirium. [27]

So it is one and the same man who sometimes appears to be on the verge of a break-through, and sometimes sinks into a depressive state out of which he is hoisted by his resentment (that Deleuze now calls 'paranoia'). This is the reason why revolutions, brought

[25] A Œ, p. 434.   [26] A Œ, p. 408.   [27] A Œ, p. 451.

about by authentic desires, are always betrayed, in politics and art alike. They go amiss from the start.[28] The greater the refinements in Deleuze's schizo-analysis of the difference between schizoid and paranoiac, the less it is able to specify what is ordered under either heading. In contradiction with his most explicit intentions, his *empiricist* project, Deleuze finds himself measuring *that which is* according to the standard of *that which is not*, but *which ought to be*. The negative, which had required eliminating, is thus reintroduced in two steps, as Deleuze explained so well in 1962,[29] with reference to Nietzsche.

1. An ideal is posited, and then opposed point by point to the reality of the present (the 'sovereign individual' is everything the 'last man' is not; schizophrenia as a process is what the psychiatric entity is not).

2. This ideal, though itself guilty of not existing, of being no more than an ideal, now permits us to accuse the present of having fallen short of it.

The Tale (of the End of the Tale) of the End of History

Jean-François Lyotard attempted to avoid this pitfall in his *Economie libidinale* (1974). The title of the book, like that of the collection of articles which had been leading up to it from 1968, *Dérive à partir de Marx et Freud* (*Casting adrift from Marx and Freud*) makes it clear that Lyotard's premises are similar to those of Deleuze in the *Anti-Oedipus*.

For someone like Lyotard, from the tradition of 'philosophy of *praxis*' – 'Man is the work of his works,' he once wrote[30] – who was for a long time a militant of the *Socialisme ou Barbarie* group, the nihilism diagnosed by Nietzsche has, among others, the following meaning: the revolutionary militant imagines that his struggle against the current state of affairs is founded upon *truth*. He avails himself of a revolutionary theory that tells him, as an established truth, that the existing mode of production, together with its entire superstructure, is condemned by the contradiction within it, and that the future of this present will be catastrophic (war, generalised fascism), unless mankind takes the initiative and

---

[28] AŒ, p. 419.   [29] NPh, p. 170.

[30] 'Note sur le marxisme', *Tableau de la philosophie contemporaine* (Fischaber, 1956), p. 57.

changes to another mode of production. But then, as a militant, he makes two discoveries.

1. He believed he had been speaking in the name of truth, whereas he had unwittingly expressed no more than a moral ideal. Hence the collapse of revolutionary values, now identified as religious (the search for the *salvation* of humanity, by means of a *revenge* upon the guilty) and clerical (the intellectual is to the masses as the good shepherd is to his flock).

2. This new lucidity ricochets into the discovery that, precisely because it is a religious 'device' or 'figure', socialism is far less revolutionary than capitalist reality, for the latter is cynical, believes in nothing and destroys all beliefs on the surface of the globe.

The truth offered by knowledge of revolutionary theory was only an ideal. It was therefore not *the truth* at all, but only the expression of a *desire for truth*. It issued from the same belief in truth as had religion.[31]

Having reached this point, we might wish to interrupt Lyotard, and say that perhaps the militant's truth was ill-founded; he was led by a desire to accept Marxist pronouncements as true, when they were perhaps quite simply untrue. Alas! Already off on his course, he cannot hear us, but races on to cross at one bound the distance that separates his own disenchantment from a polemic against truth as such. From the observation that this truth was only the expression of a desire, he passes to the interpretation – that the desire expressed in terms of this alleged 'truth' was the desire for truth. We have our doubts ... But this is the result: if there were a truth, it would be Hegelian, or, if we prefer, Marxist. If Marxism is not true, this is not because it is false, but because nothing is true.

In any event, the fundamental issue becomes that of nihilism. Is the collapse of all beliefs a liberation or a disaster? Will modern man find in incredulity the incentive for a gay science or for a depressive prostration? Like Deleuze, Lyotard considers it reactionary or reactive to protest against the state of the world, against 'capitalism', if we like. There should be no question of reproaching capitalism for its cynicism and cruelty; on the contrary, that tendency should be stoked. Capitalism *liquidates* everything that

---

[31] 'Le désir nommé Marx', in *Eco. lib.*

mankind had held to be most noble and holy; such a liquidation must be rendered 'still more liquid'. [32] For the Good Old Days will not be coming back (barring the supposition of eternal recurrence). Here is how the programme of active nihilism (which has on the whole been received as scandalous) may be understood: that which is noble and holy ceases to be so as soon as it is believed in not from naivety, but out of calculation. For example, religion (or, which for Lyotard comes to the same thing, revolutionary commitment) being neither true nor false, there is no great point in 'demystifying' it. However, this same religion, which in an age of faith was holy, became somewhat tainted after the age of criticism, when the Romantics sought to restore it, out of a nostalgia for childhood, as did the political thinkers, so that the people might have morality, and the religious thinkers themselves, in order to avoid despair. In more general terms, no sooner do we become aware that truth is only the expression of a will for truth than we must face the fact that this 'truth' betrays a timid rejection of the world inasmuch as it is not a 'true world' (stable, ordered and just). *Barring the supposition of eternal recurrence* – it is on this point, decisive for the new French Nietzscheanism, that Lyotard parts company with Deleuze. The supposition of eternal recurrence has a major role to play in the speculations of the Nietzscheans. Klossowski indicates why. Such a supposition means above all that there has never been a *first time* (no origin) and that there will never be a *last time* (no end of history). The theory rings cruelly in phenomological ears and we have already seen its effects, in Derrida's deconstructions – whence the paradoxes so obligingly developed by Klossowski: there being no *original*, the model for the copy is itself a copy, and the copy is the copy of a copy; there is no *hypocritical mask*, for the face covered by the mask is itself a mask, and any mask is thus the mask of a mask; no *facts*, only interpretations, and any interpretation is itself the interpretation of an older interpretation; there is no *meaning proper* to words, only figurative meanings, and concepts are therefore only dissembled metaphors; there is no *authentic version* of a text, there are only translations; *no truth*, only pastiche and parody; and so on. [33] In an article originally entitled 'Renverser le platonisme' ('For the

---

[32] *Disp. puls.*, p. 47.

[33] See text of Klossowski's lecture, 'Nietzsche, le polythéisme et la parodie' (1957), reprinted in *Un si funeste désir* (Gallimard, 1963).

Overthrow of Platonism'), Deleuze proposed to call *Platonism* the will – one of a moral order (the morality of resentment) – to terminate this endless flow by distinguishing the good copies (those which admit to being only the copy of an absent model) from the bad copies, or *dummies* (those which, contriving to pass for the model of which they are the copies, suggest that the model itself is only a copy, an *n*th edition, and that the original is a deception).[34] But Klossowski goes much further. *The liquidation of the identity principle* which lies behind this negation of all assignation of an origin, or an original, implies that the appearances of identity or regularity which confront us are masks. All identity is a sham. The *same* is always an *other* posing as the *same*, and it is never the same *other* that is concealed behind the *same* mask. The mask we think of as the same is indeed never really the same mask; nor is anyone who thinks it is the same, the same, etc. Precisely because this is so, the doctrine of eternal recurrence can in no way propose a *principle of difference*, opposable to the principle of identity. As Klossowski explains, the Nietzschean supposition boldly opposes the principle of identity with the *appearance* of a principle, a false principle masquerading as a true one. The doctrine of eternal recurrence, he says, is the parody of a doctrine.[35] The philosopher of difference is therefore an *impostor*, his philosophy is a *mystification*. There can be no question of entrusting him with the task of demystification.

'If we demystify, it is in order to mystify more thoroughly.'[36] This is why the Deleuzian quest for a genuine difference, one which would separate the Master from slavery, or true desire from distorted desire, proceeds from an ingenuous, if not feigned belief in the virtues of criticism. The definition of philosophy as *critique* belongs to the pre-1789 'Enlightenment'. By denouncing the impostor-priest whose lies support the despot, philosophy aims to open the innocent eyes of the people, to restore to them their ancient virtues. But the critique of all authority has omitted to examine the authority of the critique itself. It freely indulges its suspicions, while continuing to believe in the innocence of the critique. In reality, the difference between the critique of imposture and the imposture itself is a sham. Likewise the

---

[34] 'Platon et le simulacre' in LS.   [35] *Un si funeste désir*, p. 226.
[36] *Nietzsche et le cercle vicieux*, p. 194.

difference between active and reactive strength: each simulates the other, by definition, and has always done so. Sickness produces the illusion of health, while superior states of health, an excess of vitality, are always accompanied by symptoms resembling those of sickness. Klossowski writes:

> Modern catastrophies always coincide – more or less
> immediately – with the '*glad tidings*' of a false 'prophet'. [37]

Philosophy from Plato to Hegel, then, is far from being one long mystification (metaphysics, etc.) against which the rare free thinker courageously revolts from time to time. On the contrary, philosophy, that is to say the belief in truth, has been nothing but a long *demystification*, a long decline of the power to mystify, to fabulate, to produce gods. Nietzsche's mysterious words in *Twilight of the Idols*, that the *real world* has become a *fable*, do not mean that a supra-sensible world is no longer believed in, but more disturbingly, that:

> the world becomes fable, the world as such is only a fable.
> A fable is something which is told, having no existence
> outside the tale. The world is something which is told, an
> event which is narrated; it is therefore an interpretation.
> Religion, art, science, history are so many diverse
> interpretations of the world, or rather, so many variants
> of the fable. [38]

The end of history now signifies that humanity is preparing to emerge from historical time, in order to re-enter 'the time of myth'. [39] Eternal recurrence consists in leaving history, that is, in the active forgetting of the past; such is the prerequisite for the creation of new gods (or if we prefer, of new 'histories', of new legends).

This being the case, Lyotard concludes that philosophy should remove the ancient mask it had worn under the reign of the single truth (the monotheistic, Christian age) and put on the mask of paganism, polytheism. The virtuous apparel of the critic is no longer appropriate:

> So, you would challenge Spinozist or Nietzschean ethics,
> which separates the movements of being-more and those

---

[37] *Ibid.*, p. 13.   [38] *Un si funeste désir*, p. 193.   [39] *Ibid.*, p. 194.

of being-less, of action and reaction? —— Yes, let us
beware of an entire morality and an entire politics, with
their sages, militants, courts and jails, taking advantage of
these dichotomies to appear again.... We do not speak as
liberators of desire.[40]

The world is a fabulous tale. And how is the emergence from
historical time to be effected? During the course of history, for as
long as there was history, the world was no fable, but a truth
offered up to a single *logos*. How are we to return from *logos* to
muthos? By showing that the *logos* itself was already a *muthos*.
Philosophy was constructed as a measure against 'tales' and 'tall
stories'. Plato had closed the gates of his city to poets, whom he
accused of spinning seductive yarns, foreign to truth. It is now
necessary, then, to show that Plato is also something of a story-
teller; that philosophy, too, is a seductive tale. Philosophers
opposed the theoretical and the narrative discourse. The former
asserts, 'This is *always and everywhere* the case, in all places and
from all time.' The latter begins, 'Once upon a time ...' (where-
upon everyone supposes that it never happened). As long as such
an opposition subsists between the particular and the universal,
theory will dominate the mind, and 'anecdotes' and 'tales' will be
considered as harmless entertainment:

> In my opinion, theories are themselves narratives, but
> disguised; one should not be deceived by their claim to
> omnitemporality.[41]

In order to substantiate this theory, Lyotard relies upon the
rehabilitation of the *logic of occasion*, as it is found in the Greek
sophists. The curious feature of this logic is its claim to give the lie
to the logic of the one and universal truth, by showing that the
latter is only a particular case of the logic of the particular, of the
special case, the unique occasion. However, while this logic of
particularity dominates and includes the logic of universality, it is
not presented as a *more universal* logic, nor a *truer* truth.

If all discourse is considered to be narrative, whoever were to
claim that his discourse was absolute would invite mockery, for
the properties of the narrative are as follows:

[40] *Eco. lib.*, pp. 54–5.
[41] *Instructions païennes* (Galilée, 1977), p. 28.

1. It has always already begun, and is always the story of a previous story; the referent of narrative discourse is never the crude fact, nor the dumb event, but other narratives, other stories, a great murmur of words preceding, provoking, accompanying and following the procession of wars, festivals, labours, time.

> And in fact we are always under the influence of some narrative, things have always been told us already, and we ourselves have always already been 'told'.[42]

2. It is never finished, for in principle the narrator addresses a listener, or 'narratee', who may in his turn become the narrator, making the narration of which he has been the 'narratee' into the *narrated* of a fresh narration.

Thus it is that the story (history) never ends. Or perhaps, one story (one history) does; *one narrative comes to an end*, the dialectical 'narrative'. But several versions of this account already exist, several accounts of this ending, several accounts of these accounts. The 'Discourse on Universal History' was only a powerful myth. Or alternatively, it was merely a myth – but what power it must have had, to have hypnotised its narratees for so long!

The end of history is not the end of the account. The many accounts of this ending are preparing a future in which several variants on the fable of the world will reign 'again' – and for the *n*th time.

Final Remarks

My subject has no conclusion. It would be presumptuous to 'infer the lessons' from these years that are still so close: already past, since we are commenting them, but not yet for us *the past*. As for the *future*, there is little point in speculating. We all know that in predicting a brilliant future for such and such a school, we are above all expressing our own preferences. However, I would feel guilty of side-stepping the issue that my subject has been holding in store for me, here at the end of this study, if I did not reply to the question posed at the beginning of Chapter 3. Has the 'haemorrhage of subjectivity' announced by Jean Beaufret in 1947 been staunched – more especially over the course of these recent years

---

[42] *Ibid.*, p. 47.

during which 'anti-humanism', the 'liquidation of identity' or the 'disappearance of the subject' have played the leading roles? We may observe that the condition has grown worse. In 1945, there was *only one subject*, only one sovereign, whose sovereignty moreover was extremely precarious. Either the Subject reigned as absolute Monarch, with all the prerogatives attached to the 'Myself = Myself', but with its absolutism valid within the sole limits of the *for-oneself*: I am absolute for myself, but only for myself, and the *in-itself* eludes me, as do *others*. Or else the Subject possessed a certain affinity or kinship with the *in-itself*, and a concurrence between subject and object was discernible; but the more features that the *for-itself* discovered it had in common with the *in-itself*, the less the *for-itself* was for itself; 'one', the 'impersonal', the 'anonymous' overran the Subject from within.

After 1960, the sovereign subject is not 'overcome', as Merleau-Ponty, prompted by his love for nature and later by his reading of Heidegger, had wished,[43] but *multiplied*. Instead of being subjected to a single *ego*, the world must now manifest itself to a mass of small *supposita*, each one tied to a *perspective*.

The entire generation of 1960 declared itself in favour of perspectivism. But the word 'perspective' protests against the use to which it is put. For French Nietzscheanism, perspectivism has the following meaning: when the repentant phenomenologists agreed to question the equation of *being* and *being-for-myself*, they willingly sacrificed *being* – a measure of how little they were prepared to renounce the *for-myself*. We are giving the orders! Perspectivism destroys the unity of the subject, but not the subject itself. We have seen how the position of a *subject* (of the *ego*, identical to itself as origin of truth) led inevitably to the rivalry of consciousnesses, the strife of the pretenders around the throne of the absolute *ego*. As Pascal said, each person unjustly makes himself the centre of the world. Perspectivism sought to avoid the dialectic of Master and Slave (I am, therefore you are not) by pacifying the contenders: you are fighting over a non-existent prize! You all want to be the centre of the world! You must learn that there is neither centre nor world! All that is merely a game, a pretence. The Kings are drawn on Twelfth Night, but so that

<hr />

[43] PP, p. 408.

there may be no squabbling among the guests, everyone will be King – for after all, it was only a kingship conferred in jest.

As Serres reminds us, perspectivism is the same thing as phenomenology.[44] The aim of descriptive geometry is to determine the unvarying properties of any figure *for all perspectives*, i.e. for all projections of this figure on a plane (where it 'appears'). If we vary the plane of projection, the figure will also vary, but in a corresponding fashion, and retaining certain properties ('of position', as they are known). For example, a circle may become an ellipse, but along the circumference of all the conical sections that may thus be obtained, a point B, situated between A and C, will conserve its intermediate position. By definition, perspectivism means to find *order* in diversity, *invariables* in change, *identity* in difference. It tells how, in such and such a case, such and such an 'appearance' is produced.

Merleau-Ponty used the word 'perspective' in the strict sense when he saw in it the solution to the problem posed by human diversity; irrational discourse (myth, delirium) is no aberration, but

> a projection of existence and an expression of the human condition.

He added:

> If all myths are true, it is in so far as they can be set into a phenomenology of mind which shows their function in arriving at awareness, and which ultimately bases their own significance on the significance they have for the philosopher.[45]

Perspectivism and phenomenology are thus indeed equivalent.

The French Nietzscheanism of the last twenty years has tried to understand perspective in precisely the opposite way – not to impose order upon variety, not to find the invariable in variation, but on the contrary, to make of order one possible figure of variety, or to see the invariable simply as one perspective among others. Leibniz, says Deleuze, gave expression to classical perspectivism by forcing the perspectives that are monads to *converge*

---

[44] *Le système de Leibniz*, I, p. 168.   [45] PP, pp. 338–9.

upon a single object; monads are like vantage points overlooking a single city. The perspectivism of Nietzsche is different:

> it is another town that corresponds to each point of view, and each point of view is another town.... And always another town within the town. [46]

Not only do these vantage points differ from one another, but all that they have in common is their difference. There are as many cities as there are vantage points; they are dissimilar, they do not communicate, and they are set at a distance from one another.

Here, perhaps, the word *perspective* plays a trick on those who employ it as the fancy takes them. Sooner than they can divert it from its meaning, it might itself lead them where they do not wish to go. For in the *Monadology* we read:

> And just as a single city, observed from different sides, appears quite different, as if multiplied according to the perspectives, so in the same way by virtue of the infinite multitude of simple substances, there seem to be as many different universes, which are however simply the perspectives on a single one, according to the different vantage points of each Monad. (§ 57)

French Nietzscheanism claims to overcome the subject when in fact it suppresses the *object* (the city, that object common to those observing it 'from different sides'). It declares that the text has no referent outside itself, that the historical account relates no event exterior to the account, that interpretation has no bearing upon fact as distinguishable from interpretation, and that the different vantage points do not look out upon a world which is common to all perspectives. In this way, the single Centre, the first Principle, the sovereign Identity are taken to have been defeated.

Each vantage point is a city; the vantage points do not overlook the same city. Is this not precisely what Leibniz held? *And just as* ... (he writes), ... *so, in the same way: Just as the same city* is multiplied according to the perspectives, *so in the same way the universe* is multiplied by the profusion of monads. What do the monads see? Do they see *the same city*? Not at all. For them, there is no one object observed from without, from the summit of a

---

[46] LS, p. 203; see also DR, pp. 79 and 94.

neighbouring mountain by one, by another from the opposite bank of a river. The monads see the universe, which is the universe of the monads. Each monad having its vantage point, *there are apparently as many different universes, which, however, are only perspectives on a single one*: namely *the infinite multitude of single substances*. The city seen by observers is now the sum of those very observers. Leibniz conforms, then, to the requirements of Deleuzian perspectivism; a different city corresponds to each vantage point, each vantage point is a different city, always a different city within the city. To which he does not omit to add that all these cities are, however, only perspectives on a single one, for here, there is no other city than the sum of cities, the system of monads.

No doubt the time will come when the initial hypothesis – of renouncing *being* and preserving the *for-myself* – will have to be reconsidered. And the other possibility envisaged – of jettisoning the *for-myself* in order to preserve *being*.

Index